# Optimise

## Student's Book



B1+

macmillan education

| LISTENING | SPEAKING | USE OF ENGLISH | WRITING |
|---|---|---|---|
| Listening for agreement (1)<br>Multiple choice (extracts) | Talking about habits<br>Interview<br>Talk2Me | Word patterns (verb phrases)<br>Sentence transformation | Agreeing and disagreeing<br>An essay |
| Predicting missing information<br>Sentence completion | Comparing<br>Photo task<br>Talk2Me | Verbs (1) (auxiliaries, modals, particles)<br>Open cloze | Giving advice<br>A letter / An email |
| Identiying attitude (1)<br>Multiple matching | Making suggestions<br>Collaborative task<br>Talk2Me | Nouns (1) (suffixes, spelling changes)<br>Word formation | Using good descriptions<br>A review |
| Understanding responses to questions<br>Multiple choice (single extract) | Agreeing and disagreeing<br>Discussion<br>Talk2Me | Collocations<br>Multiple-choice cloze | Giving examples<br>An essay |
| Listening for agreement (2)<br>Multiple choice (extracts) | Talking about hopes and ambitions<br>Interview<br>Talk2Me | Prepositions and short adverbs<br>Open cloze | Giving reasons<br>An article |
| Identifying attitude (2)<br>Multiple choice (extracts) | Expressing preference and giving reasons<br>Photo task<br>Talk2Me | Adjectives and adverbs<br>Word formation | Engaging the reader<br>An article |
| Predicting synonyms<br>Multiple matching | Asking for clarification<br>Collaborative task<br>Talk2Me | Verbs (2) (tenses)<br>Sentence transformation | Using narrative tenses<br>A story |
| Listening for opinion<br>Sentence completion | Expressing and justifying opinions<br>Discussion<br>Talk2Me | Nouns (2) (suffixes, negatives)<br>Word formation | Explaining<br>A letter / An email |
| Taking notes<br>Sentence completion | Expressing uncertainty and speculating<br>Photo task<br>Talk2Me | Idioms<br>Multiple-choice cloze | Making recommendations<br>A review |
| Distractors (1)<br>Multiple choice (single extract) | Talking about experiences<br>Interview<br>Talk2Me | Conditionals<br>Sentence transformation | Creating a good plot<br>A story |
| Identifying attitude (3)<br>Multiple matching | Organising your ideas<br>Photo task<br>Talk2Me | Phrasal verbs<br>Multiple-choice cloze | Using formal and informal language<br>A letter / An email |
| Distractors (2)<br>Multiple choice (single extract) | Reaching a decision<br>Collaborative task<br>Talk2Me | Verbs (3) (phrasal verbs)<br>Open cloze | Drawing conclusions<br>An essay |

► USE OF ENGLISH p 144–145 ► WRITING p 146–147

**Student's Resource Centre**

- *Talk2Me* videos (flipped classroom)
- Speaking test videos
- *Optimise your grammar* worksheets
- *Optimise your vocabulary* worksheets
- *Say it right* pronunciation worksheets
- Culture and CLIL worksheets
- Class and Workbook audio

# 1 Can't live without it

## READING | Multiple choice | A magazine article

**1 In pairs or as a group, answer the questions.**

1 What modern technology do you use more than once a week? Make a list and compare answers.

2 Which things on your list do you think existed in 1986? How have those things changed since then?

**EXAM SKILL**

### Understanding purpose

- Every text is written for a particular purpose or reason – to inform, to entertain, to persuade, to describe, to advise, etc.
- Thinking about the language the writer uses can help you decide what the purpose is.

**2 Read the first paragraph of the article opposite and choose the best answer.**

1 The writer is describing

**a)** something that happened. **b)** a typical scene.

2 The writer is saying that

**a)** we shouldn't use technology.

**b)** we all use technology every day.

3 The writer uses mainly

**a)** present tenses. **b)** past tenses.

**3 Read the rest of the article and choose T (True) or F (False). If you choose T, underline the words or phrases that helped you decide.**

1 In the second paragraph, the writer wants us to think about life in the past. **T / F**

2 In the third paragraph, the writer describes what some people did. **T / F**

3 In the fourth paragraph, the writer advises parents not to worry. **T / F**

4 In the fifth paragraph, the writer describes the effect of the experience. **T / F**

**OPTIMISE YOUR EXAM**

### Multiple choice

- Read the title and the text first for general meaning and think about how the language and tenses connect to the writer's purpose.
- Then read the questions and find the part of the text that they refer to.
- Carefully read the questions again and all the options before you choose your answer.

# 1986
## A YEAR WITHOUT TECHNOLOGY

The next time you're out in a public place, like a park or a restaurant, look around you. What is happening? Some people are **surfing the internet** on their phones. Others are wearing headphones, listening to music on their MP3 players. Perhaps others are watching a film on a tablet or playing a game with friends halfway round the world. That's just the way life is today. We all spend a fair amount of our time connected to technology, even very young children, who want nothing more than to play with the latest **app** on their big brother or sister's tablet.

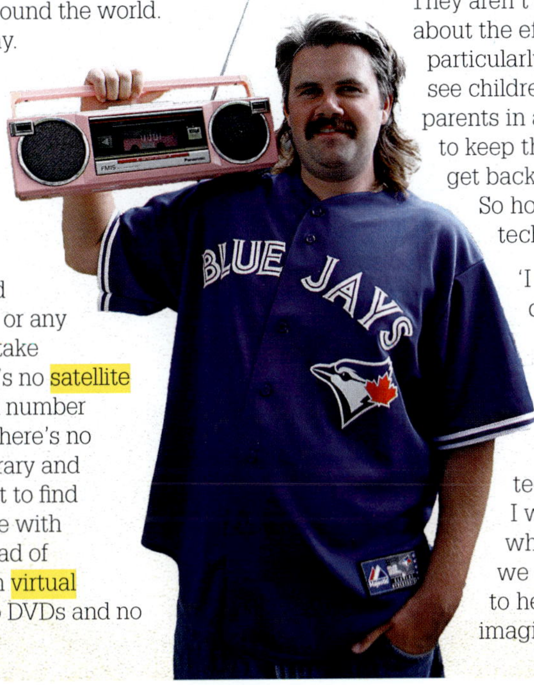

Now imagine living in a world without smartphones, tablets or any of the electronic **gadgets** we take for granted these days. There's no **satellite** TV and you only have a small number of channels to choose from. There's no internet and you go to the library and look at a book when you want to find anything out. You play outside with friends in the real world instead of playing online video games in **virtual** worlds. There are no **texts**, no DVDs and no email. Welcome to 1986!

That's the world the McMillan family from Ontario, Canada, decided to live in for a year. Blair, 27, Morgan, 28, and their two sons Trey and Denton, aged five and three, got rid of their **cable** TV, smartphones, internet, new games console, digital camera, DVD player and satnav, and instead used an old TV, a radio, old telephones, a VHS video player, an old games console and maps. They even got hairstyles just like the ones people had in 1986!

They decided to try it after seeing how their young children were becoming **dependent** on technology. They aren't alone. More and more parents today worry about the effect technology is having on their children, particularly very young children. It's not unusual to see children as young as two or three sitting with their parents in a restaurant with a tablet in front of them to keep them occupied. The McMillans decided to get back to basics to see how things have changed. So how did they find their year without modern technology?

'I thought Blair was mad when he suggested doing this whole thing,' says Morgan, 'but it's made me realise how much time we wasted. We seem much more relaxed now, not checking in on email or Facebook all the time.' The McMillans are now back in the present with a different attitude to today's technology. Blair said, 'I'm not anti-technology. I wanted to taste, and I wanted my kids to taste, what it would be like without it, and to see if we could actually do it.' From now on, they hope to help their kids spend more time using their imagination and less time on the smartphone.

**4** 1.01 **Read the article again. For questions 1–5, choose the answer (A, B, C or D) which you think fits best according to the text.**

1 What is the writer's purpose in the first paragraph?
   A to describe a nice day out in the park
   B to advise people against using too much technology
   C to show how much everyone uses technology today
   D to criticise people who use technology
2 What is the writer's purpose in the second paragraph?
   A to help us understand the McMillans' experience
   B to show that the present is better than the past
   C to make us realise that we don't need technology
   D to show why life today is so unhealthy
3 Which of the following does the writer **not** say the McMillans changed?
   A their appearance
   B their forms of entertainment
   C their forms of communication
   D their house
4 According to the writer, other parents
   A don't understand what the McMillans did.
   B share the same concern as the McMillans.
   C rely on technology too much in their lives.
   D don't think about their young children enough.
5 What is the writer's purpose in the final paragraph?
   A to show how the experience has changed the McMillans
   B to suggest that other families do the same as the McMillans
   C to explain a mistake that the McMillans made
   D to show why we need technology more these days

**5** **Complete the sentences with highlighted words or phrases from the article.**

1 If you've got ________ or ________ TV, you can watch channels from all around the world.
2 I haven't received any ________ on my phone this week. Maybe there's a problem.
3 I've got a great ________ on my phone. It shows you exactly where you are in the world.
4 Do you think young people are ________ on technology these days?
5 I can't live without my ________ , like my phone, my tablet and my MP3 player.
6 You're always ________ the ________ .
Why don't you read a book instead?
7 To play this game, you go into a ________ world online and control a character.

# 1 GRAMMAR 1 | Tense review: present simple and continuous, stative verbs

## Grammar in context

**Find and underline these words in the text on page 5. In each case, explain why the writer has used this tense.**

Some people ***are surfing*** the internet on their phones.

We all ***spend*** a fair amount of our time connected to technology, …

We ***seem*** much more relaxed now …

### REMEMBER

- The present simple is used for facts, habits, routines and permanent situations.
- The present continuous is used for actions happening now and temporary or changing situations.
- Stative verbs describe states and are not normally used in continuous tenses. Common stative verbs include: *seem, like, believe, own.*
- Some verbs can be either stative or action verbs, depending on the meaning:

*I **think** your new phone is amazing.* think = believe (stative)

*I'**m thinking** of buying a new phone.* thinking (of) = considering (action)

▶ **See Grammar reference, Unit 1,** page 148

**1 Choose the correct word or phrase.**

1 Right now I **watch / 'm watching** TV with my brother.
2 Do you agree that people **rely / are relying** on technology too much these days?
3 How often **do you use / are you using** microblogging services like Twitter?
4 Gadgets **become / are becoming** more and more a part of everyday life.
5 **Do you have / Are you having** satellite TV at home?
6 I **don't post / 'm not posting** to Facebook as much as my friends do.
7 I'm sure your parents **have / are having** a good reason for limiting your use of technology.
8 I **use / 'm using** this phone while my smartphone is being repaired.

**2 Complete the dialogue with the correct form of the verbs in the box. Use contractions where possible.**

| call \| come \| get \| have got \| look |
|---|
| not joke \| queue \| sell \| stand \| want |

**Jake:** Hello.

**Oscar:** Jake. It's me, Oscar. Listen – I **(1)** ______________ you from town. I **(2)** ______________ outside PhoneLand, and they **(3)** ______________ the new Samsung in the shop. I seriously **(4)** ______________ !

**Jake:** No! Really? Wow! What **(5)** ______________ it ______________ like?

**Oscar:** Really cool. And they **(6)** ______________ really fast. I mean, people **(7)** ______________ round the block to get one. Everyone **(8)** ______________ one!

**Jake:** OK – I **(9)** ______________ ready right now and I **(10)** ______________ down there to meet you. I have to see this!

**Oscar:** OK – and hurry up!

**3 Find and underline eight mistakes with tenses in the text. Write the correct form above each mistake.**

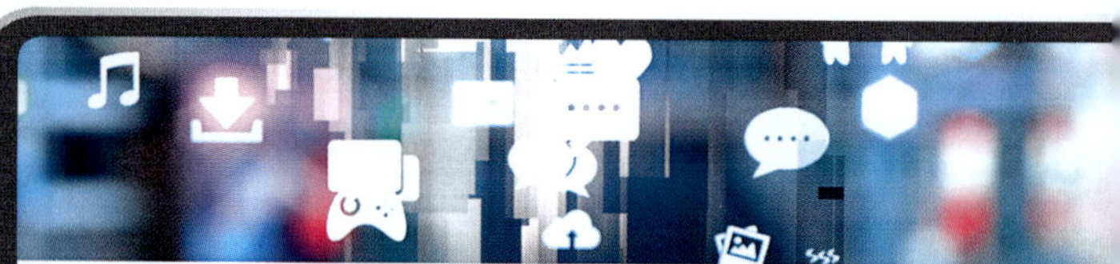

HOME | ABOUT | LINKS | ARCHIVE

## One hour a day

Posted at 18:45 on 17 September

I am owning quite a few gadgets: a smartphone, a games console, a tablet and others. My parents are thinking that I spend a bit too long on them, at the moment. Now I am having one hour of screen time a day during the week, and two a day at weekends. I am choosing what I want to spend that time on, but when the time is being up, my parents are switching all devices off. I am supposing I do spend quite a bit of time on them, so I've decided to give it a go. Wish me luck – it isn't going to be easy!

**SAY IT RIGHT**

**Resource centre: Unit 1**
Emphatic stress

THINK | RESEARCH | CULTURE | LEARN | **ME**

How important is it to keep up with the latest technology, such as new smartphones, tablets and software updates?

## Adjectives with *-able* / *-ible*

**1** 1.02 **Write the adjective form of each word in the correct column. Make any necessary spelling changes. Listen and check.**

~~access~~ | ~~admire~~ | advice | believe | fashion | horror | identify | permit | reason | reverse | sense | terror

| adjectives with *-able* | adjectives with *-ible* |
|---|---|
| *admirable* | *accessible* |

**2** **Write an adjective from Exercise 1 in each gap to complete the sentences. Sometimes there is more than one answer.**

1 Your parents don't let you surf the internet! That sounds ___________ !
2 It is ___________ for parents to limit screen time for young children.
3 I think setting limits on children's use of technology is very ___________ .
4 Playing video games has affected your eyesight, but don't worry – the effect is ___________ .
5 Make sure your phone is ___________ by getting a case for it that no-one else has.
6 Most ___________ people accept that you can't spend all your time online.

## Collocations with *come, do, make* or *take*

**3** 1.03 **Complete the phrases in italics with the correct form of *come, do, take* or *make*. Listen and check.**

1 My parents and I have ___________ *to an agreement*. I'm only going to use my games console at the weekend.
2 You should ___________ *my advice* when I tell you to spend less time on your smartphone.
3 Could you ___________ *me a favour* and lend me your tablet for five minutes?
4 I do ___________ *your point* about very young children and limiting screen time, but I disagree when it comes to teenagers.
5 I'm really ___________ *my best* to use the internet less. I've deleted my Facebook account.
6 I have ___________ *to the decision* that I will only use electronic gadgets at the weekend.
7 I spend too much time online, but I'm ___________ *progress*. I've got it down to three hours a day!

**4** **Explain the meanings of the collocations in Exercise 3.**

## Words connected with *technology*

**5** 1.04 **Choose words from the box that are synonyms for the words in bold. Listen and check.**

fix | gadgets | limit | mend | online | posted on | switch off

1 She **uploaded** some photos **to** her Facebook page. ___________
2 If our computer freezes, we usually **turn** it **off** and restart it because that often solves the problem. ___________
3 I am addicted to my electronic **devices**, especially my tablet. ___________
4 How much did it cost to **repair** your computer? ___________ ___________
5 Many parents want to **control** how much time their children spend playing games **on the internet**. ___________ ___________

**6** **Match these words to their antonyms in Exercise 5.**

1 break ___________ ___________
2 turn on ___________ ___________
3 offline ___________ ___________
4 download ___________ ___________

▶ Vocabulary reference, page 162 ▶ **Workbook Unit 1:** Vocabulary, pages 6–7, exercises 1, 2, 3

# 1 LISTENING | Multiple choice (extracts)

**1** **Ask and answer the questions.**

1 When was the last time you disagreed with someone? Describe what happened.

2 Do you ever disagree with people in your family? If you do, what do you disagree about? If you don't, what things do you think families often disagree about?

**EXAM SKILL**

## Listening for agreement (1)

- In listening tasks, you often need to decide if one speaker agrees or disagrees with another, or what they agree/disagree about.
- Listen for agreement and disagreement phrases, but also listen to the different points the speakers make. A speaker may agree with one point but disagree with another.

**2** 1.05 **Listen and decide if each speaker is agreeing or disagreeing. Make a note of the phrase they use.**

Speaker 1 is **agreeing** / **disagreeing**.
Phrase used: ______________________

Speaker 2 is **agreeing** / **disagreeing**.
Phrase used: ______________________

Speaker 3 is **agreeing** / **disagreeing**.
Phrase used: ______________________

Speaker 4 is **agreeing** / **disagreeing**.
Phrase used: ______________________

Speaker 5 is **agreeing** / **disagreeing**.
Phrase used: ______________________

**OPTIMISE YOUR EXAM**

## Multiple choice (extracts)

- Always read the questions before you start listening so you know what you are listening for.
- In this multiple-choice exam task (Exercise 4), some questions test listening for agreement and disagreement.
- Check that the phrases show agreement or disagreement about the main point in the question and not something else.

**3** **Look at the questions in Exercise 4. Which ones are about agreement or disagreement?**

**4** 1.06 **You will hear people talking in five different situations. For each question, choose the best answer (A, B or C).**

1 You hear a boy and his mother talking. What do they disagree about?
**A** the amount of time he spends online
**B** how much fun social networks are
**C** whether he should see his friends more

2 You hear two friends talking about an app they are creating. What do they disagree about?
**A** how popular the app will be
**B** how much the app should cost
**C** what the app should be called

3 You hear a man and a woman talking. What do they agree to buy?
**A** a new games console
**B** a new television
**C** a new computer

4 You hear two people on the radio reviewing a smartphone. What do they disagree about?
**A** how hard the phone is to use
**B** how fast the phone is
**C** how fashionable the phone is

5 You hear two friends talking about a new product. What do they agree about?
**A** how popular it'll be
**B** how useful it'll be
**C** how expensive it'll be

THINK | RESEARCH | CULTURE | LEARN | **ME**

What do your parents feel about young people spending time online or playing video games?

Are there rules in your family about how much screen time you're allowed?

Do you think rules like that are a good idea?



▶ **Workbook Unit 1:** Listening, page 8, exercises 1, 2

# GRAMMAR 2 | *-ing* and infinitives

## Grammar in context

**Match these sentences from the audio in the listening lesson to the verb patterns they use.**

1 *They **expect people to pay** a lot for them.*
2 *Turning it on **involves pressing** two buttons.*
3 *I think I should **make you spend** more time in the real world.*
4 *I'm not sure **I want to try** them.*

**a)** verb + full infinitive ____
**b)** verb + object + full infinitive ____
**c)** verb + *-ing* ____
**d)** verb + object + bare infinitive ____

### REMEMBER

- Some verbs or phrases are usually followed by either the *-ing* form of the verb, the full infinitive or the bare infinitive. There may or may not be an object after the verb. Learning patterns like this is very important in English.
- Be careful! Some verbs and phrases can use more than one structure. For example, the verb *want* can be used with two structures:

  *I **want to buy** a new tablet.* (verb + full infinitive)

  *He **wants me to buy** a new tablet.* (verb + object + full infinitive)

▶ **See Grammar reference, Unit 1,** page 148

**1** **Tick the correct sentences. Underline the mistakes in the other sentences and correct them.**

1 Jake attempted to set a new record on the game, but failed. ____________
2 I plan inviting a social media blogger to talk to students at my school. ____________
3 I watched my brother to play video games for a while. ____________
4 You'd better not leaving your new smartphone on your desk. ____________
5 She pretended being working but I could see she was chatting online. ____________

**2** **Complete the sentences with the correct form of the verbs in brackets. Add other words if necessary.**

1 Do you ____________ the laptop on the floor? (**deny**, **drop**)
2 My mum ____________ the laptop off and do my homework. (**make**, **turn**)
3 Do you ____________ your phone to look for something on the internet? (**mind**, **use**)
4 I ____________ the app when suddenly my phone went dead. (**start**, **use**)
5 Can I ____________ for ten more minutes and then going to do something else? (**suggest**, **play**)

**3** **Complete the text with the correct form (*-ing* or infinitive) of the verbs in the box. Use one verb twice.**

| be \| check \| limit \| play \| set<br>spend \| take \| use \| watch |
|---|

## Screen time

Next time you feel like (**1**) ____________ TV or playing a video game, think about your screen time. Add up the total time you spend looking at tablet screens, phone screens, computer screens and TV screens and you might be surprised. We all tend (**2**) ____________ more and more time using technology these days, and we'd all better (**3**) ____________ it seriously or we'll face health problems later. Experts suggest (**4**) ____________ your screen time. You might dislike (**5**) ____________ limits, and you might miss (**6**) ____________ your favourite games, but there are many other things you can do. Here are a few tips.

- Avoid (**7**) ____________ technology for more than two hours a day. This involves putting your gadgets away where you can't use them. Put your phone in a drawer in the evening and read a book instead of watching TV.
- Maybe you enjoy (**8**) ____________ Facebook just before going to sleep, but don't do it. It affects your sleep and you don't get enough rest.
- Take the TV out of your bedroom. It might seem (**9**) ____________ difficult at first, but you'll soon get used to it. Find something else to do instead, such as a hobby.

Don't put off (**10**) ____________ control of your screen time. Your body and your mind will both thank you for it!

THINK | RESEARCH | CULTURE | **LEARN** | ME

Use a dictionary to find out what structures these verbs take: *agree, dislike, imagine, refuse*. Write an example sentence for each verb.

▶ **Workbook Unit 1:** Grammar 2, page 7, exercises 1, 2

# 1 SPEAKING | Interview

Talk2Me *I tend to…*

**Flipped classroom**

**1** ▷ **Watch the *Talk2Me* video and answer the questions.**

1 Who has the most / the least amount of free time per day?
2 Which activities do the people say they do in their free time?
3 How many people play video games every day?

**2** ▷ **Watch the video again. Underline the time expressions in the *Phrase expert* box that you hear on the video.**

> **PHRASE EXPERT**
> a/per day | from time to time | hardly ever | I tend (not) to | my usual routine | now and again | up to (an hour / two hours)

**EXAM SKILL**

### Talking about habits

❍ When you talk about your own routines and habits, you may need to use adverbs of frequency. As well as the common adverbs like *sometimes*, *usually*, and *never*, you can use phrases like *hardly ever*, *from time to time*, *now and again*, etc.

**3** **In pairs or groups, answer the questions.**

- Do you have a daily routine or is each day different?
- What are the good and bad things about having a routine?

**4** **Look at the chart below, showing someone's typical use of leisure time in a day. Describe what it tells you and say what you find interesting or surprising about it.**

**5** **Complete the sentences with a word or phrase from the *Phrase expert* box.**

1 _______________ get distracted, and I stick to what I have planned.
2 You'll _______________ find me just sitting around watching TV, for example.
3 _______________ is to get up around seven and check my texts.
4 Sometimes I spend an hour _______________ online.
5 I guess _______________ two or three hours on a Saturday is _______________ .

**OPTIMISE YOUR EXAM**

### Interview

- An examiner may ask you to talk about yourself, your life, your interests, etc.
- Listen carefully to the question and give an appropriate answer.
- Be honest – the examiner wants to hear you talk about yourself in a relaxed, natural way.

**6** **In pairs, ask and answer these questions.**

- How much free time do you have?
- What do you like doing in your free time?
- How much time do you usually spend online?
- What are your favourite online activities?
- How often do you play video games?
- Do you do much sport?

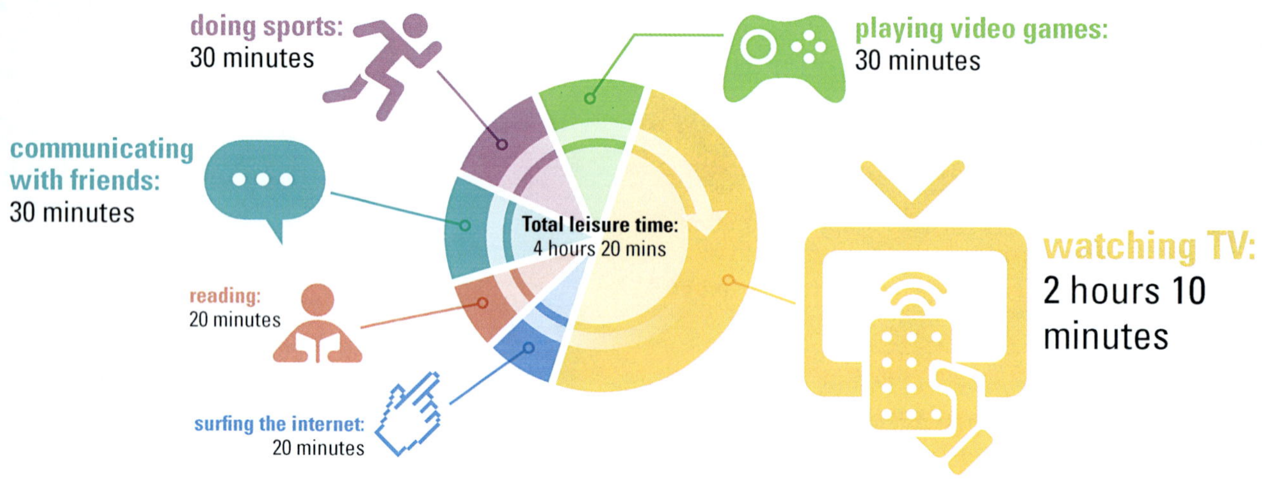

# USE OF ENGLISH | Sentence transformation

**1** **In pairs, agree on two advantages and two disadvantages of young people playing video games.**

**EXAM SKILL**

## Word patterns

- Many exam tasks test your knowledge of word patterns, the grammar associated with particular words or phrases. In Grammar 2, we looked at word patterns with certain verbs and phrases.
- In the *Vocabulary reference*, page 162, you can find more examples of the word patterns from this level.

**2** **Choose the correct sentence endings. Sometimes there is more than one answer.**

1 He denied ________
**a)** losing my phone. **b)** that he lost my phone.
2 Kelly suggested ________
**a)** playing a game. **b)** to play a game.
3 I finally succeeded ________
**a)** in fixing my tablet. **b)** to fix my tablet.
4 Would you mind ________
**a)** lending me a DVD? **b)** to lend me a DVD?
5 Are you planning ________
**a)** getting a laptop? **b)** to get a laptop?
6 I'd rather ________
**a)** have a smartwatch. **b)** to have a smartwatch.
7 Would you prefer ________
**a)** this app? **b)** to buy this app?
8 You'd better not ________
**a)** stay up too late. **b)** to stay up too late.

**OPTIMISE YOUR EXAM**

## Sentence transformation

- Read the instructions for the task carefully.
- Make sure you don't write more than five words for each question and don't change the word given.

**3** **Look at each pair of sentences in Exercise 4 and answer these questions.**

1 What word pattern is used with *able*?
________
2 What verb means 'say you didn't do something' and is followed by *-ing*?
________
3 What word pattern is used with *tend*?
________
4 What word patterns are used with *suggest*?
________
5 What phrase using *make* means 'force someone to do something'?
________
6 What is another word for *manage* which is followed by *in*?
________

**4** **Complete the second sentence so it has a similar meaning to the first. Do not change the word given. Use two to five words, including the word given.**

1 Some people can't stop themselves playing video games for hours on end. **ABLE**
Some people ________ themselves playing video games for hours on end.
2 Oliver says he didn't break your phone. **BREAKING**
Oliver ________ your phone.
3 Older people often find it hard to understand technology. **TEND**
Older people ________ it easy to understand technology.
4 Playing a video game was my idea. **SUGGESTED**
I ________ play a video game.
5 You can't force me to play games if I don't want to. **MAKE**
You can't ________ games if I don't want to.
6 I finally managed to solve the mystery at the end of the video game. **IN**
I finally ________ the mystery at the end of the video game.

THINK | RESEARCH | **CULTURE** | LEARN | ME

How popular are video games with young people in your country?
How much of a problem is video game addiction in your country?

## 1 In pairs or as a group, answer the questions.

1 Are there any children under five in your family? How much screen time do they have?

2 What are the possible negative effects of young children having too much screen time?

**EXAM SKILL**

### Agreeing and disagreeing

- In some writing tasks, you might need to express agreement or disagreement with different ideas.
- Try to use a range of phrases for agreeing or disagreeing, such as *I am for/against the idea that …* or *I agree/disagree with the argument that …*, etc.

## 2 Read the statement and the essay. Does the writer agree or disagree with the statement? Do you agree or disagree with the writer?

**Parents should limit the amount of time very young children spend using gadgets.**

**Do you agree?**

It is very common today to see children as young as two playing games on tablets or smartphones. It is my belief that this has some negative effects and I completely support the idea that parents should set limits on screen time for very young children.

It is important that young children develop social skills by playing with other children. They cannot do this while they are playing with apps on their own. I totally agree with the idea that the colours and music of most games are attractive but young children need to learn to develop real relationships with people.

I do not accept the argument that children can set limits themselves. At this age, young children have no idea how playing games may affect them later. In my opinion, only a child's parents, with their experience of life, can decide how much screen time is appropriate.

Of course, parents should discuss the situation with their child. I am not in favour of setting limits when the child does not understand the reason. Parents should also make sure that their child does activities with other children, such as visiting playgrounds.

## 3 Find and underline places in the essay where the writer agrees or disagrees with something.

## 4 Complete each phrase with a word from the box.

| accept | against | convinced |
|---|---|---|
| favour | support | totally |

**Agreeing**

1 I completely __________ (+ noun / *-ing* / *the argument/idea/suggestion that …*)

2 I am in __________ of (+ noun / *-ing* / *the argument/idea/suggestion that …*)

3 I __________ agree with (+ noun / *-ing* / *the argument/idea/suggestion that …*)

**Disagreeing**

4 I do not __________ (+ noun / *the argument/idea/suggestion that …*)

5 I am __________ (+ noun / *-ing* / *the argument/idea/suggestion that …*)

6 I am not __________ by (+ *the argument/idea/suggestion that …*)

**OPTIMISE YOUR EXAM**

### An essay

- When you write an essay, remember that the purpose is to present your opinion in a clear way, with reasons for that opinion.
- Start a new paragraph for each main point. Make the main point clearly in the first sentence of the paragraph then give reasons and examples.
- Always plan your writing and check your finished work.

## 5 Choose the correct words to complete the opinion phrases.

1 It is my **belief** / **believe** that …

2 I **tend** / **intend** to think that …

3 **From** / **In** my point of view …

4 As far as **my** / **I'm** concerned …

5 **In** / **On** my opinion …

6 **To** / **From** my mind …

**6** **Look at this writing task. Do you agree or disagree with the statement? Briefly say why.**

In your English class, you have been talking about teenagers and their use of modern technology. Now your English teacher has asked you to write an essay for homework.

Parents should limit the amount of time their teenage children spend online. Do you agree?

NOTES Write about:

1. school
2. friends
3. .................. (your own idea)

**7** **Read these sentences and explain why you agree or disagree with each idea.**

1. Parents should trust teenagers to set their own limits.
   *I agree/disagree because* ______________________________.
2. Teenagers today are too dependent on modern technology in their social lives.
   *I agree/disagree because* ______________________________.
3. Teenagers should have limits on their screen time during the school week.
   *I agree/disagree because* ______________________________.
4. Teenagers should be free to do whatever they want at the weekend.
   *I agree/disagree because* ______________________________.
5. Teenagers are old enough to be in control of their own lives.
   *I agree/disagree because* ______________________________.

**8** **Plan** **Make a paragraph plan.**

| Part | Purpose | Useful phrases | My notes |
|---|---|---|---|
| **Paragraph 1** | give your general opinion on whether parents should limit teenagers' time online | *One important issue today is …*<br>*Many people argue that …* | |
| **Paragraph 2** | give your opinion in connection with school | *In my view, it is important to remember that …*<br>*School is a time when …* | |
| **Paragraph 3** | give your opinion in connection with weekends | *We all need time to relax and …*<br>*After a busy week at school …* | |
| **Paragraph 4** | give your opinion on a third area of your own choice | *A third area that may be affected is …*<br>*People are also concerned about the effects on …* | |

**9** **Write** **Write your essay in an appropriate style. Write 140–190 words.**

**10** **Check** **Before you hand in your essay, complete this checklist.**

**Checklist**

- ◯ I've clearly agreed or disagreed with the statement.
- ◯ I've used an appropriate style for an essay.
- ◯ I've started each paragraph with a main point.
- ◯ I've given reasons for my opinion.
- ◯ I've written at least four paragraphs.
- ◯ I've checked my spelling and grammar.

▶ **Writing reference,** page 174 ▶ **Workbook Unit 1:** Writing, page 10, exercises 1, 2, 3, 4 and Progress check 1, page 11

# 2 Live and learn

## READING | Gapped text | Blog posts

**1** **In pairs or as a group, answer the questions.**

1 What things did you learn to do between the ages of (**a**) one and five, and (**b**) five and ten?

2 Is there anything that you've tried to learn but didn't manage to get the hang of?

**EXAM SKILL**

### Understanding pronoun references

- Pronouns are words like *she*, *his*, *them*, *it*, etc. They connect ideas in a text.
- To understand a written text, you often have to understand exactly what the pronouns refer to (*Who is she? What is it?*, etc.).

**2** **Look at these sentences. For each underlined word, guess what it might refer to. Make notes.**

It's great fun when you finally get the hang of it!

**Example:** *perhaps it's skateboarding or whistling*

1 While he was studying, I stood in front of the mirror and practised.

_______________

2 My older sister Emily was doing them at school.

_______________

3 Our parents always made us write them on our birthdays.

_______________

**3** **Read the text quickly to get a general idea of what it's about. Add more information to your notes in Exercise 2.**

**OPTIMISE YOUR EXAM**

### Gapped text

- In this task, you need to decide which sentences are missing from a text.
- Underline any pronouns in the missing sentences (e.g. *I*, *he*, *she*, *our*, etc.).
- Look carefully at the sentences before and after the gaps for people, places, things, etc. that might correspond to the pronouns in the missing sentences.

# What did you learn out of school?

We learn things at school – of course! But we also gain a whole load of skills beyond the school gates. What skill or ability did you acquire from friends or family? Was it easy to learn? How old were you when you first learnt it? Tell us your stories!

525 people like this | 27 comments | share

**Adrian**

10 October - 17.32

When I was about 14, I went to stay with my older brother, who was at university. He had a set of juggling balls, and he taught me how to juggle. The thing about juggling is that learning how to do it is not enough. You have to practise a lot before you can do it well. It was OK, though – I had the time as my brother had quite a lot of studying to do. [ 1 ] It was really difficult at first, and I kept dropping the balls instead of catching them, but after three or four days, I started to get better.

**Stephanie**

10 October - 17.54

My skill's a bit like Adrian's because I had to practise for ages until I could do it properly, too. I suppose I was about eight when some older kids in the neighbourhood showed me how to do an 'ollie' on a skateboard. It's all about pushing the back of the skateboard down to the ground, and then lifting your front leg and bending your knee and your ankle. [ 2 ]

**Alexandra**

10 October - 18.23

Most people learn their times tables at school when they're about seven, but I learnt them at home – when I was three! [ 3 ] In the evenings, while my mum was getting dinner ready, she tested my sister. I just sat there quietly listening. I wasn't trying to learn them, but I did! One day a few weeks later, my mum was buying some new books for my sister and me. She was working out the prices of something and she said, 'So, that's seven times eight. Seven eights are ...' [ 4 ] The shop assistant was totally amazed!

**Daniel**

10 October - 18.25

You might think this is a bit boring, but one significant thing I learnt when I was quite young was the importance of writing a thank-you letter when someone gives you a present. [ 5 ] Now I'm older, it's great to get a short card or email from one of my young nieces or nephews when I've given them a present. It doesn't have to be long – just a few sentences saying thank you and sharing your news.

**Ed**

10 October - 18.28

Stephanie's post reminded me of what I learnt last summer, when we went on holiday to the north coast of Cornwall. For those of you who don't know it, it's famous for its waves. They're perfect for surfing. I was really lucky, because my cousin Bruce from Canada, who was with us, is a bit of an expert. [ 6 ] He was also responsible for deciding if the waves were right for a beginner like me, or if it was too dangerous. I learnt a huge amount in two weeks, and can't wait to go surfing again one day. I just wish everything we learn at school was as much fun!

**4** 1.07 **Read the text again. Choose which sentence A–G fits each gap 1–6. There is one extra sentence you do not need.**

A Before she could finish her sentence, I shouted out, '56'!
B It's great fun when you finally get the hang of it!
C While he was studying, I stood in front of the mirror and practised.
D He chose the boards we used and where to go.
E My older sister Emily was doing them at school.
F I took quite a few notes while she explained exactly what to do.
G Our parents always made us write them on our birthdays.

**5** **Write the highlighted words or phrases from the text which match these definitions.**

1 someone who knows a lot about a subject ______
2 similar to ______
3 lots of ______
4 made me remember ______
5 for a long time ______
6 correctly, the right way ______
7 learn, gain, get ______
8 completely ______

THINK | RESEARCH | CULTURE | LEARN | **ME**

Write your own short comment in response to the blog post and other comments in the text above.

## Grammar in context

**Look at the introduction and Adrian's post (including the removed sentence) on page 15 and do the following:**

1 Find eight verbs in the past simple affirmative.

2 Find an example of a question in the past simple.

3 Look at this sentence from the text. *In the evenings, while my mum was getting dinner ready, she tested my sister.*
Explain why we use the past continuous for the underlined words, not the past simple.

### REMEMBER

We use the past simple for:

- a single completed action or a series of completed actions – *I **wrote** her a thank you letter and she **replied** a week later.*
- a habit or repeated action – *She **practised** on her skateboard every day.*
- emphasis or to contradict something; in this situation, we use the auxiliary verb *did* + bare infinitive – *I **did finish** my homework last night, but I forgot to bring it to school.*

We use the past continuous for:

- an action or situation in progress – *The sun **was shining** when we arrived at the beach.*

▶ **See Grammar reference, Unit 2,** page 149

**1 Put the verbs into the correct tense, past simple or past continuous. Be careful! In some sentences, the verbs can be in the same form.**

1 We ____________ (**watch**) a video on YouTube when I ____________ (**realise**) I ____________ (**want**) to learn the guitar.

2 My dad ____________ (**not learn**) how to do up a tie until he ____________ (**go**) to work in a bank.

3 Pete ____________ (**learn**) that magic trick while he ____________ (**stay**) with his best friend, Simon.

4 I ____________ (**know**) how to make a sandwich but my little brother ____________ (**not know**).

5 Who ____________ (**teach**) you to tie your shoelaces?

6 ____________ (**you / wear**) a helmet when you ____________ (**fall off**) your bike?

7 When ____________ (**you / learn**) how to solve a Rubik's Cube?

8 Yes, I ____________ (**clean** [emphatic]) my teeth after breakfast, I promise!

**2 Complete the text with the past simple or past continuous form of the verbs in the box.**

| ask \| be \| decide \| get up |
|---|
| lead \| not realise \| practise |
| rain \| say \| suggest \| tickle |

### Tongue Twisters

When I (**1**) ____________ yesterday morning, it (**2**) ____________ heavily. My sister Tammy and I were bored because we couldn't go out, and because our internet was down, we couldn't chat with our friends either. We (**3**) ____________ Mum for suggestions and she (**4**) ____________ that when she was younger (in the days before the internet), she and her sister would play games on days like this to pass the time. She (**5**) ____________ we practise some tongue twisters:

'She sells seashells by the seashore.'
'How much wood could a woodchuck chuck if a woodchuck could chuck wood?'
'Fred fed Ted bread and Ted fed Fred bread.'
'Red lorry, yellow lorry.'

I (**6**) ____________ how difficult they were. Tammy (**7**) ____________ much better than me, so I (**8**) ____________ to make things a bit more difficult for her. While she (**9**) ____________ them, I (**10**) ____________ her! It's very difficult saying a tongue twister when you're being tickled too! And that (**11**) ____________ us to make up a new tongue twister: 'Tickling talkative Tammy made Tammy's tongue twisters trickier.'

THINK | RESEARCH | **CULTURE** | LEARN | ME

1.08 Listen to the tongue twisters in Exercise 2 and then try them yourself.

What tongue twisters do you know in your own language? Practise saying them in pairs.

## Words connected with *education/ learning*

**1** 1.09 **Write a verb from the box in the correct form to complete each sentence. There may be more than one correct answer for some gaps. Listen and check.**

| beat \| manage \| progress \| succeed |
|---|

1 The driving test was tough, so she was surprised that she __________ to pass it.
2 It's amazing. It's the first time we've __________ that team in five years.
3 After a lot of practice, I finally __________ in doing an 'ollie' on my skateboard.
4 At first I was terrible at juggling, but after two weeks I was __________ well.

| accomplish \| achieve<br>come first \| overcome |
|---|

5 The explorers __________ a lot of problems before they reached the South Pole.
6 I was pleased that Julia __________ in the class test because she had done a lot of revision.
7 I __________ a new best time for swimming 1000m at the weekend.
8 We __________ a lot this morning because everyone worked really hard.

| come last \| fail \| lose \| suffer |
|---|

9 Some of the players started crying when they __________ the final match.
10 I felt awful. I didn't expect to win the race but I didn't think I would __________ either.
11 Jack was really disappointed when he __________ his French exam for the second time.
12 My team __________ a painful defeat to England in the World Cup Final.

## Adjectives with *-ful / -ive*

**2** 1.10 **Write the adjective form of each word in the correct column. Listen and check.**

| ~~act~~ \| attract \| create \| effect<br>~~harm~~ \| pain \| play \| product<br>secret \| stress \| thank \| use |
|---|

| adjectives with *-ful* | adjectives with *-ive* |
|---|---|
| *harmful* | *active* |

**REMEMBER**

All the adjectives in Exercise 2 can become adverbs by adding *-ly*. Remember that adjectives usually describe things, but adverbs usually describe the verb or the whole sentence, and can also describe adjectives (***extremely** clever*) and other adverbs (***very** quickly*):

**3** **Write the correct form of the word (adjective or adverb) in each gap to complete the sentences.**

1 It's important for parents to encourage their kids to be __________ (**create**) from an early age.
2 Our puppy's really __________ (**play**) and lively.
3 I found surfing difficult at first but __________ (**thank**) it got easier the more I practised.
4 Being able to read a map is a very __________ (**use**) skill.
5 I'm not __________ (**act**) looking for a new guitar teacher but if you hear of a good one, let me know.
6 Do you think some video games are __________ (**harm**) to children's development?

## Phrasal verbs

**4** 1.11 **Look at the phrasal verbs in italics in these sentences and choose the best meaning. Listen and check.**

1 Learning some musical instruments helps you *build up* muscle strength.
**a)** decrease **b)** increase
2 I understood the instructions, but it was difficult to *carry* them *out* in practice.
**a)** follow **b)** remove
3 Sarah used to need arm-bands when she went swimming, but she's learnt to *do without* them now.
**a)** survive without having **b)** use in a different way
4 I didn't listen to Dad's directions and we *ended up* in the wrong place.
**a)** had to stop **b)** eventually arrived
5 The instructor told them to stop talking and *get on with* packing their equipment.
**a)** make progress **b)** have a good relationship
6 I don't know how you *put up with* such an annoying neighbour.
**a)** like, enjoy **b)** accept, allow
7 What did you *get up to* last night? Anything interesting?
**a)** do **b)** buy
8 I've no idea how you *go about* teaching a dog to dance!
**a)** travel around **b)** start and continue in the right way

# 2 LISTENING | Sentence completion

**1** **In pairs or as a group, look at the photo and answer the questions.**

1 The teenagers in the photo were on an 'adventure weekend'. What activities do you think they did? Come up with as many as possible.
2 Have you ever done activities like this? If yes, did you enjoy yourself? If no, would you like to?

**EXAM SKILL**

## Predicting missing information

- Predicting what you are listening for can help you decide on the correct answer.
- Before you listen, look at the gaps and decide what kind of word might complete each one. For example, question 1 in Exercise 4 is almost certainly a number. Question 2 might be an adjective.

**2** **Look at sentences 1–4 in Exercise 4. For each gap, cross out the options that you think <u>couldn't</u> fill the gap, and add one more option that could.**

1 fifteen ten happy many ________
2 cold old excited uncomfortable ________
3 teacher teachers guards tutor ________
4 stone stones metal weapon ________

**3** **Look at sentences 5–8 in Exercise 4. Write down as many words and phrases as possible that might fill each gap.**

5 ________________
6 ________________
7 ________________
8 ________________

**OPTIMISE YOUR EXAM**

## Sentence completion

- In this exam task you have to complete the sentences with the exact words you hear.
- You usually complete the sentence with between one and three words.
- Always read your completed sentences to make sure they make sense.

**4** 1.12 **Listen to teenager Julie Spencer talking about an adventure weekend. Complete the sentences with a word or short phrase.**

1 Julie spent the weekend with approximately ________ other teenagers.
2 The large hut they slept in was ________ .
3 Kelly was one of the ________ at the camp.
4 Julie says that 'flint' is a kind of ________ .
5 Julie now knows how to help someone with an ________ .
6 They would climb a rock face and then come down again ________ .
7 Julie describes the water in the lake as ________ .
8 Another skill they learnt was how to safely use ________ .

**5** 1.12 **Listen again and check your answers. Don't leave any gaps empty.**

**THINK** | RESEARCH | CULTURE | LEARN | ME

Imagine you could design a summer/weekend camp to teach you skills you want to learn. What kind of camp/skills would you choose?


▶ **Workbook Unit 2:** Listening, page 16, exercises 1, 2, 3

# GRAMMAR 2 | *Would, used to, be used to*

## Grammar in context

**Match each sentence from the audio in the listening lesson with its description.**

1 *They would take us into the forest.*
2 *I used to be in the Girl Guides.*
3 *I'm used to swimming in a swimming pool.*

**a)** This describes a situation which the speaker is familiar with at the moment. ____
**b)** This describes a repeated action in the past. ____
**c)** This describes a state which was true but isn't true anymore. ____

### REMEMBER

- To talk about past habits we can use *would / used to* + bare infinitive:
  *When I was young, I* ***would*** *always* ***go*** *swimming on Saturdays.*
  *When I was young, I always* ***used to go*** *swimming on Saturdays.*
- To talk about past states we can use *used to* but we can't use *would*:
  *I* ***used to*** *like playing the trumpet, but I'm not so keen now.*
- To talk about something that is familiar/normal or not strange to us, we can use *be used to* + *-ing* form/noun:
  ***I'm used to writing*** *thank-you letters so they don't take me long.*
  *She****'s used to cold water*** *so swimming in the ocean doesn't bother her.*

▶ **See Grammar reference, Unit 2,** page 149

**1 Choose the correct word or phrase. Be careful! Sometimes both words and phrases are correct.**

1 I'm not used to **make** / **making** my own breakfast.
2 My mum **used to** / **would** help me get dressed in the morning.
3 When I was younger, I **would always** / **always used to** sleep with a light on.
4 Lucas never used **listen** / **to listen** to rap music before Emma lent him a CD.
5 **Are** / **Did** you used to getting up at five in the morning or is it still difficult?
6 In the holidays, we **didn't use** / **wouldn't** go to bed until about 11 o'clock at night!
7 The girls **would** / **used to** spend hours every day riding their bikes.
8 I help mum at home and I **used** / **'m used** to washing and ironing my own clothes.

**2 Rewrite the underlined words using *used to*, *be used to* or *would*. Sometimes there is more than one answer.**

1 When Diana was a teenager, she was quite shy.
______________________________
2 But secretly, Diana dreamt of being a famous comedian.
______________________________
3 She spent hours reading joke books, and practising telling jokes in front of the mirror.
______________________________
4 She didn't tell any jokes at school though, because of her shyness.
______________________________
5 Today, she is a famous and successful comedian; she feels comfortable telling jokes in front of thousands of people!
______________________________
6 She still feels strange when people recognise her in the street and ask her to tell them a joke.
______________________________

**SAY IT RIGHT**

**Resource centre: Unit 2**
Pronunciation of *use(d)*

THINK | RESEARCH | CULTURE | LEARN | **ME**

In pairs, discuss two things:
- you used to do but don't do now.
- you're used to doing.

▶ **Workbook Unit 2:** Grammar 2, page 15, exercises 1, 2

Talk2Me

One key difference is …

**Flipped classroom**

**1** **Watch the *Talk2Me* video and answer the questions.**

1 Who prefers learning at school? What reasons do they give?
2 Why do some people prefer to be taught by a person NOT in their family?
3 Who prefers working in a small group? What reasons do they give?

**2** **Watch the video again. Underline the time expressions in the *Phrase expert* box that you hear on the video.**

**PHRASE EXPERT**

Another way they are similar is … | Both types of … are … | … is far … than … | It isn't as … as … | One key difference is … | One obvious similarity between them is … | One way they differ is …

**3** **In pairs, answer the questions.**

- Write a list of some of the things you've learnt at school and things you've learnt at home.
- What are the key differences between learning at school and at home? Which do you prefer?

**EXAM SKILL**

**Comparing**

- In speaking exams, you sometimes have to compare photos. This means using appropriate language to talk about similarities and differences between them.
- Focus on the main ideas represented by the photos, not small irrelevant details.

**4** **Complete the sentences with a word from the box.**

as | both | differ | key | similarity | whereas

1 One obvious ___________ between them is that you can learn things at home and at school.
2 To start with, you need to be motivated for ___________.
3 One ___________ difference between them is who decides what you learn.
4 In the classroom, the teacher does all the planning, ___________ for self-study you have to do it all.
5 Another way in which they ___________ is that teachers are experts in their subject.
6 Studying on your own isn't ___________ formal as studying with a teacher.

**5** **In pairs, look at these two photographs which show people learning in different ways. Make notes to answer the questions.**

A

B

1 What are the similarities between the photos?
___________
2 What are the differences between the photos?
___________
3 What might be good about the way the people are learning in Photo A?
___________
4 What might be good about the way the person is learning in Photo B?
___________

**OPTIMISE YOUR EXAM**

**Photo task**

- Don't worry if you don't know or can't remember a particular word or phrase, for example, in Photo B the game 'chess'.
- It's fine to say you don't know something – try to find another way to express it . For example: *This picture shows two people playing a game. I can't remember the name but it is a board game with black and white pieces, and strategy is very important.*

**6** **Talk on your own for about a minute. Compare the two photographs in Exercise 5 and say what might be good about learning in these ways.**



▶ **Workbook Unit 2:** Speaking, pages 16–17, exercises 1, 2, 3

## EXAM SKILL

### Verbs (1)

- Some exam tasks test your understanding of different verb forms, e.g. specific tenses, auxiliary verbs, participle forms, phrasal verbs and their particles, and modal verbs.
- When you need to complete a gap in a text, check if part of a verb or verb pattern is missing.

**1 Complete the sentences with the correct word or phrase. Then choose the correct words in the explanations in italics.**

1 ______________ you going to take the exam next week?
*This is talking about the future, so we need a(n)* ***auxiliary / modal*** *verb in the present simple to fill the gap.*

2 Dan, ______________ you help me repair my bike, please?
*This is a request for help, so we need a* ***positive word / modal verb*** *to fill the gap.*

3 When my grandparents were young, they ______________ used to wear seatbelts, but now it's compulsory.
*This is contrasting the past with now, so we need a(n)* ***auxiliary verb / negative word*** *to fill the gap.*

4 I ______________ several mistakes in the test, but thankfully I still passed.
*Although there were several mistakes, we see making them as a single, completed action in the past, so we need a(n)* ***main / auxiliary*** *verb in the past simple to fill the gap.*

5 Elaine ______________ hoping they'd ask her to sing a solo, but they didn't.
*This is the past continuous, so we need a(n)* ***modal / auxiliary*** *verb in the past simple to fill the gap.*

6 I don't know how you put ______________ with Phillip's constant complaining!
*This is a phrasal verb, so we need a* ***particle / verb*** *to fill the gap.*

**2 Write down any other words that could fill each gap in Exercise 1.**

1 ______________________________
2 ______________________________
3 ______________________________
4 ______________________________
5 ______________________________
6 ______________________________

## OPTIMISE YOUR EXAM

### Open cloze

- This task tests range of grammar, including verbs and set phrases.
- Other parts of speech tested include prepositions, articles, pronouns, possessive adjectives and quantifiers.

**3 Read the task in Exercise 4 and decide:**

**a)** which gaps need verbs / verb forms. ________
**b)** which gaps needs other parts of speech. ________

**4 Write one word in each gap.**

**My dancing dog**

It was when I **(1)** __________ watching a documentary about animals with strange skills when I decided I could try to teach our dog Topsy to dance! The problem was I had no idea how to go **(2)** __________ it. I knew it would probably take a long time for us to make **(3)** __________ , and that I had to do it right. I'm **(4)** __________ used to teaching animals, so I did some research first. It turns out there's a whole load **(5)** __________ information online about it. You have to build **(6)** __________ the dog's skills slowly by teaching one move at a time. At first Topsy was resistant and **(7)** __________ not carry out any of my instructions. It was really frustrating! Then I decided that she needed rewards to motivate her, so I ended **(8)** __________ giving her a biscuit every time she learnt a move. That did the trick and she soon took to it like a duck to water. She knows loads of tricks now. Who knows? Maybe we'll be as famous as Ashleigh and Pudsey one day. They won Britain's Got Talent!

**THINK** | RESEARCH | CULTURE | LEARN | ME

Make a list of animals that humans can train.
What can we train them to do?

## 2 WRITING | A letter / An email

**1** **In pairs or as a group, answer the questions.**

1. When was the last time you gave someone some advice? Who was it?
2. What was the situation? What was the advice? How did you give it (in an email, by text or by talking to them)?
3. Did they take your advice? What happened in the end?

**EXAM SKILL**

### Giving advice

- For some writing tasks you have to imagine that someone you know has asked for your advice.
- Use a variety of advice words, phrases and grammatical structures. Some of these appear in exercises 2 and 7.
- Try to give sensible advice and explain your suggestions.

**2** **Read this letter then choose T (True) or F (False) for the statements.**

*Dear Molly,*

*It was great to hear from you! I'm so glad you had a good birthday. I loved the photos!*

*Anyway, you asked for my advice on choosing a language school in the UK. I agree that it'll really help your English, and you'll have great fun too. One thing you should do is think about where in the UK you want to go to. Why not make a list of all the things you'd like to see and do there? You might find that it'll help you choose between, say, London and Edinburgh!*

*If I were you, I'd do a lot of research. Make sure you check how much they charge, as some schools are more expensive than others. One idea is to contact some local language schools and ask them about costs.*

*Finally, my advice is to not make the decision on your own. Ask your English teacher and your parents to help you, and see what other students say online about their experiences.*

*I hope these ideas help. I have to go now because dinner is ready. Write soon!*

*Lots of love,*

*Hannah*

1. Hannah starts the letter by giving the first piece of advice. **T / F**
2. She refers to something that Molly wrote in her last letter. **T / F**
3. She gives three main pieces of advice. **T / F**
4. Each main piece of advice is given in a separate paragraph. **T / F**
5. She just gives her main advice without any further explanation. **T / F**

**3** **Find and underline all the words/phrases in the letter which give advice. Tick which of the following are used:**

1. a modal ☐
2. a question ☐
3. a conditional ☐
4. a causative ☐
5. an imperative ☐

**OPTIMISE YOUR EXAM**

### A letter / An email

- The letter you need to write in this exam task is to an English-speaking friend, so your overall style needs to be friendly and chatty.
- As well as answering the question, look for ways to include the kind of informal language that you would use if you were writing to a real-life friend.

**4** **Look at the writing task below. In pairs or as a group, discuss the problem. What advice would you give Lucy?**

You have received a letter from an English-speaking friend.

*Also, I need your advice. I'm in a band with two other friends from school. We usually just play for fun at home. Now the other two want us to enter a talent show on TV, but I'm not sure if I want to. Do you think it's a good idea? If I say 'no', I think my friends might be very unhappy.*
*What do you think I should do?*

*Write soon,*
*Lucy*

Write your **letter**.

**5** Complete with your advice for Lucy.

I think Lucy should:
1)
2)
3)

**6** Read the model text in Exercise 2 again and answer the questions.

1 What is the purpose/function of each paragraph?

___

2 Which phrases/expressions in the model text could you use for the exam task in Exercise 4?

___

3 Can you think of any other phrases that you could use to begin or end an informal letter?

___

## 7 Plan

**Complete the paragraph plan.**

| Part | Purpose | Useful phrases | My notes |
|---|---|---|---|
| **First line** | greet the person you are writing to | *Dear* ____ *,*<br>*Hi* ____ *!* | |
| **Paragraph 1** | thank the other person for their letter and refer to a piece of news | *Thanks for your letter.*<br>*It was great to hear from you.*<br>*I'm glad you had a good party / passed your test,* etc. | |
| **Paragraph 2** | give your first piece of advice | *You asked for my advice on/about …*<br>*You asked me about …* | |
| **Paragraphs 3/4** | give further advice | *One thing you might/should do is …*<br>*Have you thought about …?*<br>*You could always …*<br>*Why not …? How about …?*<br>*If I were you, I'd …*<br>*You should also think about …* | |
| **Closing expressions 1** | say you hope it helps and offer to help further / ask them to reply | *Hope that helps! Let me know if you need …*<br>*Write soon!* | |
| **Closing expressions 2** | express love, etc. | *Love,*<br>*Lots of love,*<br>*Best wishes,* | |
| **Your name** | first name | | |

## 8 Write

**Write your letter in an appropriate style. Write 140–190 words.**

## 9 Check

**Before you hand in your letter, complete this checklist.**

**Checklist**

- ◯ I've started with an informal greeting.
- ◯ I've thanked the person for their letter / referred to their news.
- ◯ I've given three or four main pieces of advice.
- ◯ I've used good phrases to give advice.
- ◯ I've written at least four paragraphs.
- ◯ I've ended the letter in an informal way.
- ◯ I've checked my spelling and grammar.

PROGRESS CHECK **UNITS 1–2**

## GRAMMAR AND VOCABULARY

**1** **Write a form of the word in capitals in each gap.**

**TECHNOLOGY AND EDUCATION**

| | |
|---|---|
| It has become very (**1**) ___________ to claim that technology is going to | **FASHION** |
| completely change education. It's an (**2**) ___________ idea. It seems that | **ATTRACT** |
| technology appeals to younger people, so it's not (**3**) ___________ to think | **REASON** |
| that technology will help young people learn. However, there may be | |
| (**4**) ___________ effects of relying on technology to learn. Young people | **HARM** |
| these days are often (**5**) ___________ on their gadgets in many ways and | **DEPEND** |
| find it (**6**) ___________ to be without them. This would be even worse if the | **STRESS** |
| gadgets played an (**7**) ___________ role in their education. We have to ask if | **ACT** |
| students will be as (**8**) ___________ with gadgets in the classroom as they | **PRODUCE** |
| are without gadgets. | |

__/8

**2** **Write one word in each gap.**

1 I've been waiting ___________ ages! Where have you been?
2 I think you should ___________ my advice and speak to her.
3 Do you find that certain songs remind ___________ of different people?
4 I've finally ___________ to a decision! I'm going to the USA!
5 Do you think skateboarding is a ___________ like snowboarding?
6 Have you ___________ any of your holiday photos on Instagram?
7 Make sure you ___________ off your laptop before you go upstairs.
8 Could you ___________ me a favour and pass me the dictionary?
9 We've made excellent ___________ with our IT project this week!
10 Tess ___________ to have a whole weekend without using any of her gadgets!

__/10

**3** **Write each verb in the correct tense in each gap.**

1 I can't talk now because I ______________ . I'll call you back. (**study**)
2 ______________ any pets when you were little? (**you / have**)
3 What ______________ ? Oh, yes! I'm having a party! (**I / say**)
4 Leo and I both ______________ at school at the same time each morning. (**arrive**)
5 We ______________ dinner and then sat down to watch TV together. (**eat**)
6 What ______________ when I texted you last night? (**you / do**)
7 This time last year, I ______________ with my aunt in Paris. (**live**)
8 My brother ______________ as a waiter until he finds a permanent job. (**work**)
9 I ______________ when the teacher told us that the exam was over. (**still / write**)
10 My parents ______________ married two years before I was born. (**get**)

__/10

## 4 Put the verbs into the correct form to complete the sentences.

1 After an hour's studying, I stopped ______________ a break. (**take**)
2 I really regret ______________ to do my French homework last night. (**forget**)
3 You did remember ______________ on the alarm, didn't you? (**turn**)
4 Do you prefer ______________ games on your tablet or PC? (**play**)
5 I really tried ______________ the article, but it was too complicated for me. (**understand**)
6 Do you mind my ______________ the door? (**close**)
7 I don't feel like ______________ anything today, do you? (**do**)
8 My teacher's promised ______________ us know our exam results as soon as she can. (**let**)
9 Everyone attempted ______________ a small robot. (**make**)
10 I didn't mean ______________ you. (**disturb**)

__/10

## 5 Complete the second sentence so it has a similar meaning to the first. Do not change the word given. Use two to five words, including the word given.

1 Let's try to agree before the end of the meeting. **COME**
Let's try to ____________________ before the end of the meeting.
2 You should stop playing games and continue to do your homework. **GET**
You should stop playing games and ____________________ your homework.
3 I hope you're making good progress with your revision. **ON**
I hope you're ____________________ well with your revision.
4 I understand what you're saying, but I disagree. **TAKE**
I ____________________ , but I disagree.
5 My mum often drove us to school in the morning. **DRIVE**
My mum ____________________ us to school in the morning.
6 I don't know how you allow your cat to bite you like that. **PUT**
I don't know how you ____________________ your cat biting you like that.

__/12

**Total score** __/50

## EXAM SKILLS

**Tick the statements that are true for you. Review the skills in the unit if you need more help.**

| I can ... | Unit/page |
|---|---|
| ☐ understand the writer's purpose in an article | Unit 1 p4 |
| ☐ listen for agreement in conversations | Unit 1 p8 |
| ☐ talk about habits | Unit 1 p10 |
| ☐ recognise some word patterns and use them in sentence transformations | Unit 1 p11 |
| ☐ use phrases for agreeing and disagreeing in an essay | Unit 1 p12 |
| ☐ understand pronoun references in blog posts | Unit 2 p14 |
| ☐ predict missing information in a short talk | Unit 2 p18 |
| ☐ compare pictures in a photo task | Unit 2 p20 |
| ☐ understand different forms of verbs and apply them in an open-cloze exercise | Unit 2 p21 |
| ☐ use the correct language to give advice in a letter / an email | Unit 2 p22 |

# 3 Viral video

## READING | Multiple matching | An online article

**1 In pairs or as a group, answer the questions.**

1 Do you ever watch videos online? What kind of videos do you like?

2 Describe a video you have seen online. Say why you like it.

3 Do you follow or subscribe to any online video channels?

> **EXAM SKILL**
>
> ### Scanning
>
> - Scanning means reading a text in order to find a specific piece of information. You don't need to read every word. You just need to find the relevant section with the information you want.
> - Make sure you understand exactly what information you are looking for.
> - Read the text by jumping quickly from paragraph to paragraph, looking for key words related to the information you want. Then read that part more carefully to find the specific information.

**2 Scan the article as quickly as you can to answer the questions.**

1 What online names do Emiliano and Bunny use?

____________________

2 When did Greyson and Jack first post videos?

____________________

3 Which countries are Bunny and Jack from?

____________________

**3 In pairs, say what these numbers represent.**

1 16
2 1,400
3 190,000
4 500,000
5 6,000,000
6 8,000,000

> **OPTIMISE YOUR EXAM**
>
> ### Multiple matching
>
> - Read the text quickly once to get the general meaning.
> - For each question, underline the specific information you are looking for. For example, in the first option in the exam task opposite, you would underline 'energetic personality'.
> - Then scan the text to find key words or phrases related to the underlined words.

# YouTube STARS

We know you love watching YouTube, but did you know that you can make serious money through it? Get enough people watching your channel, or upload a video that goes viral, and you might make a lot of money from the ads on your page. Here are a few people who've made it. And so could you!

## A JACK HARRIES

Jacksgap is a successful YouTube vlog (video blog) channel, started in July 2011 by Jack Harries from the UK to record his travel experiences during his gap year. He was soon joined by his twin brother, Finn, and by September 2012, the channel had 190,000 subscribers and over 8 million views. In fact, the advertising revenue they made covered the cost of the boys' travels in Thailand. With over 4 million subscribers and an official website, Jacksgap now includes vlogs that encourage social and environmental awareness, and raises money for various charities.

## B GREYSON CHANCE

To be successful as a musician, you have to spend years practising and playing small concerts before you make it big, right? Wrong! Back in 2010, someone uploaded a video onto YouTube of a 12-year-old boy playing piano and singing at a school concert in the US. The boy was Greyson Chance, and the song in the video was a cover of Lady Gaga's Paparazzi. Initially, only a few people saw the video, until chat show host Ellen DeGeneres heard about it. What followed next was a dream come true for Greyson: an appearance on the TV show, a phone call with Lady Gaga, millions of views of his videos, money, fame and awards, tours of the US and Asia, and a recording contract. And it all started on YouTube!

## C BUNNY MEYER

It's increasingly common to see vloggers reviewing everyday products and one of the most popular is Bunny Meyer from Texas, USA, also known as grav3yardgirl, who has 6 million fans. Bunny is known for her series 'Does this thing really work?', where she tests beauty products that have been advertised on TV. Some of her videos have been viewed almost 5 million times each and her fans (the 'swamp family'!) love her excited, crazy style and attitude, and often comment on her videos. And no wonder she loves her fans – they help her make around half a million dollars a year!

## D EMILIANO RODOLFO ROSALES-BIROU

'Let's Play', or 'LP', is a term that gamers use for videos of someone playing a video game. LPers record themselves playing the game and talking about it at the same time. They edit their videos, put them online, and their viewers watch them to learn what they should do in the game, or maybe just for fun! Chuggaaconroy (real name Emiliano Rodolfo Rosales-Birou) from the USA is a good example. Starting in 2006 aged 16, and specialising in Nintendo games, Emiliano's videos quickly gained popularity. By the end of 2013 he had posted over 1,400 videos and he remains popular today with over 1 million subscribers. If you're a really keen gamer, you ought to think about making some videos of your own!

**4** 1.13 **Read the article. For each question, choose from the people A–D. The people may be chosen more than once.**

**Which person**

- is liked for their energetic personality? 1 ____
- cooperates with a family member? 2 ____
- has left their country to perform? 3 ____
- wants their channel to make the world a better place? 4 ____
- gives their opinion about things you can buy? 5 ____
- paid for a holiday with the money earned? 6 ____
- has been interviewed on a chat show? 7 ____
- probably discusses strategy and gives viewers tips? 8 ____

**5 Find words and phrases in the article to complete these sentences. Change the form of the word or phrase where necessary.**

1. Your page on YouTube where people go to watch your videos is called your ____________ . (intro)
2. When a video ____________ ____________ , it becomes suddenly very popular online. (intro)
3. ____________ is the money/profits you make in a business. (para A)
4. People who play video games very often are known as ____________ . (para D)
5. When you ____________ a video, you take out parts you don't want and make the final video. (para D)
6. People who watch an online video or a TV show are known as ____________ . (para D)
7. When you ____________ a video to YouTube, you put it there for other people to see. (para B/D)
8. When you ____________ on something online, you write something that expresses your opinion. (para C)

THINK | RESEARCH | **CULTURE** | LEARN | ME

What YouTube and/or Vimeo videos are popular with you and your friends?

What vlogs do you know about or follow?

# 3 GRAMMAR 1 | Modals (1): review

## Grammar in context

**Look at the introduction on page 27 and find two modal verbs.**

1 What are the verbs? __________ __________

2 Which of the following do they express? ___

**a)** criticism

**b)** possibility

**c)** obligation

**d)** permission

**REMEMBER**

- Modals are auxiliary verbs which express ideas such as ability/possibility (*can, could*), advice or criticism (*should(n't), ought (not) to*), obligation (*must, have to*) and permission (*can, could, may, be allowed to*). They are followed by the bare infinitive.

▶ **See Grammar reference, Unit 3,** page 150

**1 Choose the best modal to complete each sentence.**

1 You __________ click 'upload' when you finish recording, to put your video online.

**a)** have to **b)** may **c)** shouldn't

2 I __________ watch videos online at home because the connection is too slow.

**a)** mightn't **b)** can't **c)** don't have to

3 You __________ watch this Vimeo video – it's really funny!

**a)** should **b)** might **c)** could

4 __________ I borrow your tablet to check something online?

**a)** Ought **b)** Could **c)** Must

5 Twenty years ago, you __________ go to one single website to watch lots of videos.

**a)** mightn't **b)** shouldn't **c)** couldn't

6 Hey! You __________ press the screen like that.

**a)** shouldn't **b)** couldn't **c)** haven't

7 Editing videos __________ be difficult at first.

**a)** should **b)** has to **c)** can

8 Tom's new video __________ be online now. Let's check.

**a)** can **b)** should **c)** mustn't

**2 Complete each sentence with a modal from the box. Sometimes there is more than one answer.**

| can't | could | might | ought | should |
|---|---|---|---|---|

1 Young people __________ to spend less time watching things online and __________ get out and do something more active.

2 People __________ watch online videos to learn new skills as an alternative to TV.

3 It __________ be interesting to try to make a living from uploading videos.

4 You __________ expect to have a career on YouTube, so it's OK as a hobby, but you really have to focus on getting a good job.

**3 In pairs, look at the sentences in Exercise 2 again. Compare and discuss your answers.**

**4 Complete the blog post with appropriate modal verbs. Sometimes there is more than one answer.**

## Bea's blog

I (**1**) __________ admit it – I am addicted to YouTube. In particular, watching video game walkthroughs. You know, when people video themselves playing a game, giving a commentary, to show you how to do it. I (**2**) __________ get enough of them. I spend about two hours a day watching. I suppose I (**3**) __________ cut down. My sister makes fun of me, but they are so entertaining. In fact, I think I (**4**) __________ record my own videos. I mean, I have completed lots of games and I think I have a good sense of humour. How hard (**5**) __________ it be? It (**6**) __________ even be the start of a new career. Some of the people who upload these videos make money out of them. The only problem is time. The videos (**7**) __________ take hours to make and with all the homework I (**8**) __________ do for my final exams, I simply don't have the time.

▼ read more

THINK | RESEARCH | CULTURE | LEARN | **ME**

In pairs, discuss three examples for each of the following:

- things you should do more often
- things you can do well
- things that you have to do but don't enjoy doing

*I should upload photos from my phone to my Instagram account more regularly.*



▶ **Workbook Unit 3:** Grammar 1, page 22, exercises 1, 2, 3

## Nouns with *-ity* / *-ness*

**REMEMBER**

Be careful! Sometimes when we add a suffix like *-ity* or *-ness*, we need to make other changes to the spelling. For example, *active – activity*.

**1** 1.14 **Write the noun form of each adjective in the correct column. Make any necessary spelling changes. Listen and check.**

~~active~~ | ~~aware~~ | clever | complex | creative | happy | open | original | popular | simple | weak | youthful

| nouns with *-ity* | nouns with *-ness* |
|---|---|
| *activity* | *awareness* |

**2** **Write a noun from Exercise 1 in each gap to complete the sentences.**

1 We've put a video on the internet raising ___________ of bullying at school.
2 She talks about her personal problems with incredible ___________ .
3 I'm not surprised by the ___________ of video sites such as Veoh and Vimeo.
4 My mum has a real ___________ for funny cat videos.
5 Most good music videos combine ___________ and ___________ .
6 I love the ___________ of vlogging, with just one person talking to a camera in their bedroom.

## Collocations with verbs

**3** 1.15 **Complete each phrase or collocation in italics with the words in the box. Listen and check.**

do | find | go | have | make | take (× 2) | tell

1 It will ___________ *you good* to get out and meet your friends once in a while.
2 I watched his Vube channel, but I didn't ___________ *it funny*.
3 It was fun to ___________ *part in* my friend's latest video.
4 I often ___________ *friends round*, and we play games or watch videos online.
5 You should ___________ *a break* and do something fun, like watching a DVD.
6 Why don't we ___________ *online* and see if there are any funny videos to watch?
7 I can't really ___________ *jokes* very well, so I wouldn't be a very good comedian.
8 You shouldn't ___________ *fun of* people in your videos. It's not nice.

**4** **Explain the meaning of the collocations above.**

## *TV programmes*

**5** 1.16 **Match the TV shows in the box to the extracts. Listen and check.**

chat show | cookery show | documentary | game show | music show | reality show | sitcom | soap opera | talent show | the news | weather forecast | wildlife programme

1 … tell us about your new film … ___________
2 … they're hiding! That's so funny! ___________
3 … we'll learn about the origins of … ___________
4 … and you might win a new car! ___________
5 … and the thief got away with over a million euros! ___________
6 … I don't love you anymore. I love Tom and … ___________
7 … the amazing Clare and her dancing dog! ___________
8 … deep in the forest the tiger is hunting … ___________
9 … in the studio tonight we've got Adele and … ___________
10 … a lot of rain in the south, and winds of … ___________
11 … stir in the mushrooms then bake … ___________
12 … one of the housemates will leave the house … ___________

# 3 LISTENING | Multiple matching

**1** **In pairs, imagine you are going to interview someone who has a successful video channel. Decide what questions to ask.**

## EXAM SKILL

### Identifying attitude (1)

- In some listening tasks, you need to listen for a speaker's view or their attitude towards something.
- Look for questions asking you about opinions, where speakers are more likely to express a view or an attitude.
- Remember that the words speakers use are often different from the ones in the questions.

**2** **Look at the task in Exercise 4 and read the statements A–H. Circle the letter of the statements which refer to a speaker's opinion.**

**3** **Match the correct synonym from the list below for each word/phrase.**

| | |
|---|---|
| 1 not easy ____ | a) annoying |
| 2 feel like a different person ____ | b) surprised |
| 3 get bored ____ | c) hard/difficult |
| 4 amazed ____ | d) have a different personality |
| 5 really interested ____ | e) enjoy |
| 6 have fun ____ | f) lose interest |
| 7 be yourself ____ | g) fascinated |
| 8 frustrating ____ | h) act naturally |

## OPTIMISE YOUR EXAM

### Multiple matching

- The first time you listen, make a note of which statement you think matches the speaker you are listening to. If you're not sure, make a note of all the possible answers.
- The second time you listen, focus on the differences between these possible answers, and choose the answer you think fits best.

**4** 1.17 **You will hear five extracts about YouTube. Choose from A–H what each speaker says about it. There are three extra letters you do not need.**

**A** I don't make any money from my videos.
**B** One of my videos became really popular.
**C** Making videos for YouTube wasn't as easy as I thought.
**D** I think people who perform on YouTube should be themselves.
**E** I don't have the time to create my own videos anymore.
**F** I feel like a different person when I'm making videos.
**G** Lots of people enjoy my vlog about my life and my friends.
**H** I prefer watching videos to making them.

**Speaker 1:** ☐
**Speaker 2:** ☐
**Speaker 3:** ☐
**Speaker 4:** ☐
**Speaker 5:** ☐

**5** 1.17 **Listen again and check your answers. Note down the words and phrases which help you choose the answer.**

**Speaker 1:** ____________________
**Speaker 2:** ____________________
**Speaker 3:** ____________________
**Speaker 4:** ____________________
**Speaker 5:** ____________________

THINK | **RESEARCH** | CULTURE | LEARN | ME

Go online and find information about someone who has a YouTube channel.

Tell the class what you find out.


▶ **Workbook Unit 3:** Listening, page 24, exercises 1, 2, 3

# GRAMMAR 2 | Modals (2): deductions about the present

## Grammar in context

**Look at this sentence from the audio in the listening lesson and answer the questions.**

*People must be interested in that because the video went viral!*

1 Does the speaker think people are interested in the thing they're talking about?
2 Why does the speaker think that?
3 Which other modals do we use to make deductions?

**REMEMBER**

- We use modals to make deductions. That means we look at some evidence and we decide that something is certainly or possibly true (or not true).
- When we are certain, we use *must* or *can't*. When we think something is possible but we are not certain, we use *can*, *could* or *might*.

▶ **See Grammar reference, Unit 3,** page 151

### 1 Complete the sentences with an appropriate modal.

1 I hope you get millions of viewers on your new video channel! You __________ make a lot of money from it!
2 Liam's posts on Facebook __________ be very popular, or he'd have more 'likes'.
3 I'm not sure what's wrong with my tablet, but this button __________ be broken. It doesn't seem to do anything.
4 Today it says that over a million people have watched my video, but that __________ be right. It was only 10,000 yesterday!
5 Your phone just made a noise. Someone __________ be trying to contact you.
6 Did Freddie really spend four hours uploading videos? His eyes __________ be tired from looking at the screen for so long!

### 2 Write what you would say.

1 You are sure that the person in the video isn't Josh because he wasn't there.

**A:** Is that Josh in your video?
**B:** __________

2 You are sure that Amy is here because you saw her car.

**A:** Have you seen Amy?
**B:** __________

3 You think it's possible that your friend's tablet is in the classroom.

**A:** I can't find my tablet!
**B:** __________

4 You think that the bag your friend has found belongs to Sophie.

**A:** Do you know whose this bag is?
**B:** __________

5 You are sure your friend Harry is ill in bed at home.

**A:** I've just seen Harry in the school library.
**B:** __________

### 3 Write one word in each gap.

New Topic | Add to Favourites | Mark as Read | Close

**Ruth** ★★★★
Posts: 692 | Join time: 04/03/16 15:12

***Posted:*** *18:35 on 15th June*

**I finally discovered ooVoo!**

I've just discovered ooVoo and if you're like me, and you enjoy messaging friends, this is an app you (**1**) ____ really like.

As with all apps, you (**2**) ____ download it before you can actually use it, but it's free so it doesn't cost anything to give it a try.

OoVoo can be used for video calls – and I love the fact that with this app I can chat to up to 12 friends anywhere in the world at the same time. Of course, you (**3**) ____ prefer not to use video while you're chatting. That's not a problem. Using ooVoo doesn't mean you (**4**) ____ use video to chat; it just means you have the option.

You can also make ordinary voice calls and send texts. And it's very easy to use – my friend's brother (**5**) ____ be more than six years old and he uses it to chat to his grandparents in Australia!

Post Reply — Page 1 of 3 ▶

THINK | RESEARCH | CULTURE | LEARN | **ME**

Write three present deductions using modals related to your life.

In pairs, compare and discuss your answers.

*It's three o'clock, so my mum must be at work.*

Talk2Me
Why don't we …?

Flipped classroom

**1** ▷ **Watch the *Talk2Me* video and note down which of the questions below the students talk about, and their opinions.**

1 What useful skills can you learn from playing games online?
2 What can you learn from chatting to people around the world?
3 Do you learn any useful skills from making videos online?

**2** ▷ **Watch the video again. Underline the phrases in the *Phrase expert* box that you hear on the video.**

**PHRASE EXPERT**

How about | I suggest we | might choose | One thing we | What about | Why don't we

**3 Note down things you might learn or gain from doing each activity in the list.**

making videos for sites like YouTube
*how to edit videos using a computer* __________
researching information online
__________
playing games online
__________
chatting online to people around the world
__________
using social networking sites
__________

**EXAM SKILL**

## Making suggestions

- In speaking exams, you sometimes have to make suggestions when you are talking to another candidate.

**4 Choose the correct words.**

1 One thing we **might** / **shall** consider is making Youtube videos.
2 How **about** / **for** chatting to people around the world?
3 So **which** / **what** about using social networking sites?
4 Why **not** / **don't** we talk about online games then? I am not sure you learn anything from them.
5 In fact, I suggest we **choose** / **choosing** playing online games as the number one way to learn skills via the internet.

**5 In pairs, take turns to make suggestions for YouTube videos you could make together.**

**OPTIMISE YOUR EXAM**

## Collaborative task

- In collaborative tasks, you should express your opinions and suggestions clearly and say whether you agree or disagree with your partner.
- Don't worry if your partner's English is not as good as yours, or if they don't speak much. You are marked on your own performance separately from the other candidate.

**6 Talk in pairs for two minutes. Follow the instructions.**

Here are some things that students might do online and a question for you to discuss. Talk to each other about whether students learn useful skills online.

Do students learn useful skills online?

- making videos for YouTube
- researching information
- playing games online
- chatting to people around the world
- using social networking sites

**7 In pairs, you have about a minute to decide which two things most help students learn useful skills online. Write your choices below.**

1 __________
2 __________

**SAY IT RIGHT**

**Resource centre: Unit 3**
Sentence stress

EXAM SKILL

## Nouns (1)

- Some nouns are formed using a suffix, such as *-ity*, and others by making spelling changes to the verb, e.g. *live* (v) → *life* (n).
- Sometimes more than one noun exists in a word family, e.g. *teacher* (person), *teaching* (activity).
- Nouns for people are often formed by adding *-er* to the verb (*teach* → *teacher*).

**1 Write the nouns for these words. There may be more than one.**

1 achieve ________
2 believe ________
3 capable ________
4 choose ________
5 create ________
6 decide ________
7 give ________
8 lose ________
9 natural ________
10 personal ________
11 sad ________
12 think ________

**2 Write a word from Exercise 1 in each gap.**

1 I share your ________ that most online video channels are just a waste of time.
2 The first prize in the film competition was great, but the ________ got nothing.
3 There's something about Leo's ________ I love. He always seems to have lots of fun.
4 Do you think that if sites like YouTube or DailyMotion disappeared tomorrow it would be a great ________ ?
5 I watched her talk about her problems in an online video and I shared her ________ .
6 The ________ of the Vube channel finally decided to close it down.

OPTIMISE YOUR EXAM

## Word formation

- Word formation tasks often include at least one negative word.
- Negative forms usually have a prefix at the beginning, e.g. *un-*, *in-*, *dis-*, etc.

**3 Look at the text in Exercise 4. For each gap, decide what kind of word (noun, adjective, etc.) is probably required. Then tick the gaps you think might need negatives.**

1 ________ ☐
2 ________ ☐
3 ________ ☐
4 ________ ☐
5 ________ ☐
6 ________ ☐
7 ________ ☐
8 ________ ☐

**4 Write a form of the word in capitals in each gap to complete the text.**

**So you want to be an online video star, do you?**

Many people look at the stars of YouTube and have the same (1) ________ : I could do that. **THINK** Perhaps you want to do something similar to videos you've seen online and which you really like. Or perhaps you find most online videos dull and (2) ________ but have a brand new idea that people will love. **ORIGIN** But do you really have the (3) ________ to produce fun, interesting videos that people will want to watch? **CAPABLE** It takes a special (4) ________ to really connect with people through a computer screen. **PERSONAL**

As well as being (5) ________ , you need to be able to communicate well. **CREATE** This involves developing an (6) ________ of how you come across on camera. **AWARE** Practise in front of a camera as much as you can. The (7) ________ of some of the most popular YouTube channels think carefully about their appearance and their image **CREATE** and aim to appear (8) ________ in front of the camera. **NATURE** You should too!

# 3 WRITING | A review

**1** **In pairs or as a group, answer the questions.**

1 Why do people read reviews of films, books, restaurants, etc.?
2 Have you ever read or watched a review? If so, what was it for and was it interesting? If not, how do you usually choose a book, film, restaurant, etc.?

**EXAM SKILL**

## Using good descriptions

- Good descriptions help your reader to imagine exactly what you are talking about.
- Use a range of adjectives to describe things. Don't just use simple adjectives like *good* and *bad*.
- Give reasons and details. If you think something is amazing, clearly explain why and give an example.

**2** **Read this review and choose T (True) or F (False).**

A FUTURE YOUTUBE STAR

One of the most popular new YouTube channels is Funny Girl. In it, Abigail (also known as funnygirl03) tells jokes and talks about her life. It's really taken off recently, and I decided to take a look.

Abigail produces one new video every day. She's great at making the videos and they have a professional look. Each one lasts for about five minutes, so they aren't too long. The sound quality is always excellent, and you really get a good idea of Abigail's personality from the videos.

It's true that some of the jokes she tells are old ones, but she makes them funny by the way she tells them. She talks about subjects that young people find interesting and she always has an unusual point of view. She describes things that happen to her in a very funny way. Admittedly, she sometimes refers to her close friends, but she does always explain who they are so you can understand what she's talking about.

I would definitely recommend this channel to any teenager who likes comedy. I'm sure Funny Girl is going to be very successful.

**The writer …**

| | | |
|---|---|---|
| 1 | describes what the videos look and sound like. | T / F |
| 2 | describes the content of the videos. | T / F |
| 3 | describes Abigail's appearance in detail. | T / F |
| 4 | only mentions positive things. | T / F |
| 5 | makes a recommendation at the end. | T / F |

**3** **Find and underline adjectives in the review which show that the writer has a positive view of the YouTube channel.**

**OPTIMISE YOUR EXAM**

## A review

- Remember that the purpose of a review is to describe the positive and/or negative aspects of something.
- You should finish with a recommendation so that your readers can make a decision based on your review.

**4** **Look at this writing task. Who is going to read your review if it is chosen for the website?**

You see this advert on a website aimed at teenagers.

> **Reviews wanted!**
>
> We are looking for reviews of the most popular new online video channels, whether they're about music, comedy – or something else! Your review should include information about the quality of the videos, the content of the channel and the presenter. Would you recommend this channel to other young people?
>
> The best reviews will appear on our website!

Write your **review**.

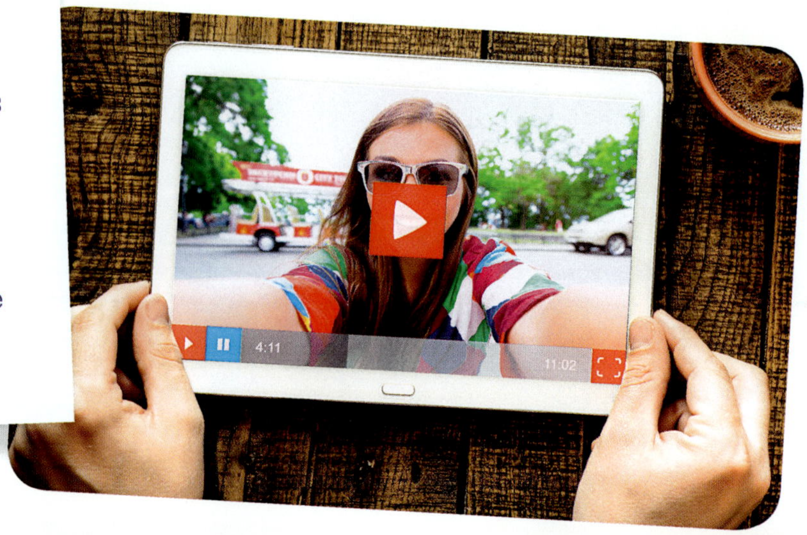

**5** **Which online channel are you going to review? Complete this information. Use your imagination!**

Name of the channel:
____________________

Content of the channel (music, comedy, gaming, etc.):
____________________

Presenter of the channel:
____________________ (real name)
____________________ (online name)

**6** **Make notes to answer each of these questions.**

1 Where did you hear about this channel? Why did you choose this one to review?

____________________

2 What is the presenter like? What kind of personality do they have? What adjectives could you use to describe them?

____________________

3 Are the videos well made? What adjectives could you use to describe them?

____________________

4 What is usually in the videos?

____________________

5 Why do you like/dislike the videos? Say as much as you can.

____________________

6 Would you recommend the channel to other young people? Why / Why not?

____________________

**7** **Plan** **Complete the paragraph plan.**

| Part | Purpose | Useful phrases | My notes |
|---|---|---|---|
| **Title** | say what you are reviewing | | |
| **Paragraph 1** | explain what you are reviewing | *One of the most popular …*<br>*I decided to have a look at …* | |
| **Paragraph 2** | describe the quality of the videos and the content and give your opinion | *The videos show …*<br>*They are generally very high/poor quality …*<br>*In my view …*<br>*It seems to me that …* | |
| **Paragraph 3** | describe the presenter and give your opinion | *The presenter comes across as …*<br>*He/She seems very confident/friendly,* etc.<br>*I find him/her entertaining/annoying …* | |
| **Paragraph 4** | say whether you would recommend this channel | *I'd be very happy to recommend …*<br>*I certainly would/wouldn't recommend …* | |

**8** **Write** **Write your review in an appropriate style. Write 140–190 words.**

**9** **Check** **Before you hand in your review, complete this checklist.**

**Checklist**

- ◯ I've clearly stated what I am reviewing.
- ◯ I've clearly given my opinion on the channel.
- ◯ I've described the channel and its content.
- ◯ I've used an appropriate style for a review, including a range of adjectives.
- ◯ I've given reasons for my opinions.
- ◯ I've written at least four paragraphs.
- ◯ I've checked my spelling and grammar.

▶ **Writing reference,** page 170 ▶ **Workbook Unit 3:** Writing, page 26, exercises 1, 2, 3, 4 and Progress check 3, page 27

# 4 Big city life

## READING | Open questions | An infographic text

**1 In pairs or groups, answer the questions.**

1 What things do you find in a city that you don't find in the countryside and vice versa?

2 Which place do you think is better to grow up in – the city or the countryside?

> **EXAM SKILL**
>
> **Skimming**
>
> - Skimming means reading a text very quickly just to get the gist – a general idea of what it's about.
> - Don't read every word. Move your eyes very quickly through the text and decide: what kind of text it is (e.g. report, blog, etc.), what it's about (e.g. life in different cities), its tone (e.g. positive or negative), and who it's aimed at (e.g. adults, students, etc.).

**2 Look at the text for one minute then cover it and then choose the correct word or phrase.**

1 The text is about a number of **different cities** / **places in one city**.

2 The tone of the text is generally **positive** / **negative**.

3 The text seems to be aimed at **adults only** / **teenagers mainly**.

4 You'd probably read this text in an online **encyclopedia** / **newspaper**.

**3 In pairs or as a group, with the text still covered, discuss your answers to Exercise 2.**

**4 With the text still covered, tick the statements that are true for you.**

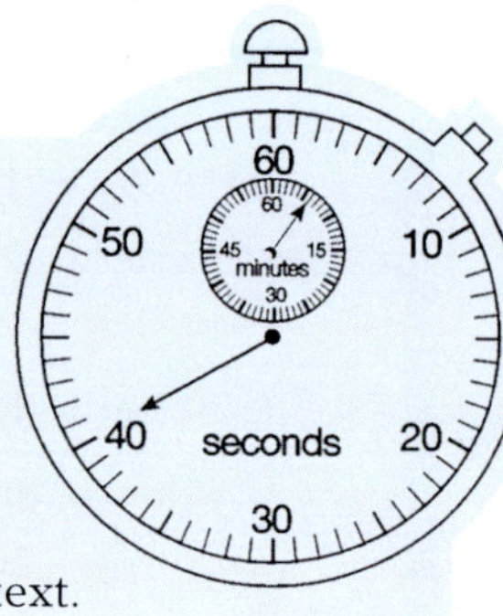


In one minute, ...

- [ ] 1 I read the text extremely quickly and managed to complete Exercise 2.
- [ ] 2 I read the text quickly but didn't have time to complete Exercise 2.
- [ ] 3 I didn't manage to skim read the whole text.

Visiting London soon? Forget boring old buildings and dusty old libraries. We've travelled the length and breadth of the city to come up with …

# 12 EXCITING, INTERESTING OR JUST PLAIN WEIRD THINGS TO DO IN ENGLAND'S CAPITAL CITY!

**1** Have you ever wanted to be James Bond? Well, there's no better way to feel like a top spy than to travel down London's famous river, the Thames, in a speedboat.

**2** Maybe you've been dying to see London from the air, and want to pretend you're a famous celebrity. If so, then a London helicopter tour could be exactly what you need. Just make sure you (or your parents) can pay for it first!

**3** For a slightly gentler (and more affordable) way to get great views of London, why not ride a cable car across the Thames on the Emirates Air Line?

**4** If speed and height are not your thing, what about learning how to make your own fashion and jewellery at the *V&A Create!* young people's events at the Victoria and Albert Museum? The V&A has been described as the world's greatest museum of art and design.

**5** Crime-lovers – never mind the TV; watch a real-life court drama unfold at the Old Bailey, a world famous criminal court where trials are open to the public. Dating from medieval times, the court has appeared in hundreds of novels, films and programmes.

**6** You've been to the Science Museum (where hopefully you experienced the 4D cinema impact of a Saturn V rocket launch). You've done the British Museum. So now you're looking for something with even more of the wow factor. Here it is! Feel the incredible force of an earthquake (simulated, of course!) at the Natural History Museum.

**7** If you're a football fan, tread in the footsteps of football legends at Wembley Stadium, Stamford Bridge (Chelsea) or The Emirates Stadium (Arsenal).

**8** Be part of the table tennis craze at Bounce in Farringdon (before 6 pm), or on one of the free Ping-Pong tables spread around the capital (you'll need your own bats and balls though).

**9** Discover what punishment was like in the old days by a visit to The Torturer at the London Dungeon. See some of the very scary 'tools' he used. **Warning**: this attraction is not for the squeamish!

**10** Do you like puzzles? Find your way out of the famous garden maze at Hampton Court Palace. And once you've managed to get out of the maze, head over to Cluequest or HintHunt for another challenge … getting out of a locked room.

**11** Are you a Sherlock Holmes or Doctor Who fan? If so, take the Sherlock Holmes Tour or Doctor Who Tour of London with Brit Movie Tours.

**12** The Unicorn Theatre, near Tower Bridge, has been putting on shows specifically for teenagers for decades – so they know what they're doing. Don't miss one of their fantastic productions while you're in town!

For more information, visit www.visitlondon.com

## OPTIMISE YOUR EXAM

### Open questions

- For this type of task, you'll mainly use the skill of scanning (see Unit 3).
- However, you should always skim the text first to understand the general idea. This will help you scan more effectively as you will know where to look for answers in the text.

**5** 1.18 **Read the text again. Write a short answer for each question. Use a maximum of four words.**

1 Financially, how does the cable car differ from a helicopter tour? ____________

2 What can you produce yourself at one of the attractions? ____________

3 Which description of the Old Bailey applies to all of the attractions mentioned here? ____________

4 What other museum re-creation is as realistic as the rocket launch at the Science Museum? ____________

5 Which people are advised not to visit a frightening exhibition? ____________

**6** **Find these words and phrases in the text. For each one, choose the best meaning.**

1 the length and breadth of (introduction)
**everywhere in** / **for a very long time in**

2 dying to (paragraph 2)
**feeling ill about** / **really looking forward to**

3 not your thing (paragraph 4)
**doesn't belong to you** / **not what you like**

4 the wow factor (paragraph 6)
**something** that will really **amaze** / **scare** you

5 craze (paragraph 8)
**very popular** / **unusual** hobby or activity

6 head over to (paragraph 10)
**think about** / **go to**

THINK | **RESEARCH** | CULTURE | LEARN | ME

Choose one of the attractions mentioned in the text and find out more about it online.

Give a short presentation about what you've found out.

▶ **Workbook Unit 4:** Reading, page 28, exercises 1, 2, 3

# 4 GRAMMAR 1 | Tense review: present perfect simple and continuous

## Grammar in context

**Look at the text on page 37 and do the following:**

1 Underline the verbs in the present perfect simple (active or passive) in the introduction and the first four paragraphs.

2 Find and circle these phrases.

*Maybe you've been dying to see London from the air …*

*The Unicorn Theatre has been putting on shows specifically for teenagers for decades …*

Why has the writer chosen to use present perfect continuous rather than present perfect simple?

### REMEMBER

- We use the present perfect simple to talk about situations or experiences that connect the past with the present because they began in the past and are still true in the present (*I've trained as a helicopter pilot.*) or have recently finished (*I've just finished my pilot training.*).
- We use the present perfect continuous to emphasise the continuing nature of situations that connect the past with the present because they began in the past and are still continuing in the present (*I've been working as a pilot for two years now.*).
- We sometimes use the present perfect simple to emphasise a completed action or situation, and the present perfect continuous when the action is unfinished:

*She **has read** a book about London.* (She finished reading the book.)

*She **has been reading** a book about London.* (She is still reading this book.)

▶ **See Grammar reference, Unit 4,** page 151

**1 Write *yes* or *no* to answer the question about each sentence.**

1 *They've been building that new multi-storey car park since last December.*
Have they finished building it yet? ___________

2 *They've built a multi-storey car park just down the road from here.*
Have they finished building it yet? ___________

3 *I've just parked the car in the multi-storey car park.*
Is the car in the multi-storey car park now? ___________

4 *We've been looking for a parking space for more than 15 minutes.*
Have they found a parking space yet? ___________

**2 Choose the correct word or phrase.**

Have you (**1**) **ever** / **before** wanted to build your own city? Have you heard of the video game Minecraft? Duncan Parcells, a student in the USA, has (**2**) **became** / **become** an expert user of the game and (**3**) **have** / **has** done just that. He's created a 'virtual city', which (**4**) **he has** / **it is** constructed online out of 4.5 million Minecraft 'building blocks'. Called Titan City, Duncan got the original idea for his creation from the buildings in New York, a city Duncan has always (**5**) **been admiring** / **admired**. Duncan has been (**6**) **worked** / **working** on the project (**7**) **for** / **since** the past two years, and has plans to expand it further. 'I've (**8**) **always liked** / **liked** always architecture,' said Duncan in a recent interview.

**3 Put the verbs into the correct tense (present perfect simple or continuous). Be careful! Sometimes both tenses are possible.**

1 Helen _______________ (**enjoy**) her new life since she moved to Amsterdam.

2 Your aunt lives in Paris now. How long _______________ (**live**) there?

3 We got to the airport six hours ago and _______________ (**wait**) for our flight announcement since then.

4 _______________ (**you** / **buy**) the plane tickets yet?

5 We only arrived a few minutes ago so we _______________ (**not even** / **check in**) to the hotel yet.

6 I _______________ (**not** / **go**) to Switzerland since I was a child so I can't wait to go back again!

7 Finally we've booked plane tickets to go to London. We _______________ (**plan**) this trip for more than a year!

8 _______________ you _______________ (**work**) in the same place ever since you left college?

THINK | RESEARCH | CULTURE | LEARN | **ME**

What famous or amazing buildings are there in your area / capital city / country? What do you think of them?

If you had to choose between being an architect or working in the building industry, which would you do?

## Places in the city

**1** 1.19 **Replace the word or phrase in bold with words from the box. Listen and check.**

| a block of flats \| city centre \| parking space |
|---|
| services \| shopping centre \| the subway |

1 Most of London's best tourist attractions are in the **suburbs**. ___________
2 My family live in **an office block** in the north-east of the city. ___________
3 In New York the underground train system is called **the Tube**. ___________
4 It is often hard to find a **car park** in the street outside our house. ___________
5 There are over a hundred different shops in this **department store**. ___________
6 There are excellent public **attractions** in Bristol, including libraries and public transport. ________

**2** **Write an example sentence for each of the incorrect words in Exercise 1.**

## Words + prepositions

**3** 1.20 **Look at Exercise 4. Underline the words in the first sentence which will probably have to be replaced to complete the second sentence. Listen and check.**

**4** **Complete the second sentence using the word given so that it means the same as the first sentence. Use the *Vocabulary reference*, page 163, to help you.**

1 You'll have a great time in London whatever the weather. **regardless**
You'll have a great time in London ____________________ the weather.
2 The city council has no plans to turn the playground into a car park. **intention**
The city council doesn't ____________________ turning the playground into a car park.
3 We're going to have to solve the problem of wheelchair access soon. **solution**
We're going to have to ____________________ the problem of wheelchair access soon.
4 There are beautiful plants all over the outside of the building. **covered**
The outside of the building ____________________ beautiful plants.
5 I've really had enough of living in a small village. **fed**
I'm really ____________________ living in a small village.
6 Make sure you throw all your litter away properly. **dispose**
Make sure you ____________________ properly.

## Adjectives/nouns/verbs

**5** 1.21 **Read the text in Exercise 6. For each gap, decide what kind of word fits the gap (noun, verb, adjective, etc.). In pairs or as a group, discuss your ideas. Listen and check.**

**REMEMBER**

We often form the opposite of a word by adding a prefix. Common prefixes are *dis-*, *un-* and *in-*. We may need to make other changes to the base word as well.

**6** **Write a form of the word in capitals in each gap to complete the text. All of the words are negative.**

For people without (**1**) *disabilities*, a shopping trip to the city can be fun and exciting. But many of us are (**2**) __________ of how different things can often be if you're (**3**) __________ to see or walk well. Disabled people have a (**4**) __________ sometimes, which can vary in seriousness from feeling worried, (**5**) __________, distressed or (**6**) __________ in a public place to facing something even more dreadful: the complete (**7**) __________ to enter a public building because it has not been designed with them in mind. That this can still happen in many capital cities in the 21st century is (**8**) __________, and few people would (**9**) __________ that all cities in the future should offer good facilities for disabled people. Let's all work hard until all the physical barriers in cities for people with disabilities have (**10**) __________!

**ABLE**
**AWARE**
**ABLE**
**ADVANTAGE**
**COMFORT**
**SECURE**
**ABLE**
**BELIEVE**
**AGREE**
**APPEAR**

# 4 LISTENING | Multiple choice (single extract)

**1** **In pairs or as a group, discuss the questions.**

1 Have you ever visited any cities in other countries?
2 If you have, what did you like/dislike about them? If you haven't, choose one city and say why you would like to go there.

**EXAM SKILL**

## Understanding responses to questions

- When speakers answer yes/no questions, their answer doesn't always start with *Yes* or *No*. They sometimes use other words and phrases. Some of these appear in Exercise 2.
- Whatever word or phrase they use, it's important to be able to tell if they're introducing a positive or negative response to the question, or a mixed response.

**2** **Decide whether these words and phrases are used to introduce a positive answer (P), a negative answer (N) or a mixed positive/negative answer (M).**

1 To a certain extent ___ ☐
2 Definitely ___ ☐
3 On the contrary ___ ☐
4 Quite the opposite ___ ☐
5 Absolutely ___ ☐
6 Up to a point ___ ☐
7 Yes and no ___ ☐
8 Absolutely not ___ ☐

**OPTIMISE YOUR EXAM**

## Multiple choice (single extract)

- Always read the questions and options before you start listening.
- As you listen the first time, note down words and phrases you hear that might help you answer the questions.
- Don't worry too much about choosing the correct option the first time you listen because you will hear the recording a second time.

**3** 1.22 **Read the questions in Exercise 4. Then listen to the interview and tick each word/phrase in Exercise 2 that you hear.**

**4** 1.22 **Listen again to the radio interview with Lena Callow and choose the best answer (A, B or C).**

1 What happened in the period before Lena went on her trip?
**A** She had to persuade her father to let her go on her own.
**B** It was hard to choose between this trip and a beach holiday.
**C** Many of the accommodation arrangements were made.

2 What does Lena say about where she'd like to live?
**A** She doesn't want to live in another country.
**B** She prefers living in a rural environment.
**C** She'd love to live in Montreal one day.

3 What surprised Lena about Athens?
**A** how old some of the buildings were
**B** how different it was from Istanbul
**C** how it was nicer than she had imagined

4 What was Lena's view of New York?
**A** It's actually a city you can relax in.
**B** She prefers cities that are less busy.
**C** It's too big to see all the main sights.

5 What does Lena say about visiting Mexico City?
**A** It has elements of the other cities.
**B** She spoke Spanish there.
**C** She went to lots of museums.

THINK | RESEARCH | CULTURE | LEARN | ME

Imagine you're going on a similar trip to Lena's. Where would you go and what would you see? In pairs, plan a trip together.


▶ **Workbook Unit 4:** Listening, page 32, exercises 1, 2

# GRAMMAR 2 | Question review: question tags and question forms

## Grammar in context

**Write one word or contraction in each gap to complete these extracts from the audio in the listening lesson.**

1 So, Lena, you've just come back from visiting five major cities, __________ you?
2 So __________ cities did you get to see?
3 What __________ you like – or not like – about Athens?
4 __________ it what you expected?
5 I imagine __________ quite similar though, aren't they?

### REMEMBER

- Question tags are used to check or confirm information and are formed using the verb or the auxiliary verb + subject + *?*
- If the verb or auxiliary verb is positive, the question tag is negative and vice versa.
- For imperatives, use *will you?* and for phrases that begin *Let's*, use the question tag, *shall we?*

▶ **See Grammar reference, Unit 4,** page 151

**1 Write the question tags.**

1 It's a huge city, __________
2 They're going to Moscow as well as St Petersburg, __________
3 I'm meeting them outside the library, __________
4 You haven't been to New York, __________
5 Jack doesn't live in Dublin, __________
6 Let's go to the cinema this evening, __________
7 Pass me the map, __________
8 Don't lose the guide book, __________

### REMEMBER

- With some questions, which form of the verb you need to use depends on whether you're asking a subject question or an object question.
- Subject question: *Who stayed with Emma?* Someone stayed with Emma. Who? *Lily stayed with Emma.* Lily is the subject of the sentence.
- Object question: *Who did Emma stay with?* Emma stayed with someone. Who? *Emma stayed with Lily.* Lily is the object of the sentence.
- Questions that begin *How come* are followed by subject + verb, like in an affirmative sentence.

▶ **See Grammar reference, Unit 4,** page 151

**2 If a phrase in bold is correct, put a tick. If it's incorrect, rewrite it correctly.**

1 Do you know **who founded** the city of Barcelona? __________?
2 Which city **Romulus and Remus founded**? __________?
3 **How come you've never heard** of Brussels? __________?
4 Who **does go** to London and doesn't see Big Ben? __________?
5 Where **goes that bus** to, do you know? __________?
6 **Isn't it** a perfect day to go sightseeing? __________?

**3 Read the text and write a question for each answer.**

# NEW AMSTERDAM

**Have you heard of the city New Amsterdam?**

In the 1600s, New Amsterdam was a small Dutch settlement on the island of Manhattan. The Dutch did a deal with the English, where they swapped the city for control of some islands. In 1664, the English changed the name of the city. They named it after the Duke of York, and it became what it's known as today: New York City.

1 __________
On the island of Manhattan.
2 __________
With the English.
3 __________
They swapped the city for control of some islands.
4 __________
The English did.
5 __________
The Duke of York.

**SAY IT RIGHT**

**Resource centre: Unit 4**
Intonation in question tags

THINK | RESEARCH | **CULTURE** | LEARN | ME

What myths, legends or interesting stories are there about how cities in your country were founded?

# 4 SPEAKING | Discussion

Talk2Me
That's a good point.

**Flipped classroom**

**1** **Look at questions 1–5. Watch the *Talk2Me* video and note down who answers which of the questions below and what their opinion is.**

1 When you're older, do you think you'll want to live in a city or somewhere smaller?
2 Do you think children who grow up in the countryside learn different things to children who grow up in cities?
3 Would you rather live near the top or the bottom of a big block of flats?
4 What are the most important things to think about when choosing which part of a town or city to live in?
5 How do you think cities in the future will be different to cities today?

**2** **Watch the video again and number the phrases in the *Phrase expert* box in the order you hear them.**

> **PHRASE EXPERT**
> don't entirely agree | I agree (with that) to a certain extent | I'm not sure I agree with that | I think the opposite | That's a (very) good point | That's true/right up to a point | There's something in that

**3** **In pairs or groups, answer the questions.**

- What are the three best things about the area where you live?
- What would you change or introduce to improve the area?

> **EXAM SKILL**
> ### Agreeing and disagreeing
> - In exams, you sometimes have to listen to someone else's opinion and agree or disagree with them.
> - To agree or disagree, you might say what you think (e.g. *I think you're right.*), or you might tell someone else (e.g. *I think Mason's right.*).

**4** **Complete the sentences for agreeing and disagreeing with the words in the box.**

| entirely \| extent \| in \| opposite |
|---|
| point \| right \| sure \| true |

1 Yes, I think you are ___________ about that.
2 That's a very good ___________ .
3 There's something ___________ that, I suppose …
4 That's ___________ up to a point.
5 Yes, I agree with that to a certain ___________ .
6 I don't ___________ agree with you about that.
7 I'm not ___________ I agree with that.
8 I think the ___________ .

> **OPTIMISE YOUR EXAM**
> ### Discussion
> - In a discussion, listening is as important as speaking. Listening carefully means you can respond appropriately and have a proper discussion.
> - It's fine to agree, or disagree, or partly agree – but always do it politely.

**5** **As a class or in groups, carry out the following task.**

- Start with the first question in Exercise 1.
- One person in the group should express their opinion.
- They then nominate the next person to speak.
- That person agrees or disagrees as appropriate, and then nominates someone else.
- Continue until several people have expressed an opinion.
- Then move on to the next question.

▶ **Workbook Unit 4:** Speaking, pages 32–33, exercises 1, 2

# USE OF ENGLISH | Multiple-choice cloze

**1** **In pairs, describe this photo. What do you think are the benefits of having a garden like this?**

**EXAM SKILL**

## Collocations

- Some words often appear with other words to make phrases. These are called 'collocations'.
- There are lots of different types of collocations, including: noun + noun (e.g. *city centre*), verb + noun (e.g. *make a mistake*), adjective + noun (e.g. *detached house*).
- Exams often test collocations, so it's important you don't just learn vocabulary as one-word items. You also have to learn which words are used together in collocations.

**2** **Choose the correct word to complete the collocations from this unit.**

1 **make** / **have** sure
2 **earth** / **world** famous
3 football **fan** / **admirer**
4 **take** / **make** a tour
5 **multi-storey** / **multi-level** car park
6 shopping **trip** / **journey**
7 **recent** / **fresh** interview
8 wheelchair **access** / **admission**
9 **make** / **do** arrangements
10 **view** / **see** the sights
11 **incompletely** / **partly** agree
12 department **store** / **shop**
13 **virtual** / **almost** city
14 parking **room** / **space**
15 get a **general** / **whole** idea
16 **society** / **public** building
17 **capital** / **head** city
18 up to a(n) **point** / extent
19 tower **block** / **building**
20 wow **factor** / **issue**

**OPTIMISE YOUR EXAM**

## Multiple-choice cloze

- This task often tests your knowledge of collocations.
- Decide if the collocation starts before the gap or in the gap and say all the possible answers to yourself, e.g. for Exercise 4, question 7, you'd say *fresh studies*, *recent studies*, *latest studies*, *unused studies*.
- Cross out any answers that are definitely wrong, then think carefully about the ones that are left.

**3** **Skim the text in Exercise 4. In pairs or as a group, discuss what you think the main points of the text are.**

**4** **Choose the correct word or phrase for each gap.**

### Green roofs – an urban solution?

Are you **(1)** __________ up with living in a building that's baking hot in the summer and freezing cold in the winter? Have you had **(2)** __________ of expensive electricity bills? **(3)** __________ of whether you live in a detached house or a tower **(4)** __________, environmentalists, ecologists and gardeners might have **(5)** __________ up with the solution to all your problems: a green roof. Green roofs – roofs that are **(6)** __________ with plants – are becoming increasingly popular. They're great in terms of turning an otherwise under-used space into a lovely garden, providing insulation and creating an eco-system in an urban environment. What's more, **(7)** __________ studies have shown that if the majority of buildings in a typical city **(8)** __________ had green roofs, the average temperature on the hottest days could come down by several degrees.

| | A | B | C | D |
|---|---|---|---|---|
| 1 | **A** given | **B** fed | **C** drunk | **D** eaten |
| 2 | **A** much | **B** adequate | **C** sufficient | **D** enough |
| 3 | **A** Despite | **B** Regardless | **C** Not | **D** No matter |
| 4 | **A** block | **B** skyscraper | **C** structure | **D** building |
| 5 | **A** come | **B** found | **C** made | **D** set |
| 6 | **A** poured | **B** laid | **C** covered | **D** filled |
| 7 | **A** fresh | **B** recent | **C** latest | **D** unused |
| 8 | **A** middle | **B** heart | **C** core | **D** centre |

THINK | RESEARCH | **CULTURE** | LEARN | ME

Do you think green roofs will/should become more popular in the future?

▶ **Vocabulary reference,** page 163 ▶ **Workbook Unit 4:** Use of English, page 33, exercises 1, 2

# 4 WRITING | An essay

**1** **In pairs or as a group, answer the questions.**

1 Have you ever been to the top of a skyscraper?
2 If yes, did you enjoy the experience? If not, would you like to?

**EXAM SKILL**

## Giving examples

- Giving examples helps the reader understand your arguments. Without them, your ideas can seem too vague and general, and less convincing.
- These might be examples of advantages, disadvantages, problems, solutions, etc. Some might be examples from your own experience.

**2** **Read this essay and make notes to complete the chart.**

*Many big cities like Dubai and New York have skyscrapers. There are problems with living and working in such tall buildings, but I believe on the whole they're wonderful things.*

*Skyscrapers do have disadvantages. Firstly, being so high up can make life difficult. For instance, you can't just open the window wide on a hot day if you're on the 90th floor. Secondly, they rely on technology and electricity, which is not ideal if there's a problem such as a power cut and the lifts stop working. Thirdly, they can be dangerous. For example, if there's a fire, it might be difficult to escape.*

*However, I believe that the advantages outweigh the disadvantages. Skyscrapers are becoming safer and stronger each year. They're also beautiful, and some are amazing works of art. The New World Trade Centre is an example of this. More importantly, they allow a large number of people to live and work in the same building space.*

*To sum up, I hope we continue to build bigger, better and safer skyscrapers. They can solve the problem of too little space in cities, and are beautiful at the same time.*

**The writer gives a number of examples. Complete the table about each one.**

| | What is it an example of? | What specific example is given? |
|---|---|---|
| Example 1 | *big cities* | |
| Example 2 | | |
| Example 3 | | |
| Example 4 | | |
| Example 5 | | |

**3** **Each of the words in bold is incorrect. Write the correct word.**

1 Some cities, **as** example New York, have a large number of skyscrapers. ____________
2 Some buildings, for **instant** the Burj Khalifa in Dubai, are more than 150 storeys high. ____________
3 The Shard in London is a good example **for** a beautiful modern skyscraper. ____________
4 Some cities, **much** as Athens, have very few really tall buildings. ____________
5 Films **as** *The Tower* show how dangerous skyscrapers can be. ____________

**OPTIMISE YOUR EXAM**

## An essay

- Good essays are balanced and examine both sides of an argument/situation.
- For the exam task in Exercise 4, write about the advantages and the disadvantages in the middle paragraphs.
- Your conclusion (final paragraph) should then express which 'side' of the argument you support.

**4** **Look at this writing task. In pairs or as a group, think of as many advantages and disadvantages as possible.**

In your English class, you have been talking about the advantages and disadvantages of living in a city. Now, your English teacher has asked you to write an essay for homework. Write an essay using all the notes and give reasons for your point of view.

**Are there more advantages or disadvantages to living in a city?**

**Notes**

Write about:

1. events and facilities
2. cost of living
3. ............................ (your own idea)

**5** **Complete the chart.**

| Advantages | Examples | Disadvantages | Examples |
|---|---|---|---|
| *lots of events* | *concerts, plays* | | |
| | | | |
| | | | |
| | | | |

**6** **In one or two sentences, summarise your position.**

*I believe that there are more* ***advantages/disadvantages*** *to living in a city than* ***advantages/disadvantages*** *because* ________________________________________________ .

**7** **Plan** **Complete the paragraph plan.**

| Part | Purpose | Useful phrases | My notes |
|---|---|---|---|
| **Paragraph 1** | introduce the subject | *Millions of people live …*<br>*For example,* | |
| **Paragraph 2** | agree or disagree with the statement, give reasons and explain why OR describe (dis)advantages | *Firstly,*<br>*One (dis)advantage of living … is …*<br>*Because of this,*<br>*As a result,*<br>*For this reason,*<br>*However,*<br>*For example, …,*<br>*such as* | |
| **Paragraph 3** | give further reasons OR describe (dis)advantages (whichever you didn't describe in paragraph 2) | | |
| **Paragraph 4** | come to a conclusion | *To sum up,*<br>*To conclude,*<br>*In conclusion, I believe that …*<br>*It seems to me …* | |

**8** **Write** **Write your essay in an appropriate style. Write 140–190 words.**

**9** **Check** **Before you hand in your essay, complete this checklist.**

**Checklist**

- ◯ I've used the two notes in the question.
- ◯ I've come up with my own idea as an additional point to write about.
- ◯ I've given reasons and examples to support my opinions.
- ◯ I've written four main paragraphs.
- ◯ I've checked my essay makes sense logically.
- ◯ I've checked that my essay doesn't sound too informal.
- ◯ I've checked my spelling and my grammar.

▶ Writing reference, page 174 ▶ **Workbook Unit 4:** Writing, page 34, exercises 1, 2, 3, 4 and Progress check 4, page 35

# PROGRESS CHECK UNITS 3–4

## GRAMMAR AND VOCABULARY

**1 Write a form of the word in capitals in each gap.**

**WHAT MAKES A GOOD VIDEO BLOG?**

The best and most popular video blogs come in all sorts of styles. Some are funny, some are serious. Their (1) __________ is never due to just one factor, but most of the most successful ones share certain characteristics. How the blogger talks to the audience is central. No-one wants to watch someone who looks (2) __________ , as if they don't want to be there. Viewers respond to (3) __________ and honesty. A good blog doesn't have to be complicated. Often, (4) __________ is better, which is why many great blogs are of people just talking to a camera in their bedroom. However, even those contain elements of (5) __________ on the part of the presenter. Without some (6) __________ , they would be boring and people would stop watching. The top bloggers have an (7) __________ of this. It's actually (8) __________ how they manage to combine all these different things so successfully.

**POPULAR**
**COMFORT**
**OPEN**
**SIMPLE**
**CREATIVE**
**ORIGINAL**
**AWARE**
**BELIEVE**

__/8

**2 Write one word in each gap.**

Have you (1) __________ thought about making a vlog? I've (2) __________ making them (3) __________ the past two years. It's great fun! One thing you ought (4) __________ consider before you start is who you expect to watch them. That will help you decide what to focus on. Having said that, people other than your friends and family (5) __________ see your videos too, so never say or do anything that (6) __________ get you into trouble. Most vloggers never become famous but a few lucky ones (7) __________ made lots of money from talking to camera. It (8) __________ be great if you were the next one, wouldn't it?

__/8

**3 Choose the correct word.**

1 Getting some fresh air this afternoon will do you **well / good**.
2 I wonder if our video will **go / make** viral!
3 You shouldn't **make / do** fun of someone because of where they live.
4 We played a joke on Matt but he didn't **find / take** it very funny.
5 I'm not very good at **telling / speaking** jokes.
6 Let's **make / take** a ten-minute break and then do some more filming.

__/6

**4 Write a word from the box in each gap.**

| check | come | dispose | have | head | set |
|---|---|---|---|---|---|

1 No-one should __________ out to be a star immediately – it takes lots of hard work.
2 Let me know if you __________ across any interesting places to visit.
3 Make sure you __________ out Carrie's new video on YouTube.
4 When we finish here, let's __________ over to the café for some lunch.
5 How are we going to __________ of all this rubbish?
6 Do you often __________ friends round to watch videos and things like that?

__/6

## 5 Write a word or short phrase in each gap.

1 You haven't seen my camera anywhere, ______________ you?
2 ______________ old were you when you moved to Moscow?
3 You don't ______________ watch this, but you can if you like.
4 Adrian likes living in a big city, ______________ he?
5 Did you know that Sue ______________ ride a bike until she was 16 years old?
6 ______________ time does the film start this evening?
7 I think we ______________ each make a vlog this week, don't you?
8 You ______________ go to that neighbourhood at night – it's dangerous.
9 I'm allowed to stay up till the end of the film, ______________ I?
10 You ______________ never drink liquid from a bottle without a label.
11 ______________ do you think is going to watch your vlogs?
12 Kyle ______________ get up at half past six because he lives so far away from school.

__/12

## 6 Complete the second sentence so it has a similar meaning to the first. Do not change the word given. Use two to five words, including the word given.

1 Simon, I'm sure Zara's not on holiday in Berlin – I saw her earlier! **BE**
Simon, ______________________ on holiday in Berlin – I saw her earlier!
2 Joel doesn't have any plans to move to the countryside. **INTENTION**
Joel has ______________________ to the countryside.
3 I think you should enter the competition. **PART**
I think you ought ______________________ the competition.
4 You should always be careful when you throw batteries away. **OF**
You should always be careful about ______________________ batteries.
5 I imagine it's incredible living in New York. **BE**
New York ______________________ incredible city to live in.

__/10

**Total score** __/50

## EXAM SKILLS

Tick the statements that are true for you. Review the skills in the unit if you need more help.

| I can … | Unit/page |
|---|---|
| ☐ scan an online article to find specific information | Unit 3 p26 |
| ☐ identify speakers' attitudes in short extracts | Unit 3 p30 |
| ☐ make suggestions in a collaborative task | Unit 3 p32 |
| ☐ understand how nouns are formed and use them in word-formation exercises | Unit 3 p33 |
| ☐ use good descriptions in a review | Unit 3 p34 |
| ☐ skim an infographic text to get the gist | Unit 4 p36 |
| ☐ understand responses to questions in an interview | Unit 4 p40 |
| ☐ agree and disagree with someone else's opinions in a discussion | Unit 4 p42 |
| ☐ form some collocations and apply them in a multiple-choice cloze exercise | Unit 4 p43 |
| ☐ give examples in an essay | Unit 4 p44 |

# 5 The weekend starts here!

## READING | Multiple choice | An historical article

**1 In pairs or as a group, answer the questions.**

1 How do you like to spend your free time at the weekend?
2 Describe your ideal weekend.

**2 Decide whether you think these statements are true or false. Then quickly read the article to check your answers.**

1 Everyone's weekend falls on the same days around the world. **T / F**
2 The weekend has existed for thousands of years. **T / F**
3 In most countries, people work 48 hours a week. **T / F**

### EXAM SKILL

#### Understanding references

- We saw how pronouns connect ideas in a text in Unit 2. Other important references include possessive adjectives (*my*, *her*, *our*, etc.) and demonstratives (*this*, *that*, etc.).
- They usually refer to things mentioned earlier in the text, but can also include things later in the text.
- Sometimes they refer to a whole sentence or paragraph.

**3 Find and underline these phrases in the second and third paragraphs of the text. Write what the words in italics refer to.**

1 … where *it* originated … ____________________
2 And how is *the concept* going to change … ____________________
3 *Their* working lives … ____________________
4 … *they* had managed to reduce … ____________________
5 *This* meant that working people … ____________________

### OPTIMISE YOUR EXAM

#### Multiple choice

- Some questions ask what a specific word or phrase in a text refers to, e.g. Exercise 4, question 5.
- Read the sentence that includes the word or phrase and the sentences before and after it.
- Choose the best answer then read the sentence again to check your choice makes sense.

# History *of the* weekend

What are you doing this weekend? Perhaps you're spending time with family, hanging out with friends, or maybe you're going to play a sport. All around the world, people chill out at the end of the working week and take part in leisure activities. In many countries, the weekend consists of Saturday and Sunday, while in others Friday and Saturday are the days of rest. In Afghanistan, Thursday and Friday form the weekend, while in one country, Brunei, Friday and Sunday are the days off.

Have you ever stopped to wonder, though, exactly where it originated? And how is the concept going to change? The modern weekend took shape during the Industrial Revolution. In the early 19th century, in areas such as the north of England, people began to leave the countryside to work in towns and cities. There, new factories were springing up. Their working lives were once ruled by nature, with the amount of work depending on the changing seasons. Now, their employers demanded a different rhythm – a six-day week of up to 12 hours a day, followed by one day of rest.

Campaigns for workers' rights appeared. By the end of the century they had managed to reduce the working week to five and a half days. This meant that working people could take an interest in hobbies such as photography, which was very new at the time. In the US in the 1920s, the industrialist Henry Ford helped to create the weekend. He gave all his workers Saturday and Sunday off work. His factories manufactured cars, and he wanted to allow his employees time to purchase and enjoy the cars they were producing.

These days, in many countries, working a 40-hour week is normal. Many people have a nine-to-five job, but even that is rapidly changing. Technology enables more people to work from home and plan their own use of time. This means that an official period away from work is becoming less important. Perhaps in the future we will work fewer hours altogether. If we become more productive, we should be able to afford the same lifestyle by working fewer hours. It has been estimated, for example, that a worker in the US can achieve a 1950s standard of living by working just 11 hours a week. Some people have recommended a 21-hour working week to help with unemployment, climate change and inequality. However, a change like
*line 49* that may mean more leisure time but it will probably limit people's ability to earn money to enjoy it.

**4** 2.01 **For questions 1–5, choose the answer (A, B, C or D) which you think fits best according to the text.**

**1** People's working lives began to change when they
**A** moved to the north of England.
**B** decided to ignore the climate.
**C** left England and went elsewhere to work.
**D** started working in factories.

**2** What happened as a result of campaigns on behalf of workers?
**A** People worked fewer hours overall.
**B** People worked fewer hours per day.
**C** People found employment in leisure industries.
**D** People became more inventive.

**3** The writer says an American businessman gave his workers time off so that
**A** they would enjoy working for him.
**B** they could spend money on cars.
**C** he didn't have to pay them to drive.
**D** he could produce more cars.

**4** Why does the writer suggest the weekend may be less important now?
**A** because we start work later than we used to
**B** because we have enough free time to use technology
**C** because people are more in control of their working week
**D** because nobody works over 40 hours a week

**5** What does 'like that' in line 49 refer to?
**A** reducing the hours most people work
**B** making the world a fairer place
**C** the world becoming hotter
**D** living as people did in the 1950s

**5** **Write the highlighted words or phrases in the article which match the explanations.**

**1** a phrase that refers to things you do in your free time: ______________
**2** the period of development in Europe and the USA in the 18th and 19th centuries: ______________
**3** a phrasal verb that means 'relax': ______________
**4** a phrase for a normal office job: ______________
**5** a phrasal verb that means 'appear suddenly': ______________
**6** a word for a series of actions to produce social change: ______________
**7** a verb that means 'started, began': ______________
**8** a phrase that refers to the other days apart from the weekend: ______________

THINK | RESEARCH | **CULTURE** | LEARN | ME

What is the typical working week in your country?
What do people usually do at the weekend?

5

# GRAMMAR 1 | The future (1): *will, be going to*, present simple and continuous

## Grammar in context

**Find and underline these words in the text on page 49. Match each one to a function.**

1 *Perhaps you'**re spending** time with family?*

2 *… maybe you'**re going to** play a sport.*

3 *Perhaps in the future we **will** work fewer hours altogether.*

**a)** a prediction ____

**b)** an intention ____

**c)** an arrangement ____

### REMEMBER

- We use *will* to make predictions based on our knowledge, to make offers, requests, promises and refusals. *I **will** definitely **visit** you this weekend.*
- In questions to make offers, we only use *shall.*
- ***Shall** I **get** us some tickets for the concert this weekend?*
- We use *be going to* to make predictions based on something we can see, and to talk about intentions. *What **are** you **going to do** this weekend?*
- We use the present simple to talk about things happening according to a schedule or timetable, and after phrases such as *as soon as, unless,* etc. *My train **leaves** on Saturday morning.*
- We use the present continuous to talk about arrangements. *We **are seeing** my relatives on Sunday.*

▶ **See Grammar reference, Unit 5,** page 152

**1** **Choose the correct word or phrase. Be careful! Sometimes both are correct.**

1 I'm **going to see / seeing** my cousins this weekend.

2 What **do you / are you going to** do this Friday evening?

3 I think the party **starts / is starting** at about nine on Saturday.

4 We can't meet at six because I **will meet / am meeting** Jude at five.

5 Where **are you going to play / are you playing** basketball this weekend?

6 **Will / Shall** we go away somewhere for the weekend?

7 I **'ll / 'm going to** find out when the show starts on Saturday, if you like.

8 You leave if you want to but I'm going to stay until the film **will finish / finishes**.

**2** **Complete the sentences with a future form of the verbs in brackets. Sometimes there is more than one answer.**

1 Which film ______________ at the cinema with Kyle? (**see**)

2 We'd better hurry up and get tickets before they all ______________ out. (**sell**)

3 I ______________ anything this weekend, so why don't you come over to my house? (**not do**)

4 The Wilkinsons ______________ to Paris by train for the weekend. (**go**)

5 ______________ Lauren to meet me outside the bowling alley at seven? (**you ask**)

6 We should get to the sports centre early on Saturday. What time ______________ ? (**it open**)

**3** **If a word or phrase in italics is correct, put a tick. If it's incorrect, rewrite it correctly. Sometimes there is more than one answer.**

**Evie:** Thank goodness it's Friday! (**1**) *Are you doing* __________ anything this weekend?

**Daisy:** Oh, yes! (**2**) I *will go* __________ to Morgan's party. (**3**) Everyone*'s going to be* __________ there!

**Evie:** Oh, I'm not! (**4**) We *will visit* __________ my grandparents. All my relatives (**5**) *are getting* __________ together for my granddad's birthday.

**Daisy:** I bet (**6**) that*'ll be* __________ fun! (**7**) *Is your cousin Rick being* __________ there?

**Evie:** Oh, yes. He and I (**8**) *are organising* __________ the birthday party. (**9**) I*'m going to buy* __________ a cake. Rick (**10**) *organises* __________ the entertainment. We (**11**) *will have* __________ a band that play old-fashioned music, the kind my granddad loves.

**Daisy:** Great, although I hope the music at Morgan's party (**12**) *will be* __________ a bit more modern than that!

**Evie:** Have fun, and tell me all about it on Monday!

**Daisy:** I will!

THINK | RESEARCH | CULTURE | LEARN | **ME**

How often do you get together with your extended family?

What's your next big family event?

Describe who will be there and what you expect to happen.



▶ **Workbook Unit 5:** Grammar 1, page 38, exercises 1, 2, 3

## Verbs/adjectives with *-ate*

**1** 2.02 **Most of these words form verbs or adjectives ending in *-ate*. Cross out the one which doesn't and check that you know what the verbs/adjectives for the other words are. Listen and check.**

active | affection | consider | decor | despair | equal | fortune | motive | special | stimulus | value

**2 Write a verb or adjective from a word in Exercise 1 in each gap.**

1 That's really ___________ of you to organise a weekend trip for your mum and dad's anniversary.
2 We're going to ___________ the spare room this weekend. Do you want to help?
3 You're really ___________ to have so much free time.
4 I'm ___________ to find tickets for the concert this weekend – I'll pay anything!
5 Oh, you can't ___________ me having a day off with you taking a week off!
6 What ___________ you to go to the gym and train every weekend?
7 My dog is so ___________ and loves to curl up on my feet.
8 In order to ___________ your gym membership, you have to go to their website.

## Phrasal verbs

**3** 2.03 **Match to make sentences. Listen and check.**

1 I try not to let it *get* me ____
2 When I don't *feel* ____
3 I hate it when people *put* other people ____
4 I hope that in the future, when I *look* ____
5 I can't believe my parents *let* my sister ____
6 Our boss is quite nice, but she doesn't *stand* ____
7 I'd been working so hard that I started to *drop* ____
8 It's important to *sort* ____

a) *off* when she came home really late last Saturday!
b) *down* when I have to work over the weekend.
c) *up to* seeing people, I just stay in my bedroom.
d) *for* people talking when they should be working.
e) *out* any problems before they grow into something bigger.
f) *down* just because they want to play video games all weekend!
g) *back on* my teenage years, I remember the fun times.
h) *off* when we went out at the weekend!

**4 Explain what the phrasal verbs in Exercise 3 mean.**

## *Hobbies*

**5** 2.04 **Put these hobbies in the correct category. Listen and check.**

blogging | board games | DJing | martial arts | mountain biking | online gaming | painting | photography | programming | scuba diving | social networking | yoga

| Computer hobbies | Sports hobbies | Other hobbies |
|---|---|---|
| | | |

**6 For each hobby, think of verbs connected with it.**

*online gaming: play, download, save ...*

**SAY IT RIGHT**

**Resource centre: Unit 5**
Pronunciation of *-ate*

THINK | RESEARCH | CULTURE | LEARN | ME

Have you done any of the hobbies in Exercise 5?
If so, talk about what it was like.
If not, talk about which hobbies you would most like to try.

**1** In pairs or as a group, discuss the questions.

1. Do you belong or have you ever belonged to a club connected to a hobby?
2. Why do some people like to get together with other people who have the same hobby?

**EXAM SKILL**

### Listening for agreement (2)

- Listen carefully to the type of phrases people use when they agree or disagree about something. Some of these appear in Exercise 2.
- Think carefully about what the speaker is referring to and whether you think they are agreeing, disagreeing or partially agreeing.

**2** 2.05 **Choose the correct word to complete each phrase. Listen and check. Then decide if they express agreement (A), partial agreement (P) or disagreement (D).**

1. I agree in **fact** / **principle**, but it's more difficult in practice. ____
2. That's true up to a **place** / **point**. ____
3. I agree to a **certain** / **particular** extent. ____
4. They don't see eye to **ear** / **eye** on anything. ____
5. I don't think we're on the same **frequency** / **wavelength**. ____

**OPTIMISE YOUR EXAM**

### Multiple choice (extracts)

- If you're not sure of the correct answer for a multiple-choice question, try to decide if any of the answers are definitely incorrect.
- If you can exclude one of the options, you have a better chance of getting the right answer the second time you listen.

**3** 2.06 **You will hear people talking in five different situations. For each question, choose the best answer (A, B or C).**

1 You hear two people talking about their hobby.
What do they disagree about?
**A** how much time it takes
**B** how expensive it is
**C** how interesting it is

2 You hear a woman describing a meeting.
What did the people at the meeting agree about?
**A** the venue for an event
**B** the budget for an event
**C** who to invite to an event

3 You hear a news report about a leisure centre.
Who disagrees with the local mayor?
**A** the director of the leisure centre
**B** members of the leisure centre
**C** residents near the leisure centre

4 You hear two friends talking about their camera club.
What do they decide to do?
**A** sell some equipment
**B** organise a competition
**C** hold a fundraising event

5 You hear two friends talking about a new hobby they have taken up.
What does the girl find hard?
**A** getting on with some other people
**B** doing the hobby in the right way
**C** finding the time for the hobby

**4** 2.06 **Listen again and note down the words and phrases which help you choose the answer.**

1 ____________________
2 ____________________
3 ____________________
4 ____________________
5 ____________________


▶ **Workbook Unit 5:** Listening, page 40, exercises 1, 2, 3

# GRAMMAR 2 | Comparatives and superlatives

## Grammar in context

**Look at these extracts from the audio in the listening lesson and answer the questions.**

1 *... is a better idea.*
2 *That was the worst event ever!*
3 *And it was easier than I thought, ...*
4 *I know you work hardest out of all ...*

Which extracts contain ...

**a)** an irregular form? ____
**b)** a superlative? ____
**c)** a superlative adverb? ______
**d)** a comparative? ____

### REMEMBER

- We use comparative adjectives and adverbs to show differences between things and people. We use superlative adjectives and adverbs to show that something/someone is number one in a category.
- For regular one-syllable adjectives and adverbs, we usually form the comparative and superlative by adding *-er* and *-est*. For longer adjectives and adverbs, we use *more/less* and *the most / the least*.
- Remember that there are also a number of irregular forms, including *good-better-best, bad-worse-worst*, etc.
- We can also compare people or things using *(not) as* adjective *as*.

▶ **See Grammar reference, Unit 5,** page 153

**1 Look at these two advertisements and complete the sentences using the prompts.**

**PHOTOGRAPHY MADE EASY!**

**12-week photography course for beginners**

Classes are limited to five people, so you really get the chance to practise and learn!
Course fees: £99.99

For more information, contact info@photogenius.com.

**Learn digital drawing**

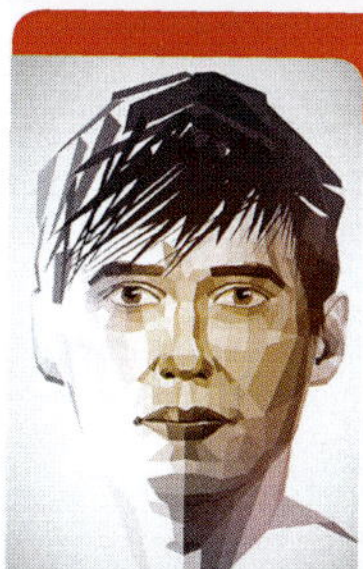

**Digital drawing course, only £120!**

The course lasts eight weeks and is a basic introduction to using your computer to create amazing drawings and pictures. In groups of around 20, you'll learn to produce digital images of people, buildings and landscapes.

Further details: learntodigidraw@artmaster.com

| big | cheap | expensive |
|---|---|---|
| ~~long~~ | short | small |

**Example:**
The photography course *is longer than* the digital drawing course.

1 The digital drawing course ______ the photography course.
2 The photography course ______ the digital drawing course.
3 The digital drawing course ______ the photography course.
4 The photography classes ______ the digital drawing classes.
5 The digital drawing classes ______ the photography classes.

**2 Write a form of the word in brackets in each gap to complete the sentences. Add other words if necessary (*the, than, less, more, as*, etc.).**

1 Thank you so much! That was ______ (**fantastic**) meal I've ever had!
2 It was a fun run, so it didn't matter if some people ran ______ (**fast**) others.
3 That was probably ______ (**interesting**) film I've ever seen. It was so boring!
4 I didn't think the weather would be quite as ______ (**bad**) it was. It rained non-stop all weekend.
5 Messi is one of ______ (**great**) footballers ever, in my opinion.
6 I definitely think geocaching sounds a lot ______ (**fun**) origami!

**3 Write a word or short phrase in each gap to complete the dialogue. Sometimes there is more than one answer.**

**Charlotte:** How was your weekend, Layla?
**Layla:** Great! I had the (**1**) ______ time ever!
**Charlotte:** What did you do?
**Layla:** Well, I had (**2**) ______ money than I usually have, so I went shopping!
**Charlotte:** Did you go to that new place? I heard it's not as (**3**) ______ as the other shops.
**Layla:** Yes, the prices were high, but the quality is (**4**) ______ than in other shops. I bought lots of clothes. What about your weekend?
**Charlotte:** I had even (**5**) ______ free time than usual. I find some of the homework (**6**) ______ to do this year than ever before. It's a bit depressing.
**Charlotte:** Poor you!

# 5 SPEAKING | Interview

Talk2Me *I'm hoping to …*

**Flipped classroom**

**1** Watch the *Talk2Me* video and for each young person, make a note of the hopes and dreams they mention.

**2** Watch the video again and number the phrases in the *Phrase expert* box in the order you hear them.

**PHRASE EXPERT**

at some point | I'd love to | I'm hoping to | I'm looking forward to | I'm not sure, but | in the future | In the future, I'd like to | My ambition is to | one day | We are planning to

**3** In pairs, discuss what the photo shows and how it makes you feel. Would you want to be like the young person in the photo, or not?

**EXAM SKILL**

## Talking about hopes and ambitions

- Your hopes and ambitions are the things you want to do or achieve in the future (education, travel, family, job).
- You can prepare for speaking exams by thinking about your hopes and ambitions. If you aren't sure, use your imagination!

**4** Make a note of your summer plans and your future hopes/ambitions. Use your imagination if necessary.

Tick your ambitions and make a note of why.

| | | |
|---|---|---|
| get a qualification | ☐ | ______ |
| get a good job | ☐ | ______ |
| buy a house | ☐ | ______ |
| become famous | ☐ | ______ |
| get married | ☐ | ______ |
| have children | ☐ | ______ |
| travel the world | ☐ | ______ |
| other: ______ | | |

**5** Use your notes from Exercise 4 and complete sentences 1–6 with your own ideas.

1 To be honest, I don't have ______.

2 My ambition is to one day ______.

3 I'm looking forward to ______.

4 I'm hoping to ______.

5 At some point, I'm planning to ______.

6 In the future, I'd like to ______.

**OPTIMISE YOUR EXAM**

## Interview

- You can prepare for the exam by thinking about how you would answer typical exam questions.
- Don't memorise complete sentences/answers because your answer might not be appropriate to the examiner's question.
- Focus instead on learning useful phrases like those in the *Phrase expert* box.

**6** In pairs, ask and answer these questions.

- Do you have any plans for when you finish school?
- What job or career interests you?
- Where do you see yourself in 10 years' time?
- Do you have any personal ambitions?

**7** Tell the class what you learnt about your partner.

# USE OF ENGLISH | Open cloze

**1** **In pairs or groups, answer the questions.**

1 What do different people in your family do to relax?

2 What do you do as a whole family when you have free time?

**EXAM SKILL**

## Prepositions and short adverbs

- Prepositions and short adverbs are often tested in exams.
- These are words that tell us, for example, when (e.g. *at, in, until, before, since*), where (e.g. *in, between, under*), or about direction (e.g. *up, down, out, towards*). They also can appear in word patterns (e.g. *in your free time, regardless of*) and as part of phrasal verbs (e.g. *go away, put up with, sort out*).

**2** **Complete the sentences with a preposition or short adverb in each gap.**

1 I like to look ___________ the CD artwork when I'm listening ___________ my favourite band.

2 I met Robin ___________ the cinema ___________ half past five ___________ going in to watch the film.

3 I've got the day ___________ work on Friday so let's go ___________ the countryside.

4 Are you interested ___________ joining the scuba diving club that meets ___________ Fridays?

5 I've been working ___________ six and I'll be here ___________ ten, so call me ___________ half past ten.

6 On Saturdays I like to go ___________ , usually ___________ friends.

7 I prefer to stay ___________ bed late ___________ the weekend, but my brother likes to get ___________ early and do exercise.

8 ___________ school I usually see if there is anything interesting ___________ TV or if I have any emails ___________ my friends.

9 **A:** 'We are going to hang ___________ at the shopping mall tomorrow.'

**B:** 'Really? I don't think I am feeling ___________ to it. I'll stay ___________ home.'

10 I have been feeling a lot fitter ___________ I took ___________ rock climbing.

**3** **Quickly read the text in Exercise 4. Which three gaps are part of a phrasal verb?**

___________ ___________ ___________

**OPTIMISE YOUR EXAM**

## Open cloze

- Read the title and whole text first for general understanding.
- Look at each gap and decide what kind of word you need, e.g. a noun, verb, etc. and write only one word in each gap.
- Check your spelling carefully – it must be correct to get full marks.

**4** **Write one word in each gap.**

### Free time choices

Whether you're a teenager looking for ways to chill **(1)**___________ or an adult who comes home after working nine **(2)**___________ five in an office job wanting to relax, you have a number of options available to you. Perhaps you're going to watch TV, listen **(3)**___________ music or go online and chat with friends or play games. Whole industries worth millions of pounds have sprung **(4)**___________ to meet our need for leisure. In fact, these days many of us are involved **(5)**___________ so many leisure activities, we are afraid we might run **(6)**___________ of time before we can enjoy them all.

It wasn't always like that. In the past, people worked longer hours and had jobs that were physically more demanding. Any time **(7)**___________ work was used to rest and to recover. Next time you ask yourself what you're doing **(8)**___________ the weekend, just remember how fortunate you are to have a weekend in the first place!

THINK | **RESEARCH** | CULTURE | LEARN | ME

Ask your parents and grandparents how they think leisure activities have changed over time.

Make a note of what people used to do in their free time in the past and tell your class what you have learnt.

▶ **Workbook Unit 5:** Use of English, page 41, exercises 1, 2

**1** **In pairs or as a group, answer the questions.**

1 Do your parents let you do whatever you want in your free time or are there some rules?
2 Do you think you should have more freedom? What would you do with more freedom?

**EXAM SKILL**

### Giving reasons

- When you give your opinion in a piece of writing, it's important that you provide reasons for that opinion.
- You can use phrases such as *The reason for this is …* and *This is because …* to help your reader to see that you are about to give a reason.

**2** **Read the article. How does the writer try to get the reader's attention at the beginning? Do you agree with the advice the writer gives?**

## Is your free time really free?

Do you have the freedom to do what you want in your free time? Many young people don't. That's because their parents want to control all their time. If this sounds familiar, here are a few suggestions for sorting out the situation.

First of all, don't blame your parents. Because they want the best for you, they sometimes put you under pressure regarding school and homework, which can affect your free time. Instead of blaming them, show them that you're doing well at school and that playing video games now and then won't affect your marks!

Secondly, show your parents how motivated you are. If you want to stop doing an activity they have chosen, show them how much you really want to do another activity of your own choice instead. They might change their minds if they can see how serious you are.

Finally, remind your parents that you need to be responsible for planning your own time to some extent. The reason for this is that in the future you will have to do that without their help. Explain that you need to start learning skills like that now.

Good luck!

**3** **Read the article again and underline any reasons the writer gives.**

**4** **In pairs, make a list of words and phrases for giving reasons in an article. Compare your ideas with another pair.**

**OPTIMISE YOUR EXAM**

### An article

- Before you write your article, think of five or six ideas you could include.
- Then decide which of these ideas are the best ones to include.
- For 140–190 words, try to choose three ideas, because you also need to give reasons, examples or explanations.

**5** **Look at this writing task and choose three ideas to write about.**

You see this notice on an English-language website for teenagers.

> **NOT ENOUGH FREE TIME!**
> We all know that teens don't have enough free time these days. But what advice do you have for young people just like you who are under pressure? Tell us in an article. The best articles will appear on our website!

Write your **article**.

- talk to your parents ☐
- talk to your friends ☐
- watch less TV ☐
- learn to manage your time better ☐
- your idea: ______________________ ☐
- spend less time online ☐
- drop some activities or hobbies ☐

**6** **For each idea you have chosen, make a note of the main reason why you think it is a good idea.**

Idea: ______________________ Reason: ______________________
Idea: ______________________ Reason: ______________________
Idea: ______________________ Reason: ______________________

**7** **Plan** **Complete the paragraph plan.**

| Part | Purpose | Useful phrases | My notes |
|---|---|---|---|
| **Title** | briefly describe what the article is about – and make us want to read it! | *We all know ...*<br>*But ...*<br>*Many young people ...* | |
| **Paragraph 1** | introduce the subject and engage the reader | *Have you ever ...?*<br>*Do you ...?* | |
| **Paragraph 2/3** | describe your ideas, giving reasons and examples where appropriate | *The reason for this is ...*<br>*Also, remember that ...*<br>*One example of this is ...,*<br>*For instance, ...* | |
| **Paragraph 4** | come to a conclusion, offer any final advice | *The most important thing ...*<br>*Follow this advice and you'll ...* | |

**8** **Write** **Write your article in an appropriate style. Write 140–190 words.**

**9** **Check** **Before you hand in your article, complete this checklist.**

**Checklist**

- ○ I've chosen three ideas to write about.
- ○ I've included reasons and examples where appropriate.
- ○ I've used a conversational style.
- ○ I've included all the information I was asked to.
- ○ I've written at least four paragraphs.
- ○ I've checked my spelling and grammar.
- ○ I've written a good conclusion and offered advice.

▶ **Writing reference,** page 169 ▶ **Workbook Unit 5:** Writing, page 42, exercises 1, 2, 3, 4 and Progress check 5, page 43

# 6 Good food, good mood

## READING | Multiple choice | A magazine article

**1** **Look at these sayings and statements. What do you think they mean? Which of them do you agree with?**

An apple a day keeps the doctor away.

Don't go outside with wet hair or you'll catch a cold.

Don't go swimming for an hour after you've eaten.

Feed a cold, starve a fever.

Chicken soup cures a cold.

**EXAM SKILL**

### Deducing meaning from context

- When you need to guess the meaning of a word/phrase in a text, think about the general idea and subject of the text.
- Then focus on the sentence/paragraph the word/phrase appears in and look for clues to its meaning.
- This context can help you to make a logical guess.

**2** **Find these sentences in the article. Choose the best word or phrase to complete each description.**

1 *But are all old wives' tales false, or does modern science back any of them up?*

The second part of the sentence begins with 'or', suggesting contrast, so the phrasal verb 'back up' here probably means **disprove** / **support** / **negate**.

2 *They say it's to avoid muscle cramps, because the body is busy digesting the food.*

The advice is aimed at avoiding something, so 'muscle cramps' are probably some kind of **exercise** / **food** / **pain**.

**3** **Choose the correct word. If you aren't sure, find the phrases in the article and deduce the meaning.**

| | | |
|---|---|---|
| 1 | fever (paragraph 3) | **low** / **high** temperature |
| 2 | dehydration (paragraph 3) | condition caused when the body has too **much** / **little** water |
| 3 | nutrient (paragraph 3) | **unhealthy** / **healthy** things we get from food |
| 4 | inflammation (paragraph 4) | red, **hot** / **cold** and/or swollen area of the body |
| 5 | inevitably (paragraph 5) | used to say that something is **unlikely** / **certain** to happen |

# Science fact or science fiction?

Chocolate makes you live longer. Carrots help you to see in the dark. If you go outside with wet hair, you'll catch a cold. These are some of the old wives' tales that have been passed down through generations. If I had a pound for every time my mum stopped me leaving the house with wet hair, I'd be rich. But are all old wives' tales false, or does modern science back any of them up? I've been to see GP, Dr Jane Turner to ask if there's any scientific proof for any of these common myths.

*By Dani Wells, Year 11*

### 'Don't go swimming for an hour after you've eaten.'

My mum and dad often say this. They say it's to avoid muscle cramps, because the body is busy digesting the food. Interestingly, Dr Turner thinks there's an element of truth to this. She told me, 'I wouldn't agree it has to be an hour – that seems too long to me – but I would say if you've had a big meal, you should at least wait until you've started to digest it. I'd say at least 15 or 20 minutes would probably be enough.'

### 'Feed a cold, starve a fever.'

I've never fully understood what it meant, so I asked Dr Turner to explain it. 'Well, this is saying: if you have a cold, eat and drink well, but if you have a fever, don't. It's totally wrong, and I believe it's based on a misunderstanding with the word "starve". Originally, the saying used to be 'feed a cold, stave off a fever'. This means eat and drink well to prevent your cold developing into a fever. That was probably sensible advice. You should try to eat and drink well as it's important to avoid dehydration. And if your body doesn't get the vitamins and nutrients it needs, it loses strength.

### 'If you have a cold, eat chicken soup.'

We've all heard this one, haven't we? And Dr Turner agreed. 'I think it's probably good advice – unless you're vegetarian or vegan, of course! A bowl of chicken soup is comforting, so it may well have a positive psychological effect. Also, I've heard of a study which suggests it may reduce inflammation, so it's worth a try.'

So what about going outside with wet hair? Does it inevitably lead to getting a cold, or can I tell my mum she's wrong? 'No, this one's not true at all. Colds are caused by viruses, not wet hair or generally "being cold". This has actually been tested several times. They've split people into two groups, one where the people were warm, and one where the people were cold. They then exposed them to a virus. There was no difference between the two groups in terms of how many people caught a cold.'

## OPTIMISE YOUR EXAM

### Multiple choice

- Always start by reading everything carefully.
- For some questions you need to refer to a whole paragraph, e.g. Exercise 4, questions 1 and 2.
- Find the correct reference in the paragraph. Some options may look correct but may refer to something different.

**4** 2.07 **For questions 1–5, choose the answer (A, B, C or D) which you think fits best according to the text.**

1 What do we learn about the writer's mother in the first paragraph?
  **A** She probably never believes in her sayings.
  **B** She only regularly tells Dani one folk saying.
  **C** She'd never let Dani go outside with wet hair.
  **D** She often says what some people call 'old wives' tales'.

2 What advice does Dr Turner give in the second paragraph?
  **A** Don't swim for more than 20 minutes with a full stomach.
  **B** Don't go swimming just after a large meal.
  **C** Completely ignore the old wives' tale about swimming.
  **D** Digest your food very quickly before going swimming.

3 Dr Turner suggests that the phrase 'stave off' in line 25
  **A** is used to mean 'starve' but doesn't mean that anymore.
  **B** means something similar to 'eat and drink well'.
  **C** changed over time into 'starve' and this made the saying false.
  **D** not heard in modern-day English.

4 Talking about chicken soup, Dr Turner says
  **A** she doesn't understand the science behind the treatment.
  **B** she always has a bowl whenever she has a cold.
  **C** it only helps us get well because it affects us psychologically.
  **D** vegetarians and vegans are at a disadvantage if they get ill.

5 The word 'exposed' in line 46 means they allowed them to
  **A** see the virus.
  **B** avoid the virus.
  **C** come into contact with the virus.
  **D** study the virus.

THINK | RESEARCH | **CULTURE** | LEARN | ME

What old wives' tales and sayings, similar to the ones in the article, do you have in your own culture/language?

▶ **Workbook Unit 6:** Reading, page 44, exercises 1, 2, 3

# 6 GRAMMAR 1 | Conditionals (1): zero, first and second conditionals

## Grammar in context

**In pairs, find and underline these conditional sentences in the text on page 59. Identify the grammar in each sentence.**

1 If you go outside with wet hair, you'll catch a cold.
2 If I had a pound for every time my mum stopped me leaving the house with wet hair, I'd be rich.
3 And if your body doesn't get the vitamins and nutrients it needs, it loses strength
4 I think it's probably good advice – unless you're vegetarian or vegan, of course!

### REMEMBER

Conditionals use different tenses depending on what we are talking about:

- We use the zero conditional to talk about general truths and scientific facts: *If you* ***don't eat*** *for a few days, you* ***start*** *to feel very weak and dizzy.*
- We use the first conditional to talk about real or likely situations now, generally or in the future: *If you* ***eat*** *four ice creams, you****'ll be*** *sick!*
- We use the second conditional to talk about hypothetical, impossible or unlikely situations now, generally or in the future: *If you* ***lived*** *at the North Pole, you* ***would*** *probably* ***eat*** *a lot of fish.*

Sometimes we use different words instead of *if* in conditionals:

- *unless* means 'if not' or 'except if': *If it is not urgent, I won't call the doctor. = Unless it is urgent, I won't call the doctor.*
- *as long as* is similar to *if* and means 'on condition that': *I will go to the doctor as long as you come with me.*

▶ **See Grammar reference, Unit 6,** page 153

**1 Match to make sentences.**

1 If you bite your tongue, it ____
2 If you yawn, ____
3 Put half an onion under your bed ____
4 If you put half an onion under your bed ____
5 If someone's nose is itchy, it means they're ____
6 The visitor will be female if ____
7 If it's the left side of the nose, the visitor ____
8 It means you might ____

**a)** if you're ill.
**b)** it's the right side of the nose that's itchy.
**c)** when you're ill, it will help you get better.
**d)** means that you've recently told a lie.
**e)** will be male.
**f)** go on a journey soon if your right foot itches.
**g)** it often means that danger is nearby.
**h)** going to have a visitor.

**2 If a word or phrase in bold is correct, put a tick. If it's incorrect, rewrite it correctly.**

1 If I have a headache, I usually **took** a couple of aspirin and it disappears. ____________
2 If you don't feel well tomorrow, you **aren't** able to play in the match. ____________
3 **I'll** make an appointment to see a doctor if I were you. ____________
4 If Carla **won't feel** well, she should lie down for a while. ____________
5 You **won't get** any cake unless you eat your vegetables.____________
6 If I told you to put half an onion under your bed, **will** you do it? ____________

**3 Complete each second sentence so that it means the same as the first sentence. Use zero, first or second conditionals.**

**Example:** Eat more fruit and you'll feel better.
*If you eat more fruit, you'll feel better.*
*Unless you eat more fruit, you won't feel better.*
*As long as you eat more fruit, you'll feel better.*

1 Don't go swimming on a full stomach or you might get cramp.
If ______________________________.
2 The only thing that will make my headache go away is drinking a lot of water.
Unless ______________________________.
3 Ellie has a lot of energy when she gets enough sleep.
As long as Ellie ______________________________.
4 It's not weird that doctors don't believe most old wives' tales.
It would ______________________________.
5 People who eat carrots regularly have great eyesight.
If you ______________________________.
6 Take my advice and you'll recover very soon.
If you ______________________________.
Unless you ______________________________.
As long as you ______________________________.

THINK | RESEARCH | CULTURE | LEARN | **ME**

In pairs, decide which of the sayings and ideas in Exercise 1 you think are sensible and which you think are silly.

## Words + prepositions

**1** 2.08 **Write one preposition in each gap to complete the phrases. Use the words in italics to help you. Listen and check.**

1 Do you think you might be *addicted* ___________ chocolate?
2 When would you *advise* ___________ going swimming?
3 Do you know any sayings that *date back* ___________ the old days?
4 Do you ever do anything that's *based* ___________ an old wives' tale?
5 Do you know anyone who's *allergic* ___________ penicillin?
6 Do you *approve* ___________ people eating crisps for breakfast?
7 What diseases do you think they will have found a *cure* ___________ by 2050?
8 If you had to *get rid* ___________ one thing from your diet, what would you choose?

**2** **In pairs, decide what the phrases in italics mean then ask and answer the questions in Exercise 1.**

## Adverbs formed from adjectives

**3** 2.09 **Write the adverb form of each adjective in the correct column. Listen and check.**

~~accidental~~ | anxious | ~~automatic~~ | basic | cheerful | comfortable | current | day | early | easy | extraordinary | fast | frequent | good | gradual | happy | hopeful | regular | relative | remarkable | short | surprising | traditional | true | unbelievable

| adverb is adjective + *-ly* | adverb is not just adjective + *-ly* but does ends with *-ly* | adverb does not end with *-ly* |
|---|---|---|
| *accidentally* | *automatically* | |

**SAY IT RIGHT**

Resource centre: Unit 6
Pronunciation of adjectives ending with *-ly*

## Words connected with *health*

**4** 2.10 **Choose the correct word to complete the sentences. Use a dictionary if necessary. Listen and check.**

1 Joe picked up a very hot pan that was in the oven and there's a nasty **burn** / **cut** on his hand.
2 I've felt ill for ten days. I think I must have a **cramp** / **virus**.
3 40.1 degrees is a very high **allergy** / **temperature**. You should go to the doctor.
4 Anna **sprained** / **cut** her finger with a knife in the kitchen. I think she needs a plaster.
5 Lots of people catch **flu** / **burns** in the winter.
6 One of the symptoms of flu can be a **sore throat** / **virus**.
7 Max has got a headache and a **fever** / **bruise**. I think he's got flu.
8 Beatrice can't walk very well. She **burnt** / **sprained** her ankle playing tennis today.
9 I've been sitting down all day and now I've got **an allergy** / **a cramp** in my leg.
10 You've got a bad **sprain** / **cold** so make sure you wear some warm clothes and take some tissues with you.
11 My eyes are sore and my skin is red. I think I've got **an allergy** / **a virus**. It must be your cats.
12 David had a nasty **bruise** / **fever** on his arm after he fell off his bike.

# LISTENING | Multiple choice (extracts)

**1** **Say the phrase below, using the four different emotions. Does the tone of your voice and attitude change according to the emotion?**

'It's time to go home.'

worried

happy

surprised

angry

## EXAM SKILL

### Identifying attitude (2)

- Sometimes listening for attitude involves more than just understanding the phrases speakers use.
- The same phrase can have different meanings depending on the attitude of the speaker.

**2** 2.11 **Read and listen to the extract and answer the questions.**

**Man:** It's quite an unusual job ...

**Woman:** Yes, and I'm totally addicted to it! It's not so much that people are going to benefit from the work I do – they aren't particularly. It's more that it's just absolutely fascinating. And when other people find what I discover interesting too, well, that's an added bonus.

1 When the woman says 'I'm totally addicted to it', is her attitude towards her job positive or negative?
2 Does the woman think that people will really benefit from her work?
3 Does the phrase 'an added bonus' mean 'even more important' here?

## OPTIMISE YOUR EXAM

### Multiple choice (extracts)

- Multiple-choice tasks often include a question on understanding a speaker's attitude or opinion.
- Read each question and the options carefully before you listen to identify the possible attitudes.

**3** 2.12 **You will hear people talking in five different situations. For each question, choose the best answer (A, B or C).**

1 You hear a boy talking about a school project. What did he feel most proud of?
**A** how long he worked on it
**B** what he discovered
**C** his choice of topic

2 You hear part of an interview with a social historian. How does the woman feel about her work?
**A** She loves the fact it helps people.
**B** She knows everyone will find it interesting.
**C** She thoroughly enjoys doing it.

3 You hear a doctor talking about his childhood. What is he grateful for?
**A** that he's had the opportunity to become a doctor
**B** that his family's sayings made him question things
**C** that family members taught him so many things

4 You hear two friends talking about a saying. How does the girl feel?
**A** She completely disagrees with the saying.
**B** She only disagrees with part of the saying.
**C** She thinks the saying is generally sensible.

5 You hear a customer talking to a chemist. Why is the woman unhappy?
**A** The chemist's attitude has annoyed her.
**B** She's uncertain where to go next.
**C** She's worried about plans she has made.

**4** 2.12 **Listen again and note down the words and phrases which help you choose the answer.**

1 ____________________
2 ____________________
3 ____________________
4 ____________________
5 ____________________



▶ **Workbook Unit 6:** Listening, page 48, exercises 1, 2, 3

# GRAMMAR 2 | Relative clauses

## Grammar in context

**Write one word in each gap to complete these extracts from the audio in the listening lesson.**

1 My next guest is Linda, __________ is a social historian.

2 … old sayings and various pieces of folk advice __________ people have given each other over the centuries.

3 … there were many times __________ my grandparents – and my parents to be honest – came out with …

4 I think that's the reason __________ some people say it, isn't it?

### REMEMBER

- A defining relative clause identifies which thing or person we are talking about: *The person who gave me the information is a GP.*
- A non-defining relative clause gives us extra, but not essential, information. The clause is separated from the rest of the sentence by commas: *My GP, who is called Dr Turner, told me to take antibiotics.*

▶ **See Grammar reference, Unit 6,** page 154

**1 Which sentences in the box above are defining and which are non-defining?**

### REMEMBER

- Relative clauses often begin with a relative pronoun, such as *who*, *which*, *that*, *why*, *where*, *whose*.
- The pronoun *that* can be used instead of *who* or *which*; we cannot use *that* in non-defining clauses.
- The pronoun *who* becomes *whom* for people as the object of the relative clause, but is very formal; and we can use *whom* after a preposition (*She is the doctor to whom I spoke.*).
- If the relative pronoun refers to the object of the clause, we can omit it (*She is the doctor (who) I spoke to.*).

▶ **See Grammar reference, Unit 6,** page 154

**2 Write one word in each gap. Sometimes there is more than one answer.**

1 What was the name of that health website for teenagers __________ you told me about?

2 I saw a programme about extremely unfit people and that was the day __________ I decided to exercise more and eat healthily.

3 The reason __________ I don't believe in aromatherapy is simple.

4 Anyone __________ mum or dad is a dentist will know how important it is to clean your teeth regularly.

5 The clinic __________ my mum works has more than 15 doctors.

6 The Health Minister, in __________ the Prime Minister has total confidence, will visit a hospital later today.

**3 Tick the correct sentences. Underline the mistakes in the other sentences and correct them.**

1 Acupuncture which is a treatment using needles is becoming more popular.

______________________________

2 The kind of treatment which I think is ridiculous is aromatherapy.

______________________________

3 Hypnosis, that involves putting someone into a hypnotic state, is only practised by a few doctors.

______________________________

4 To have a lovely massage once a month was the reason why I joined the health club.

______________________________

**4 Write one word in each gap.**

## Phobias

What do heights, spiders, snakes and clowns have in common? They're among British people's most common fears. A survey, (**1**) __________ was recently carried out in the UK, asked people to rate 13 common phobias. Acrophobia, (**2**) __________ is the fear of heights, was the most common. Younger people (**3**) __________ answered the survey were more afraid of spiders and public speaking, whereas older people were more afraid of snakes and heights.

Phobias are a common condition and people (**4**) __________ phobias aren't diagnosed can suffer for years. Luckily there are lots of online forums (**5**) __________ you can chat to other people (**6**) __________ suffer from the same condition. Alternative therapies are often used to treat these kinds of fears. That's the reason (**7**) __________ hypnotherapy, (**8**) __________ is the use of hypnosis to treat medical and psychological conditions, is often used in the treatment of phobias.

THINK | RESEARCH | CULTURE | LEARN | **ME**

What phobias do you have?

What things do you think people usually have phobias about?

Talk2Me

My preference would be …

Flipped classroom

**1** Watch the *Talk2Me* video and note down who answers which of the questions below and what their preferences are.

1 Would you rather have a fizzy drink, fruit juice or water?
2 Would you prefer to eat a sandwich, salad or burger?
3 Do you like eating in or out?
4 Do you usually choose a savoury or a sweet snack?

**2** Watch the video again. Underline the phrases in the *Phrase expert* box that you hear on the video.

**PHRASE EXPERT**

because (of) | due to | my preference would be | so | the reason why / for this is | would prefer (not) to do | would rather … than

**EXAM SKILL**

**Expressing preference and giving reasons**

- You may have to express a preference in a speaking exam.
- Remember to give a reason for your preference.
- Use a variety of different words and phrases for expressing preference and giving reasons.

**3** In pairs or as a group, choose one of the questions in Exercise 1 to discuss and talk about your preferences.

**4** Complete the sentences with the words in the box.

for (× 2) | (not) to | over/to | than

1 I'd never go ____________ a fizzy drink due to all the sugar they have.
2 My preference would be ____________ water because it's healthier.
3 I'd much rather have burger and chips ____________ salad.
4 I prefer eating in ____________ eating out as it's more practical.
5 I'd definitely prefer ____________ have something sweet.

**5** Match to make sentences.

1 I'd never choose to have a burger because ____
2 I'd prefer not to eat out due to ____
3 The reason why I'd never choose fizzy drinks is ____
4 The reason for me never choosing salad ____
5 I hate unhealthy food so ____

**a)** because I don't like them.
**b)** I avoid going to fast-food restaurants.
**c)** I'm a vegetarian.
**d)** is because I hate vegetables.
**e)** the fact that it's not practical.

**OPTIMISE YOUR EXAM**

**Photo task**

- After your partner has compared two photographs you have to answer a short question about them.
- You have about 30 seconds to talk so don't worry if the examiner stops you!
- In Exercise 6, the short question asks you to give a preference and explain your reasons.

**6** In pairs, look at the photos. Make notes to answer the questions.

1 What are the positive aspects of each restaurant?
______________________________
2 What are the negative aspects of each restaurant?
______________________________
3 How do you think the people in the photos feel?
______________________________
4 Which restaurant would you prefer, and why?
______________________________

**7** In pairs, look at the photos and complete the task. Then swap roles.

**Student A:** Compare the two photographs and say what the benefits are of eating in each place. (1 minute)

**Student B:** Which of the two restaurants would you prefer to eat in? Why? (30 seconds)



▶ **Workbook Unit 6:** Speaking, pages 48–49, exercises 1, 2, 3

# USE OF ENGLISH | Word formation

**1** **Look at the words in the box below that collocate with food. For each one say what the collocations means and give some examples.**

comfort | fast | fresh | junk
organic | processed

*junk food – unhealthy food that contains a lot of fat, salt and sugar.*

## EXAM SKILL

### Adjectives and adverbs

- Adjectives usually describe people/things but can also describe certain verbs (e.g. *be, stay, get*)
- Adverbs can describe a verb (e.g. *drive* ***quickly***), a whole sentence (e.g. ***Fortunately***, *I got better*) and adjectives (e.g. ***extremely*** *healthy*).

**2** **In pairs, decide whether each missing word is an adjective (adj) or an adverb (adv). Write an example for each one.**

1 adj/adv It was really ________.
2 adj/adv She ran ________ quickly.
3 adj/adv Is it ________ friendly?
4 adj/adv It's a ________ , shocking story.
5 adj/adv I ________ managed to finish in time.
6 adj/adv ________ , it's true!
7 adj/adv I find it ________ to believe.
8 adj/adv Eat it ________ .
9 adj/adv Stay ________ !
10 adj/adv Speak ________ !

**3** **Look at the text in Exercise 4. For each gap, decide what kind of word (noun, adjective, etc.) is probably required.**

## OPTIMISE YOUR EXAM

### Word formation

- If you're not sure what part of speech you need, ignore the word in capitals and think of other words that could complete the gap.
- For example, in Exercise 4, question 4, ignore 'HEALTH' and try different adjectives and adverbs (e.g. *happy/happily, strong/strongly*) to see which sound right. This can help you decide that you should change 'HEALTH' into an adjective.

**4** **Write a form of the word in capitals in each gap to complete the text.**

### Fish is brain food

For centuries, people have believed that eating fish is beneficial for the brain. (1) ________ , nutritionists and other experts now accept that there is a lot of truth to this ancient wisdom. Some essential fatty acids (EFAs) aren't produced by the human body. To get them, we have to eat things which contain them – and many oily fish do. When we eat them, our bodies (2) ________ absorb the useful EFAs. **REMARK** / **EASY**

Many (3) ________ studies have shown that these EFAs help our brains stay (4) ________ , as well as benefitting other parts of the body, such as the heart. They also help preserve the (5) ________ of our joints. But how much fish do we need to eat? Perhaps (6) ________ , not very much. You certainly don't need to eat it (7) ________ . It seems that eating fish just once or twice a week can be (8) ________ beneficial. **SCIENCE** / **HEALTH** / **STRONG** / **SURPRISE** / **DAY** / **TRUE**

THINK | RESEARCH | CULTURE | LEARN | ME

Go online and research 'super foods'.

Choose one and write a short text explaining how it is good for your health.

# WRITING | An article

**1** **In pairs or as a group, match the food sayings to their meanings.**

1 Don't cry over spilt milk.
- **a)** Don't be unhappy about something that's already happened.
- **b)** Don't be upset if you spill milk on something.

2 Take something with a pinch of salt.
- **a)** Don't have too much salt in your diet.
- **b)** Be sceptical about what you are told.

3 Don't bite off more than you can chew.
- **a)** Don't take on too much.
- **b)** Don't eat too much at mealtimes.

**EXAM SKILL**

### Engaging the reader

- A key skill when you write is to find ways to hold the attention of the reader so they will want to keep reading.
- There are a number of ways you can do this depending on the type of text.
- We will look at some in exercises 2 and 3.

**2** **Read this article and make notes to answer the questions.**

## A COMMON SAYING

You know what it's like. You're hungry and you grab some crisps or you're rushing off to school and haven't got time for breakfast.

Have you ever heard the saying 'you are what you eat'? It means that in order to be fit and healthy, you need to eat good food. I'm sure it's the kind of thing you've heard your parents say!

Although it's a common saying, I've never stopped to think about what it actually means. Apparently, nine of out ten of us eat junk food on a daily basis and we've probably all had the short-term sugar rush after snacking on chocolate. But there's a real link between what we eat and how we function. Think about smart snacking – eating healthy snacks, such as fresh fruit and popcorn instead of sweets to give us more energy and improve our concentration, which actually helps us study and perform better.

Do you know what the strangest thing is? I've started paying attention to what I eat and I think it's having a positive effect on my energy levels and my ability to study more effectively. Maybe I really am what I eat!

1 Did you find the article interesting?
2 Do you think the writer tried to make the article interesting to read?
3 If yes, what language and techniques did they use? If no, what should they have done to make it more interesting?

**3** **Look at the article again. Find these sentences and answer the questions.**

*You know what it's like.*

1 Who is 'you'?
2 By the end of the sentence, do we know what 'it' refers to?
3 What effect does this have?

*Do you know what the strangest thing is?*

4 Is the reader supposed to answer this question?
5 By the end of the question, do we know what is strange?
6 What effect does this have?

**4** **In pairs or as a group, discuss your answers to exercises 2 and 3.**

**OPTIMISE YOUR EXAM**

### An article

- An article should entertain and engage the reader so try to keep their attention throughout, starting in the introduction.
- Asking the reader questions, or saying something that surprises the reader, makes them think about what you might say next.

## 5 Look at this writing task and complete the information.

You see this notice in an international English-language magazine for teenagers.

> **ARTICLES WANTED**
>
> We're looking for articles about unusual or interesting sayings about health and fitness.
> Does anyone you know use a saying to give advice on how to stay healthy?
> Tell us about it – describe the saying and explain what makes it unusual or interesting.
> The best articles will be published in our next issue.

Write your **article**.

| | |
|---|---|
| **What is the saying in English?** It doesn't have to be a real saying. You can make one up. Use your imagination! | |
| **What is it used for?** Make sure it's connected in some way to health and fitness and staying healthy. | |
| **What makes it unusual or interesting?** What does the saying mean and how is it relevant today? | |
| **How are you going to start?** Write the first one or two sentences. Try to interest and engage the reader and make them want to read on. | |

## 6 Plan Make a paragraph plan.

| Part | Purpose | Useful phrases | My notes |
|---|---|---|---|
| **Title** | interest the reader | | |
| **Paragraph 1** | engage the reader and get them interested in the subject | *You know what it's like.*<br>*Have you ever heard ...?* | |
| **Paragraph 2** | describe the saying and when people use it | *One saying I find interesting is …*<br>*Isn't it strange when people say …?* | |
| **Paragraph 3** | explain what makes the saying unusual or interesting | *It's a bit odd because …*<br>*Do they mean …?* | |
| **Paragraph 4** | conclude | *So, next time you hear someone say …*<br>*Listen out for …* | |

## 7 Write Write your article in an appropriate style. Write 140–190 words.

## 8 Check Before you hand in your article, complete this checklist.

**Checklist**

- ◯ I've included all the information from my notes in Exercise 5.
- ◯ I've followed my paragraph plan.
- ◯ I've tried to engage the reader and make them want to continue reading.
- ◯ I've used a friendly style that's not too formal.
- ◯ I've checked my spelling and grammar.

▶ Writing reference, page 169 ▶ **Workbook Unit 6:** Writing, page 50, exercises 1, 2, 3, 4 and Progress check 6, page 51

# PROGRESS CHECK UNITS 5–6

## GRAMMAR AND VOCABULARY

**1 Write a form of the word in capitals in each gap.**

**JOINING A DANCE GROUP**

Being in a dance group isn't easy. You need to be (**1**) ___________ to have the right physical abilities, and you also need to be very hard-working. It isn't always easy to (**2**) ___________ yourself to do the long hours of practice that are necessary. However (**3**) ___________ you can dance, it's (**4**) ___________ essential to trust, and help, the other people in the group. But, if you're an (**5**) ___________ good dancer who can also be (**6**) ___________ towards the other dancers, then maybe it's the right hobby – or even career – for you.

**FORTUNE**
**MOTIVE**
**GOOD**
**TRUE**
**EXTRAORDINARY**
**CONSIDER**

__/6

**2 Choose the correct word or phrase.**

1 The weather forecast said it **is raining / is going to rain** tomorrow.
2 What do you think **will happen / is happening** if we tell him the truth?
3 I think I **have / am going to have** a party for my birthday this year.
4 You **won't see / aren't seeing** Big Ben because we're not going into London.
5 **Are you making / Do you make** dinner tonight or is it Mum's turn?
6 What **are you going to do / are you doing** if you don't pass the exam?

__/6

**3 Write a relative pronoun in each gap. Sometimes there is more than one answer.**

1 Rugby league, ___________ is a similar game to rugby union, is popular in many countries around the world.
2 Do you remember the day ___________ they knocked down the cinema to build a gym?
3 I wonder ___________ DVD this is?
4 That's the park ___________ they hold the book and film festival.
5 Do you know the reason ___________ the youth club has been closed?
6 The villages ___________ we drove through were really pretty.
7 The team captain, ___________ they gave the trophy to, lives quite near here.
8 That was the year in ___________ they didn't take part in the competition.
9 Do you know ___________ country is going to host the next World Cup?
10 Do you know ___________ the next World Cup is going to be held?

__/10

**4 Choose the correct word or phrase.**

1 What's the **more / most** difficult game you've ever played?
2 Our team played much worse **that / than** I'd expected.
3 That knife's sharp, but this one is **even / more** sharper.
4 Today you played the **better / best** you've ever played.
5 We walked a lot **further than / as far as** we'd planned to.

__/5

## 5 Match to make sentences.

1 How is your sore ____
2 These cave paintings date ____
3 Seb is ill and doesn't feel ____
4 Our teacher caught us talking but let us ____
5 You should sort ____
6 I'd love to learn scuba ____

a) up to going out tonight.
b) diving but I can't swim.
c) throat feeling now?
d) off with just a warning.
e) back thousands of years.
f) out your back problem before it gets worse.

__/6

## 6 Write one word in each gap.

1 Mum says I spend too much time on social ________ sites.
2 You're addicted ________ sweets! You eat them all the time.
3 Do you approve ________ people who drop rubbish in the streets?
4 Doctors advise ________ eating too much sugar.
5 I don't think they'll ever find a cure ________ cancer.
6 Have you taken your ________ ? I think you might have a fever.
7 We can't have a kitten because my brother's really allergic ________ cats.

__/7

## 7 Complete the second sentence so it has a similar meaning to the first. Do not change the word given. Use two to five words, including the word given.

1 The council have removed the statue from the park. **RID**
The council have ____________________ the statue from the park.
2 I think you should complain. **IF**
I would ____________________ you.
3 No-one in the group is more considerate and caring than Emma. **MOST**
Emma is ____________________ member of the group.
4 If you bring it back straight away, you can use my tablet. **LONG**
You can use my tablet ____________________ you bring it back straight away.
5 Don't ride your bike at night if it doesn't have lights on. **UNLESS**
Don't ride your bike at night ____________________ lights on.

__/10

**Total score** __/50

## EXAM SKILLS

Tick the statements that are true for you. Review the skills in the unit if you need more help.

| I can … | Unit/page |
|---|---|
| ☐ understand references in an historical article | Unit 5 p48 |
| ☐ listen for agreement phrases in short extracts | Unit 5 p52 |
| ☐ talk about my hopes and ambitions in an interview | Unit 5 p54 |
| ☐ understand prepositions and short adverbs and use them in an open-cloze exercise | Unit 5 p55 |
| ☐ give reasons for my opinions in an article | Unit 5 p56 |
| ☐ deduce meaning from context in a magazine article | Unit 6 p58 |
| ☐ identify attitude from the speaker's tone of voice in conversations | Unit 6 p62 |
| ☐ express my preferences and give reasons in a photo task | Unit 6 p64 |
| ☐ understand when to use adjectives and adverbs and apply them in a word-formation exercise | Unit 6 p65 |
| ☐ engage the reader in an article | Unit 6 p66 |

# 7 Best friends forever

## READING | Gapped text | A story

**1** **Think about a close friend of yours. In pairs, ask and answer these questions.**

- Where, when and how did you meet?
- What is your friend's personality like?
- What's the best thing about him/her?
- When are you next seeing him/her and what will you do together?

**EXAM SKILL**

### Understanding linking words/phrases

- Linking words/phrases connect ideas in a text, making it easier for the reader to follow the writer's ideas.
- They show you if the writer wants to explain, add information, contrast ideas, etc.
- Knowing a range of linking words/phrases will improve your reading comprehension.

**2** **Complete the examples with the phrases in the box.**

| apart from that \| as a result \| before long \| in other words \| to begin with |
|---|

Phrases that we use for …

1 saying when things happened: *after that,* ________ , ________ .

2 making things clear: *that is to say,* ________ .

3 giving a result: *as a consequence,* ________ .

4 introducing a contrast: *on the other hand,* ________ .

**3** **In groups, think of one more word or phrase for each category in Exercise 2.**

1 *later (on), finally,* ________

2 ________

3 ________

4 ________

# Long lost friends

When I saw her name on the screen, it took me right back to the moment she had moved away with her family, ten years before. We'd been such close friends. My dad had named us 'BFF1' and 'BFF2'. It was his idea of a joke. 'BFF' stood for 'best friends forever'. And that's what I'd thought we would be.

We'd met at primary school, where we were both in the same year, although not in the same class. [ 1 ] I'm not entirely sure why – perhaps we were both a bit shy. We'd quickly got over that, though, and as time went on, we'd become really good friends, until you almost never saw one of us without the other.

And now after so much time apart, there was her name. Lauren Mitchell had reappeared! She'd sent me a friend request on a social networking website I use. I knew she'd been living abroad, and her profile picture showed her on the beach. I'd been expecting her to look different after ten years. [ 2 ] The girl in the photo was the same old Lauren, though.

Nowadays, it's easy to find old friends and relatives thanks to social networking sites. There are lots of stories about long lost friends getting back in touch after years apart. Only the other day, I had read a story about a brother and sister who reconnected via Facebook after losing touch for 45 years! [ 3 ] It was strange because I had been thinking about our friendship too and now here she was!

A chat window suddenly popped up on my screen. It was Lauren. A single word appeared: 'Hi!' I felt a rush of emotions: excitement and happiness. I wrote 'Hi there stranger!' and then hesitated for a second before adding a smiley face and pressing send. I waited for what seemed like forever, and then her reply came. [ 4 ]

She told me about the place where she'd been living for the past ten years, and I told her about things that had happened to me. [ 5 ] Of course, true friends are loyal and listen to you when you're down. And they're the people you have fun with. But deep down, I realised that the truest friends are those you are most yourself with. And that's something that never changes.

Most of the things that happen to you in your life are just details. Of course, some changes in your life are bigger than others, and some of them might change who you are forever. [ 6 ] That's what Lauren and I learnt that day, the day we realised our friendship had never really ended in the first place.

## OPTIMISE YOUR EXAM

### Gapped text

- Look for linking words/phrases after the gaps or at the start of missing sentences.
- Think about their function and what they refer to. For example, if you see the phrase *As a result*, ask yourself *As a result of what?*

**4 Look at sentences A–G in Exercise 5. Find and underline the phrases from Exercise 2.**

**5** 2.13 **Read the text. Choose which sentence A–G fits each gap 1–6. There is one extra sentence you do not need.**

**A** As we did that, I realised what it was about our friendship that was so precious.
**B** In other words, I knew I'd changed in more ways than one and thought she would have, too.
**C** Before long, the years melted away and we were the same two girls who had spent so much time together.
**D** On the other hand, I thought she might still feel angry about what happened.
**E** Apart from that, though, events aren't as important as your basic personality.
**F** To begin with, she and I hadn't hit it off.
**G** I thought Lauren had forgotten about me but then I realised she hadn't.

**6 Find forms of the words and phrases in italics in the text or removed sentences, and choose the best definitions.**

1 (paragraph 1) If something *takes you back*, it ____
**a)** reminds you of the past.
**b)** helps you forget the past.

2 (paragraph 3) When you get a *friend request*, someone on a social networking site wants to ____
**a)** meet you in real life.
**b)** be your friend online.

3 (paragraph 5) If you *hesitate*, you ____
**a)** do something immediately.
**b)** wait for a moment before doing something.

4 (paragraph 6) If a friend is *loyal*, they ____
**a)** always support you.
**b)** often criticise you.

5 (sentence F) If two people *hit it off* when they meet, they ____
**a)** like each other.
**b)** dislike each other.

**THINK** | RESEARCH | CULTURE | LEARN | ME

Think of a story you know about long-lost friends or relatives meeting again. Tell the class.

▶ **Workbook Unit 7:** Reading, page 52, exercises 1, 2, 3, 4

# 7 GRAMMAR 1 | Tense review: past perfect simple and continuous

## Grammar in context

**Find and underline these words in the text on page 71. In each case, explain why the writer has used this tense.**

*When I saw her name on the screen, it took me right back to the moment she **had moved** away with her family, ten years before.*

*I knew she**'d been living** abroad, and her profile picture showed her on the beach.*

### REMEMBER

We use the past perfect simple for:

- an action or state that happened before another event in the past: *I **had finished** my homework by the time my friend called.*
- a completed action where the important thing is the result in the past: *Ed and I weren't talking to each other because we **had argued**.*

We use the past perfect continuous for:

- actions continuing up to or stopping just before a moment in the past: *Liam was out of breath because he **had been running**.*

▶ **See Grammar reference, Unit 7,** page 155

**1 Choose the correct answers.**

1 Before James and I met, I ____ that he was very easy to talk to.
  **a)** had heard **b)** had been hearing
2 My friend and I ____ for a few minutes when we both suddenly started laughing!
  **a)** had argued **b)** had been arguing
3 A week after they ____ with each other, Ella and Amy made up again.
  **a)** had fallen out **b)** had been falling out
4 Jake ____ Alex before so I introduced them to each other.
  **a)** hadn't met **b)** hadn't been meeting
5 I ____ with my friend for so long that I didn't realise it had got dark outside!
  **a)** had talked **b)** had been talking
6 Our teacher asked me and my friend what we ____ about.
  **a)** had whispered **b)** had been whispering

**2 Tick the correct sentences. Underline the mistakes in the other sentences and correct them.**

1 When Simon finally arrived, I had been waited for over half an hour. ______________
2 I hadn't seen Ava behind me so I jumped when she started to speak! ______________
3 Had you been working there long before you met Alicia? ______________
4 By the time the party ended, we been dancing for hours. ______________
5 When I walked into the room, I knew they had been talking about me. ______________
6 How long had you been knowing Nils before you became friends? ______________
7 I hadn't listen to the teacher, so the question came as a complete surprise. ______________
8 We had been planning the surprise party for weeks and it was fantastic! ______________

**3 Complete the text with the correct tense (past perfect simple or continuous) of the verbs in the box.**

| argue \| cry \| do \| forget \| get \| happen \| joke \| not buy \| not forget |
|---|

**A MISUNDERSTANDING**

When I walked into the room, I could see that Zoe **(1)** ______________ . Thomas was frowning, and it was obvious they **(2)** ______________ for some time. I looked at them both and asked what **(3)** ______________ . They both started talking at once. It seemed that Thomas **(4)** ______________ Zoe's birthday and **(5)** ______________ her a card or a present. And he **(6)** ______________ the same thing last year. I got them both to calm down and asked Thomas to explain. After a moment, he pulled out a card and a present! He **(7)** ______________ at all! He **(8)** ______________ and Zoe **(9)** ______________ upset before Thomas could explain! Zoe wiped her face and smiled. Then she gave Thomas a hug. It's not always easy having friends who are practical jokers!

THINK | RESEARCH | CULTURE | LEARN | **ME**

Think of a time when friends of yours argued.

In pairs, describe what had caused the argument, what happened as a result and how the argument ended.



▶ **Workbook Unit 7:** Grammar 1, page 54, exercises 1, 2, 3

## Words connected with *friendship*

**1** 2.14 **Write a verb from the box in the correct form to complete the text. Listen and check.**

| forgive \| get on \| gossip \| make friends \| rely on \| share |
|---|

I first met Nadia when she moved in next door. We **(1)** __________ really well straight away, started walking to school together and soon **(2)** __________ . We would **(3)** __________ all our secrets and **(4)** __________ about the boys in our class. Even when we argued, it never took long before one of us would **(5)** __________ the other one, and when I was having some trouble at school, I knew I could **(6)** __________ Nadia to help me get through it.

| admire \| appreciate \| confide in \| count on \| lose touch \| support |
|---|

When we were both 18, we went to different universities and then she moved to Sweden and got married. After that, we **(7)** __________ . But two years ago, I got a friend request from her on Facebook. We started chatting online and she **(8)** __________ me that she sometimes felt quite lonely in Sweden, so I suggested visiting her. A few weeks later, I flew to Stockholm to see her. I really **(9)** __________ her for moving abroad and learning a language, which I knew wasn't easy. I knew she **(10)** __________ my visit but I was just really pleased that I could **(11)** __________ her like she had done with me. After all, it's important to be able to **(12)** __________ your friends.

## Nouns with *-ance / -ence / -ment / -ship*

**2** 2.15 **Write the noun form of each word, using the endings in the box. Listen and check.**

| -ance \| -ence \| -ment \| -ship |
|---|

1 assist__________
2 develop__________
3 encourage__________
4 exist__________
5 friend__________
6 member__________
7 partner__________
8 perform__________
9 prefer__________
10 relation__________

**3** **Complete the text using words from Exercise 2. You may need to use a plural. Sometimes there is more than one answer.**

# friends

TEENAGE WORLD

As people who work with teenagers, all our advisers understand that **(1)** __________ don't always go the way you want them to. You fall out with your best friend and the most important **(2)** __________ in your life suddenly goes wrong. We're here to offer **(3)** __________ and **(4)** __________ and tell you that you can stop your friendships going wrong by following our simple advice.

* Remember that it takes two to make a friendship. It's a kind of **(5)** __________ , just like in business. Don't be lazy. Make an effort to help your friend.

* Friendship is about growing together as people. This kind of personal **(6)** __________ is very important. Think about how you can help your friend grow.

Good luck!

## Phrasal verbs

**4** 2.16 **Match to make sentences. Listen and check.**

1 For me, my heroes are people I *look* ____
2 People tell me that I *take* ____
3 I decided to *go* ____
4 It's important to try to *get* ____
5 Polly was ill, so we *dropped* ____
6 If you want to make new friends, you have to *keep* ____
7 Elena took her friend's letter, *ripped* it ____
8 When Daisy walked out of the party, I *ran* ____

**a)** *on* trying and you'll find people you like.
**b)** *round to* my friend's house to see what she was doing.
**c)** *after* my dad, but I think I'm more like my mum.
**d)** *along with* people, even if you're not close friends.
**e)** *after* her to apologise for what I had said.
**f)** *up to* and admire, such as my friend Josh, who has had a difficult life.
**g)** *in* to see her on our way home.
**h)** *up* and threw the pieces onto the fire.

**5** **Explain what the phrasal verbs in Exercise 4 mean.**

**1** **In pairs or as a group, discuss the questions.**

1 Why do some people find it difficult to make new friends?
2 How easy do you find it?

**EXAM SKILL**

### Predicting synonyms

- In many listening exam tasks, the speakers use different words from those in the questions/statements.
- Thinking about different ways to express the key words/phrases in the questions/statements before you listen can help you answer the questions.

**2** **Match the words and phrases with similar meanings.**

| | |
|---|---|
| 1 advice ____ | a) abroad |
| 2 comfortable ____ | b) relaxed |
| 3 tough ____ | c) opinion |
| 4 nervous ____ | d) start a conversation |
| 5 in another country ____ | e) anxious |
| 6 begin chatting ____ | f) difficult |

**OPTIMISE YOUR EXAM**

### Multiple matching

- Underline the key words in the statements and try to think of synonyms for them.
- The first time you listen, focus on each speaker's main idea.
- The second time you listen, focus on synonyms for the key words or phrases in the statements.
- Make sure that you put a different letter for each answer.

**3** **In pairs, look at the sentences (A–H) in Exercise 4 and underline the words or phrases that express the main idea. Think of different ways you can express those ideas.**

**Example:**

**A** *It's difficult for me to make new friends.*
*difficult – not easy / hard/complicated/tough*
*make new friends – meet new people / get to know someone new*

**4** 2.17 **You will hear five extracts about making friends. Choose form A–H what each speaker says about it. There are three extra letters you do not need.**

**A** It's difficult for me to make new friends.
**B** I've learnt to make friends because we've moved a lot.
**C** I made friends while we were on holiday.
**D** My friends usually introduce me to other people.
**E** I feel more comfortable making friends online.
**F** I follow the advice someone once gave me.
**G** My experience has made me nervous around new people.
**H** I generally wait for the other person to start a conversation.

**Speaker 1:** ☐
**Speaker 2:** ☐
**Speaker 3:** ☐
**Speaker 4:** ☐
**Speaker 5:** ☐

**5** 2.17 **In pairs, compare your choices. Listen again to check and discuss your answers.**

THINK | **RESEARCH** | CULTURE | LEARN | ME

Look up 'friend' using an online thesaurus and find five synonyms.
Make notes and be prepared to explain the exact meaning of the different synonyms in class.

 ▶ **Workbook Unit 7:** Listening, page 56, exercises 1, 2

# GRAMMAR 2 | Connectors of contrast

## Grammar in context

**Complete the missing words in these sentences from the audio in the listening lesson.**

1 I soon got better at making friends, e__________ though it can still be hard work.

2 I know everyone has to learn how to make new friends, d__________ how difficult it can be.

3 I don't seem to meet a lot of new people where I live, so making new friends doesn't happen often. H__________, it's different when I'm abroad.

### REMEMBER

- *Although, even though, in spite of, despite* and *however* are used to contrast one idea with another. *Olivia and I were close friends,* ***even though*** *we were very different.*
- With *although, even though, in spite of* and *despite*, the clauses can come in a different order. ***Even though*** *we were very different, Olivia and I were close friends.*
- *However* usually goes at the beginning of a sentence but can also go at the end or in the middle. *Olivia and I were very different. We were close friends,* ***however****.*
- *In spite of* and *despite* are often followed by either an *-ing* form, a clause that begins with *what* and *how*, or the phrase *the fact that* + clause.

▶ **See Grammar reference, Unit 7,** page 155

**1 Choose the correct word.**

1 In spite of **argue / arguing**, they remained friends.

2 We all need friends sometimes, **even though / however** they can also hurt our feelings.

3 **Despite / Although** being quite shy, Tom often makes new friends.

4 **Although / However** I've got lots of friends, I still feel lonely sometimes.

5 Liam's a good friend, **despite / spite** the fact that he lives so far away.

6 I saw Emily at the party. **Although / However**, I didn't speak to her.

**2 Rewrite the sentences in different ways using the words given.**

*Despite not having many friends, Grace is happy.*

1 **(although)** ______________________________

2 **(however)** ______________________________

*Rob is quite friendly. However, he doesn't get along with his brother.*

3 **(though)** ______________________________

4 **(spite)** ______________________________

**3 Complete the text with connectors of contrast. Sometimes there is more than one answer.**

## FRIENDS NETWORK

Is your best friend just like you, or are you very different? Tell us about it in the comments below!

Hi! I'd like to tell you about me and my friend Brandon. We get on really well, **(1)** __________ we don't really have much in common. He loves sport and exercises a lot. **(2)** __________, I'm into reading and playing video games. Still, we get on really well with each other!

**OscarM_2002,** New York, USA

My best friend is Maria. **(3)** __________ we don't look like each other at all, we have very similar personalities. I think that's what counts. Maria's tall and really good-looking, and I'm not, LOL! **(4)** __________ looking very different, we have a great relationship and spend all our time together. I wouldn't change it for the world!

**Happygirl09,** Madrid, Spain

My best friend Karl is so similar to me that people sometimes think we're brothers, **(5)** __________ the fact that we're not related at all! We look the same, have the same personality and enjoy doing the same things. **(6)** __________, I understand that some friends can be very different from each other, but Karl and I are almost like twins!

**Hans_Anders,** Berlin, Germany

### SAY IT RIGHT

**Resource centre: Unit 7**
Intonation in contrasting clauses

THINK | RESEARCH | CULTURE | LEARN | **ME**

Choose a friend and think of two contrasting ideas that are true of him/her.

Write a sentence expressing those ideas, using one of the connectors of contrast above.

▶ **Workbook Unit 7:** Grammar 2, page 55, exercises 1, 2

# 7 SPEAKING | Collaborative task

Flipped classroom

**1** ▷ **Watch the *Talk2Me* video and for each person, note down their answers.**

1 What are the qualities of a good friend?
2 How important is a good sense of humour in a friend?

**2** ▷ **Choose the correct word. Then watch the video again to check your answers.**

1 Are you **saying / telling** that you think …?
2 What do you **know / mean** when you say …?
3 Could you give me an **example / instance**?
4 **Are / Do** you mean that …?
5 Could you explain **completely / exactly** what you mean?
6 Sorry, but I don't really **see / look** your point.

**3** **In pairs or small groups, answer the questions in Exercise 1. Explain your answers using the phrases in the *Phrase expert* box.**

**PHRASE EXPERT**

Are you saying …? | Could you explain exactly …? | Could you give me an example? | Do you mean …? | I (don't) see your point | What do you mean …?

**EXAM SKILL**

**Asking for clarification**

- In a speaking exam, you might not understand what the examiner or another candidate has said. Don't just stop talking, or guess what they mean. Ask them for clarification.

**4** **Look at Exercise 5. For each of the friendship characteristics, make notes for and against each one.**

Similar tastes and interests:
have things in common to do together, have lots to talk about, but it is also good to learn new things from friends with different interests

**OPTIMISE YOUR EXAM**

**Collaborative task**

- Remember to listen carefully to what your partner says.
- Make sure you take turns – give your partner time to speak and ask them what they think.
- If you interrupt your partner, try to be polite (see the *Phrase expert* below).

**5** **Talk in pairs for two minutes. Follow the instructions.**

Here are some characteristics a friend can have and a question for you to discuss. Talk to each other about how these things can affect a friendship.

What makes a good friend?
- similar tastes and interests
- popular, fashionable or cool
- always agrees with you
- generous and helpful
- always honest with you

**6** **You have about a minute to decide together which two things are the most important characteristics in a friend.**

1 ______________________
2 ______________________

**7** **Compare your choices with another pair or with the whole class. Explain the reasons for your choices.**

▶ **Workbook Unit 7:** Speaking, pages 56–57, exercises 1, 2

# USE OF ENGLISH | Sentence transformation

**1** **In pairs or groups, answer the questions.**

1 Are you similar in appearance to any members of your family?

2 Do you have a similar personality to any members of your family?

**EXAM SKILL**

## Verbs (2)

- Many exam tasks test your ability to recognise which verb tense is needed to complete a sentence.
- To help you, look for key words that are used with certain tenses, such as *while*, *by the time*, etc.
- Other verbs in the sentence, such as different tenses and question tags, can also give you clues.

**2** **Choose the correct answers.**

1 You ____ with your best friend again, have you?
**a)** don't argue **b)** hadn't argued
**c)** haven't been arguing

2 By the time I got to the party, my friend ____ .
**a)** had left **b)** was left
**c)** left

3 I could see that Lizzie ____ .
**a)** has been crying **b)** had been crying
**c)** will be crying

4 It was the first time I ____ Matt's brother.
**a)** meet **b)** 've met
**c)** 'd met

5 I played a game on my phone while my friend ____ her homework.
**a)** finished **b)** has finished
**c)** had finished

6 Harry said I ____ his feelings by ignoring him.
**a)** am hurting **b)** had hurt
**c)** had been hurting

**3** **Look at the sentences in Exercise 4. Write the question numbers.**

1 Which sentence requires a change from the present simple to the present perfect? ____

2 Which sentence requires a change from past simple to past perfect? ____

**OPTIMISE YOUR EXAM**

## Sentence transformation

- Underline the words in the first sentence that are the same in the second.
- Then focus on the remaining words in the first sentence and decide how to express them using the given word.
- Remember that contractions, e.g. *he'd*, count as two words.

**4** **Complete the second sentence so it has a similar meaning to the first. Do not change the word given. Use two to five words, including the word given.**

1 This is my first visit to Lauren's house.
**NEVER**
I ______________________ Lauren's house before.

2 Do you know any reason why Sophie might be angry with you?
**AWARE**
Are ______________________ any reason why Sophie might be angry with you?

3 We live many miles apart but we're still good friends.
**DESPITE**
We're still good friends ______________________ miles apart.

4 I can't believe Jo blamed me for causing the argument with Evie!
**HAD**
I can't believe Jo said ______________________ the argument with Evie!

5 Although we disagreed a lot, we were very close friends.
**OF**
In ______________________ a lot, we were very close friends.

6 Kyle and his father are similar to each other in lots of ways.
**AFTER**
Kyle ______________________ in lots of ways.

# 7 WRITING | A story

**1 In pairs or as a group, answer the questions.**

1 When was the last time you got lost? Describe what happened.
2 Do you have a good or a bad sense of direction?

**EXAM SKILL**

### Using narrative tenses

- Past verb tenses are very important when you write stories or descriptions of events.
- Try to use a variety of tenses when you write a story, such as the past perfect simple and continuous, where appropriate.
- Direct speech gives you the chance to use other tenses.

**2 Read this story and explain in your own words what happens.**

*IN THE WRONG PLACE!*

*I had been waiting for my friend for ten minutes when I suddenly realised that I was in the wrong place! The train was slowly leaving the platform, and people were walking past me. I searched, but there was no sign of Emily. I found a guard to ask for assistance.*

*'The train from Glasgow.' he said. 'It arrives at West Station in ...' He looked at his watch. '12 minutes. You'll have to be quick!'*

*I ran out of the station as fast as I could. I had passed West Station earlier, so I knew how far it was. I looked at my phone. No battery! I had no way of communicating with Emily. I had to make it or she would think I'd forgotten about her!*

*I ran along the pavement, shouting 'Sorry!' and 'Excuse me!' at the people I passed. I was getting tired but I knew I had to keep on going. Finally, I saw West Station ahead. I got there just as the train from Glasgow arrived! Emily got off the train and hugged me. She couldn't understand why I was laughing!*

**3 Find and underline the first examples of these tenses in the story. In pairs, explain why the writer uses each of these tenses.**

1 past perfect continuous
2 past simple
3 past continuous
4 present simple
5 past perfect simple

**OPTIMISE YOUR EXAM**

### A story

- Story tasks often ask you to begin with a given sentence and include two details. You lose marks if you don't follow the instructions.
- If the first sentence is given, make sure you don't change it.

**4** **Look at this writing task. Explain in your own words what you have to do.**

You have seen this announcement on an English-language website for young people.

> **Star Stories!**
>
> We want your stories for the website! Your story must **begin** with this sentence:
>
> *I had been looking for my friend for an hour when I suddenly realised that I had made a mistake!*
>
> Your story must include:
> - an address
> - a secret

Write your **story**.

**5** **Make notes to answer each of these questions.**

1 Which friend had you been waiting for? Why?

2 Where had you been waiting for your friend?

3 What mistake had you made?

4 What did you do about your mistake?

5 Did you finally meet your friend? Where?

6 How did your friend react when you met?

7 What address are you going to include in your story?

8 What secret are you going to include in your story?

**6** **Write two or three sentences to describe what happens in your story.**

**7** **Plan** **Make a paragraph plan.**

| Part | Purpose | My notes |
|---|---|---|
| **Title** | briefly describe what the story is about – and make us want to read it! | |
| **Paragraph 1** | copy the first sentence and set the scene – where were you? who was your friend? what mistake had you made? | |
| **Middle paragraphs** | continue the story – what happened? (remember to include the address and the secret) | |
| **Final paragraph** | bring the story to a close – how did everyone feel? did anything interesting happen afterwards? | |

**8** **Write** **Write your story in an appropriate style. Write 140–190 words.**

**9** **Check** **Before you hand in your story, complete this checklist.**

**Checklist**

- ◯ I've used the sentence given without changing it.
- ◯ I've included an address and a secret.
- ◯ I've used different narrative tenses correctly.
- ◯ I've included direct speech.
- ◯ I've used an appropriate style for a story.
- ◯ I've written at least four paragraphs.
- ◯ I've written a good ending to my story.
- ◯ I've checked my spelling and grammar.

▶ **Writing reference,** page 173 ▶ **Workbook Unit 7:** Writing, page 58, exercises 1, 2, 3 and Progress check 7, page 59

# 8 The only way is up

## READING | Multiple matching | Blog posts

**1 In pairs or groups, imagine you're planning to climb a mountain. Make two lists.**

- Problems you could have on the way up and down.
- Things you should take with you.

**EXAM SKILL**

### Understanding implication

- Some exam tasks require you to 'read between the lines.'
- Not everything in a reading text is stated directly. Some information is implied by the writer.
- For example, in a tourist brochure, it might say, *We strongly suggest you take wet-weather clothes with you*. So we can infer that it probably rains often there.

**2 Find these sentences in the article and read the sentences around them. For each one, decide what is implied. Choose the correct word.**

1 *It's not for everyone – your feet and legs will ache.*
This trip is quite **strenuous** / **boring**.

2 *It's been described as the busiest mountain in Britain, and for good reason.*
It's busy because lots of people **visit it** / **work there**.

3 *As my mum and I are huge fans of* The Hobbit, *we went on a dream holiday to New Zealand last year.*
They went to New Zealand to **relax** / **to visit the movie locations**.

4 *The chair-lift ride to Knoll Ridge Chalet, New Zealand's highest café at 2,020 metres, is out of this world.*
The writer was **impressed** / **not impressed**.

**OPTIMISE YOUR EXAM**

### Multiple matching

- This task may include inference questions. These often include words like *suggests* and *implies*.
- For example, in Exercise 3, question 4, none of the four teenagers says explicitly that their climb was '*for educational purposes*', but one of them suggests (implies) it.

# Reaching the Top

**We asked you to send us your holiday experiences (good or bad) on the subject of 'height'. Here are some of the best posts we received.**

## A Rocio Montoya
AGED 14

### *Machu Picchu*

Machu Picchu, which in Quechua means 'old peak', is a city in the clouds close to the modern-day city of Cuzco. It is an ancient Inca city that stands 2,430 metres above sea level, and its ruins are visited by tourists from all over the world.

I visited it as part of a school project and we did 'The Inca Trail', a five-day trek along an ancient Inca path that passes through many famous Inca ruins and involves camping outdoors. It's not for everyone – your feet and legs will ache, but I found it very rewarding, in particular when we finally arrived at the Sun Gate of Machu Picchu.

If you are interested in doing the trail, book in advance as there are limited places, avoid the rainy season (October–April) and consider taking tablets to deal with the altitude.

## B Gareth Williams
AGED 15

### *Mount Snowdon*

I've climbed Mount Snowdon in Wales several times now, usually with friends. It's been described as the busiest mountain in Britain, and for good reason. Every time I have been, there have been plenty of walkers no matter what time of year it is. There are six main routes – some more difficult than others – and the climb can take five to six hours from start to finish. Apparently, Sir Edmund Hillary trained here for his amazing 1953 Everest climb. Presumably he chose some of the trickier routes, something we always do when we go up. You feel a real sense of achievement when you reach the top after a difficult ascent. And the hot soup they sell in the café there is a great reward! But if you're feeling a bit lazy, take the railway, which was built in the late 1890s, to the top. Personally, I've never been up on the train.

## C Steffi Kunstmann
AGED 14

### *Dinner in the sky*

My dad won tickets to the Dinner in the Sky restaurant in Vienna so he took the whole family, including my grandparents. Dinner in the Sky is an amazing concept. It's a gourmet restaurant that is lifted 50 metres into the air by a crane, giving amazing views of the city.

However, I can't say that I would like to repeat the experience. Every time I looked down, I felt dizzy, and as a result, I lost my appetite. I tried to be happy for my family's sake, but I only relaxed once we were back on the ground. Not surprising really – I feel the same way on the balcony of our flat on the fifth floor.

## D Sam Freeman
AGED 13

### *Mount Ruapehu*

As my mum and I are huge fans of *The Hobbit*, we went on a dream holiday to New Zealand last year. We visited many of the locations from the movies and the one that sticks in my mind is Mount Ruapehu, the setting for the Lonely Mountain, home of Smaug the dragon.

Part of me was disappointed when we got there. I had expected to see the huge film sets but of course, they were dismantled once filming had finished. However, the scenery there is breathtaking and we got to do a whole load of great activities, including skiing and snowboarding. The chair-lift ride to Knoll Ridge Chalet, New Zealand's highest café at 2,020 metres, is out of this world. I would definitely recommend a visit to Mount Ruapehu. Just don't go expecting to see film sets and pack your winter clothing!

**3** 2.18 **For each question, choose from the people A–D. The people may be chosen more than once.**

**Which person**

1 mentions a famous mountaineering expedition? [1]
2 made an effort to enjoy the trip? [2]
3 suggests the place they visited was cold? [3]
4 suggests that they visited the place for educational purposes? [4]
5 suffered from being so high up? [5]
6 had a different experience from what they imagined? [6]
7 gives advice on how to organise a trip? [7]
8 stresses how many routes there are? [8]

**4 In pairs, compare your answers to Exercise 3. If you agree, find the part of the text which gives you the answer. If you disagree, justify your choices.**

**5 Find each word in the text and write a short definition or close synonym. Use a dictionary if necessary.**

1 sea level (para A) ____________
2 altitude (para A) ____________
3 ascent (para B) ____________
4 crane (para C) ____________
5 sake (para C) ____________
6 sets (para D) ____________
7 scenery (para D) ____________
8 breathtaking (para D) ____________

THINK | **RESEARCH** | CULTURE | LEARN | ME

Find two more facts online about each of the four places in the article and turn them into eight questions. In pairs or groups, give each other a quiz.

▶ **Workbook Unit 8:** Reading, pages 60–61, exercises 1, 2, 3

## Grammar in context

**Write one word in each gap to complete these phrases and sentences. Then find them in the article on page 81 and check your answers.**

1 It's an ancient Inca city that stands 2,430 metres above sea level, and its ruins __________ visited by tourists from all over the world.
2 It's __________ described as the busiest mountain in Britain, and for good reason.
3 It's a gourmet restaurant that __________ lifted 50 metres into the air by a crane, giving amazing views of the city.
4 I had expected to see the huge film sets but of course, they __________ dismantled once filming had finished.

### REMEMBER

- We form the passive with *be* + past participle (+ *by/with/of*).
- If you're not sure what tense *be* should be in, or which past participle to use, try to imagine the active form of the sentence.
  **Active:** *Susie has brought the ropes.*
  verb = *bring*, tense = present perfect
  so we need to use the present perfect of the verb *be* (i.e. *have been*) in the passive sentence
  **Passive:** *The ropes have been brought by Susie.*
- We normally use *by* if we want to say who or what does the action of the main verb, but sometimes we use other prepositions, such as *with, for, of* and *as*, depending on the meaning.
  *Everest is now climbed* ***by hundreds of people*** *every year.*
  *My new ropes are* ***made of*** *a special material.*

▶ **See Grammar reference, Unit 8,** page 155

**1** **Complete each second sentence, using the passive, so that it means the same as the first sentence.**

1 Every year, they rescue dozens of people from the steep slopes.
Every year, ______________________________ .
2 They usually take the people they rescue to hospital by helicopter.
The people they rescue ______________________________ .
3 Ponies carried everything up the mountain.
Everything ______________________________ .
4 When did they make the path to the summit?
When ______________________________ ?
5 You should only climb the mountain in the spring and summer.
The mountain ______________________________ .

**2** **Write one word in each gap.**

1 The emergency shelter has been stayed in __________ a number of climbers.
2 These ropes are very strong and are made __________ nylon.
3 In the end, the rope was cut __________ a pair of scissors.
4 K2 is also known __________ the Savage Mountain.
5 The peak is covered __________ snow for most of the year.
6 The rare mountain flower was identified __________ a botanist.

**3** **Put the verbs into the passive to complete the text. Sometimes there is more than one answer.**

Everyone knows that Everest is the highest mountain on Earth, but what's the second highest? It (**1**) __________ (**call**) K2, and (**2**) __________ (**locate**) on the border between China and Pakistan. The summit (**3**) __________ (**never / reach**) during winter, and even during the summer the ascent is treacherous. For this reason, K2 (**4**) __________ (**often / refer**) to as the 'Savage Mountain', and (**5**) __________ (**consider**) by experts to be a lot more challenging than Everest. Because the Chinese side is particularly dangerous, climbs (**6**) __________ (**usually / attempt**) on the Pakistani side of the mountain.

K2 (**7**) __________ (**first / conquer**) in 1954, when on July 31st a group of Italian and Pakistani climbers reached the top. Since then, the peak (**8**) __________ (**reach**) by only about 300 people. Sadly, more than 80 people (**9**) __________ (**kill**) in their attempts to reach the top.

THINK | RESEARCH | CULTURE | **LEARN** | ME

What are the differences between 'active' and 'passive' sentences in your language? Are they similar to or different from the active and passive forms in English?

Do you find forming and understanding the passive in English easy, or is it confusing?

## Words connected with *geographical features*

**1** 2.19 **Work in pairs. Match the words in the box to the numbers. Listen and check.**

| a cliff \| a mountain range \| a path \| a slope \| a stream \| a summit \| a valley \| a volcano \| a waterfall \| coast |
|---|

**2** **Choose the correct words to complete the sentences.**

1 When you're in the mountains you might need to wash in a **stream** / **range**.
2 If we follow this **path** / **cliff** through the forest we will get back to the camp.
3 The **summit** / **coast** of Mount Everest is 8,848 metres high.
4 There are some excellent ski **streams** / **slopes** in the Alps.
5 The **coast** / **cliff** was very steep and we needed ropes to climb it.
6 My family usually goes on holiday to the **coast** / **stream** because we love swimming in the sea.

## Nouns formed from verbs

**3** 2.20 **Change each verb in bold into a noun to complete the sentences. Listen and check.**

1 Our ______ at the summit was greeted with cheers. **arrive**
2 Their ______ from base camp was delayed due to bad weather. **depart**
3 We've got no ______ . We'll have to turn back. **choose**
4 I want everyone on their best ______ . **behave**
5 I loved her ______ of the view from the top. **describe**
6 We'd better find a ______ soon or we'll be stuck here all night! **solve**
7 There's a huge ______ of plants and flowers on the lower slopes. **vary**
8 We need to make a ______ about our geography project. **decide**
9 I've come to the ______ that rock climbing isn't for me. **conclude**
10 You'll notice a wide ______ in temperature from day to night. **vary**

## Words + prepositions

**4** 2.21 **Complete the text with prepositions. Use the words in italics to help you. Listen and check.**

Archive

Posted 19/11/16 16.34

Well, I can't blame my mum. She *warned* me (**1**) ______ going rock climbing and abseiling. She said: 'Carol, what's the *purpose* (**2**) ______ going all the way up, just to come down again?' But when Angie picked me up, I actually felt *optimistic* (**3**) ______ it and thought we'd have a great day. What I was *lacking* (**4**) ______ experience I'd make up for with enthusiasm. I wasn't worried at all – I knew the instructors *specialised* (**5**) ______ dealing with novices.

Going up was no problem. After we'd checked there was nothing *wrong* (**6**) ______ the way I'd attached my harness, I started my descent.

Well, I've never been abseiling before. I didn't realise you've got to be careful not to *crash* (**7**) ______ the rock face as you go down, and secondly that you can get stuck. After I'd been hanging there for several minutes – with no *shelter* (**8**) ______ the driving rain – I knew I was in serious trouble.

▶ Vocabulary reference, page 165 ▶ Workbook Unit 8: Vocabulary, pages 62–63, exercises 1, 2, 3

# 8 LISTENING | Sentence completion

**1** **Imagine you have been asked to do a geography project on mountains. What different aspects might you focus on?**

*highest mountains in the world*
*definition of a mountain*
*climate*

**EXAM SKILL**

**Listening for opinion**

- Listening tasks often test your ability to distinguish fact from opinion.
- Listen out for common phrases to express opinions, as they will help you decide. Some of these appear in Exercise 2.

**2** 2.22 **Listen to someone agreeing with the statement below in eight different ways. Complete the opinion phrases.**

**Many geologists argue that we need to take** *steepness* **into account …**

1 … I __________ to think …
2 … that makes __________ to me …
3 … that __________ like …
4 I don't __________ with that …
5 To my __________, …
6 If you __________ me, …
7 __________, I agree with that.
8 My __________ is …

**OPTIMISE YOUR EXAM**

**Sentence completion**

- If you have written more than three words, listen carefully the second time and decide which words you need to cut.
- Check your answers and try to spell everything correctly.

**3** 2.23 **Listen to Sandra Atkins talking about mountains. Complete the sentences with a word or short phrase.**

Sandra says she'll describe typical mountain environments, plants and wildlife, and **(1)**__________ .

Sandra says that **(2)** __________ and countries may disagree about what a mountain is.

Sandra disagrees with the need to **(3)** __________ mountains in great detail.

Approximately 35% of **(4)** __________ is mountainous.

Sandra's opinion of 'plate tectonics' is that it is **(5)** __________ .

'Fold mountains' are frequently part of a **(6)** __________ .

Sandra describes a 'fault' as being like a channel or **(7)** __________ .

Sandra mentions a mountain higher than Everest that's over **(8)** __________ in height.

**4** 2.23 **Listen again and check your answers.**

THINK | RESEARCH | CULTURE | **LEARN** | ME

What do you think are the best strategies for making an interesting presentation?


▶ **Workbook Unit 8:** Listening, page 64, exercises 1, 2, 3

## Grammar in context

**Read this extract from the audio in the listening lesson. Write the correct word in bold next to each statement.**

*So, my **geography** project is on **mountains**, and to be honest, when I was first given this **topic**, I wasn't particularly interested by it because I thought mountains were a bit boring, but now I've done some **research**, there's a lot more to mountains than you might imagine.*

1 This is a singular countable noun. ________

2 This is a plural countable noun. ________

3 These are uncountable nouns. ________

### REMEMBER

- Uncountable nouns are often:
  abstract ideas, e.g. *truth, information, news*;
  materials, e.g. *iron, glass, water*;
  collections, e.g. *furniture, luggage*.
- Most uncountable nouns are treated as singular, even if they're describing more than one object: *All the furniture in the room **was** broken.*
- There are a few uncountable nouns which are treated as plural, even if they're describing only one thing. These include *clothes, jeans, trousers, scissors, groceries, sunglasses*.
- How you use articles (*a(n), the, no article*) and quantifiers (*few/little, much/many*, etc.) often depends on whether a noun is countable or uncountable.

▶ **See Grammar reference, Unit 8,** page 156

**1 Write the verb in the correct form to complete the sentences.**

1 All the information they gave us about abseiling ________ really useful. (**be** – present)

2 The news about the volcano ________ very worrying. (**be** – past)

3 The waterproof trousers you lent me ________ incredibly warm. (**be** – past)

4 Chocolate ________ a good source of energy when you're walking or climbing. (**be** – present)

5 Your knowledge of the highest mountains in the world ________ me! (**amaze** – present)

6 Those lambs ________ really tiny down there in the field. (**look** – present)

**2 Choose the correct word or phrase.**

Archive

Posted 14/12/16 12.50

So, for quite some (**1**) **times** / **time**, I'd been dangling off the side of a cliff. The instructor at the top was trying to give me a (**2**) **little** / **few** encouragement. The instructor at the bottom was trying to give me a (**3**) **little** / **few** instructions. I wasn't listening to either of them. I was thinking about how (**4**) **much** / **many** rain was running down my neck and under my clothes, and how (**5**) **much** / **many** times my mum has warned me not to do adventurous things. 'Only (**6**) **little** / **a few** people in the world really enjoy doing dangerous things, and you're not one of them,' she always tells me. And she's right.

**3 Write *a*, *an* or *the* in each gap to complete the text. If no article is needed, put a dash (–).**

Archive

Posted 15/12/16 10.15

Then I heard Angie give me a piece of (**1**) ________ advice. 'You're wearing (**2**) ________ pair of thick boots, Carol. Use them to kick against (**3**) ________ rock. As you do that, just move your arm that's holding (**4**) ________ rope behind your (**5**) ________ back.' I'd heard (**6**) ________ instructor below say something similar a number of (**7**) ________ times before, but Angie's tone of (**8**) ________ voice revealed (**9**) ________ anger she was feeling, so I thought I had (**10**) ________ little choice. She had (**11**) ________ car keys, after all. Less than (**12**) ________ minute later, I was back down on (**13**) ________ ground.

Despite my nerves, we had (**14**) ________ amazing time and we're going there again (**15**) ________ next week!

THINK | RESEARCH | CULTURE | LEARN | **ME**

Imagine Carol in Exercise 3 was your friend, and you could leave a comment under her blog post. What would you write?

# 8 SPEAKING | Discussion

Talk2Me
*If you ask me …*

**Flipped classroom**

**1** **Watch the *Talk2Me* video and answer the questions.**

1 Which activities do the people on the video discuss?
2 Which activities do they think are the most expensive/dangerous/exciting to watch?
3 Do you agree/disagree with what they say?

**2** **Watch the video again. Underline the expressions in the *Phrase expert* box that you hear on the video.**

**PHRASE EXPERT**

as far as I'm concerned | I agree / don't agree with you/that | I'd say | if you ask me | I'm of the opinion/view that | in my opinion/view | I tend to think | Personally, | that makes sense to me | to my mind

**3** **In pairs or groups, answer the question.**

What adventure activities do you know? Check the meaning of these and add your own ideas.

skiing
rock climbing
abseiling
scrambling

**EXAM SKILL**

**Expressing and justifying opinions**

- In the Listening section, you saw some words and phrases for expressing opinion.
- When expressing an opinion, always try to justify it. See the *Phrase expert* box in Unit 6 (page 64) for phrases giving reasons.

**4** **Complete these sentences with phrases for expressing opinions.**

1 ___________ my opinion, skiing is more expensive than rock climbing.
2 I ___________ to think that abseiling is more dangerous than scrambling.
3 **A:** If you ___________ me, skiing is much more exciting to watch than rock climbing.
**B:** I ___________ agree with that.
4 As far as I'm ___________ skiing and rock climbing are equally tiring.
5 I'd ___________ skiing is the most exciting to do.

**5** **Choose from the activities in Exercise 1. For each one, answer the question and give a reason.**

Which is the most …

1 expensive?
**Example:** *Skiing because you need all the equipment and ski resorts are often very expensive.*
2 enjoyable?
3 dangerous?
4 difficult?
5 exciting to watch?
6 exciting to do?
7 tiring?

**OPTIMISE YOUR EXAM**

**Discussion**

- When using opinion phrases, the stress is usually on the 'I/my' word, so: *in my opinion, to my mind, as far as I'm concerned*, etc.
- You can practise this further in this unit's *Say it right* activities (Resource centre).

**6** **In small groups or as a class, follow the instructions.**

1 Each of you should:
   - choose two activities from Exercise 3.
   - use your ideas from Exercise 5.
   - choose an opinion phrase from the *Phrase expert* box.
2 When it's your turn, compare the two activities you've chosen, giving a reason for your opinion.
**Example:** *If you ask me, skiing is more dangerous than rock climbing because you're going so fast. If you fall over, you can easily break a leg.*
3 When it's not your turn, agree or disagree with what the other people in the group say, giving reasons.
4 Repeat the task with different activities, phrases and reasons.

**SAY IT RIGHT**

**Resource centre: Unit 8**
Stress in opinion phrases


▶ **Workbook Unit 8:** Speaking, pages 64–65, exercises 1, 2, 3

# USE OF ENGLISH | Word formation

**1** In pairs, imagine this photo is important to you for some reason. Describe it to your partner, saying why it's important and how you feel about it.

## EXAM SKILL

### Nouns (2)

- Forming nouns correctly is an essential skill in word formation tasks in many exams.
- Unit 3 and the Vocabulary section in this unit, have both featured noun formation. Exercises 2 and 3 below look at other ways to form nouns.
- If you're not sure what the noun form is, think about common noun suffixes (endings), such as *-ity*, *-ness*, *-ment*, etc., and ask yourself which one sounds right.

**2** Write nouns from each of these words. All the nouns will end in the same two letters.

1 deep ___________
2 die ___________
3 grow ___________
4 long ___________
5 strong ___________
6 true ___________
7 warm ___________
8 wide ___________
9 young ___________

**3** Write the positive and negative nouns in the correct column.

| | positive noun | negative noun |
|---|---|---|
| mature | | |
| perfect | | |
| possible | | |
| responsible | | |

## OPTIMISE YOUR EXAM

### Word formation

- Always check your spelling carefully. If you make one small spelling mistake, your answer will be marked wrong.
- Be particularly careful when forming nouns from words that end in *-e*. Sometimes the *-e* remains (*improve – improvement*) and sometimes the *-e* is removed (*wide – width*).

**4** Write the correct noun form of the word in bold in each gap to complete the text.

**A hero on Everest**

In 2015, a powerful earthquake in Nepal caused an avalanche on Mount Everest, but in the middle of all of the **(1)** ___________ **DIE** and destruction, some people became heroes. One was Dr Rachel Tullet. She had to make a **(2)** ___________ **CHOOSE** between treating her badly injured leg or helping other people. She decided to take **(3)** ___________ for **RESPONSIBLE** dealing with the wounded in the medical tent at base camp. Her selfless **(4)** ___________ saved 23 lives, **BEHAVE** keeping the patients alive for almost 24 hours until the **(5)** ___________ **ARRIVE** of a helicopter to take them to safety and medical **(6)** ___________ in **TREAT** Kathmandu. After the **(7)** ___________ **DEPART** of the helicopter, Dr Tullet attended to her own wounds, stitching up the serious cut in her leg without anaesthetic. From the **(8)** ___________ of Dr Tullet's **DESCRIBE** amazing work by the people who witnessed it, it's clear that she really is a true-life hero.

**1** **In pairs, explain what the activities are, using the questions below.**

| astronomy \| snowboarding whitewater rafting |
|---|

1 Where is it done?
2 Who does it?
3 How is it done?
4 What do you need to do it?
5 Why do people do it?

**EXAM SKILL**

## Explaining

- In writing tasks, you sometimes have to explain things to help your reader understand better.
- '*Wh-*' questions can help you focus on giving an explanation (e.g. what something is, where/when/why/how something happened, etc.).
- When you explain, you may need to state the facts, give an opinion or include reasons.

**2** **Read this email and answer the questions.**

Bex does a lot of explaining in her email. What words does she use to say …

1 how she felt getting Alisha's email?
______________________
2 how she felt hearing about Alisha's new school?
______________________
3 how she feels about Alisha's project?
______________________
4 where she lives?
______________________
5 where Snowdon is?
______________________
6 when she went there?
______________________
7 why she likes it?
______________________
8 what people can do there?
______________________
9 which activities she did there?
______________________
10 her hope for what she's told Alisha?
______________________

To: Alisha
Subject: Your project

Hi Alisha,

Thanks for your email. It was lovely to hear from you! I'm glad you're settling in well at your new school.

So, your project on mountains sounds interesting! As you know, I live in the city but I've been to a few mountains. You asked me to pick an interesting one. I'd choose Snowdon, which is a two-hour drive from where I live. We went there on a school trip recently.

It's great because it's really high, but there's a railway up to the top so you don't have to spend hours walking and climbing to get there. The view is stunning – you can see for miles. They have lots of telescopes up there, so you can see things far away in great detail. The people and cars at the bottom look really tiny!

There are loads of things you can do there, including horse-riding, rock climbing, mountain-biking, and even whitewater rafting. We didn't do anything like that on our trip – maybe next time.

I hope that's useful for you. Let me know how your project goes!

Bye for now,

Bex

**OPTIMISE YOUR EXAM**

## A letter / An email

- Make sure you read the question information carefully. Don't start planning and writing until you're sure you understand it.
- If you forget to include key information, or include information that isn't asked for, you will lose marks.

**3** **Look at this writing task and answer the questions.**

You have received this email from your English-speaking friend, Alex.

> **From:** Alex **Subject:** class project
>
> Can you help me with a class project? I have to write about activities which people do on mountains. Can you tell me about a mountain activity that you like? Explain what it is, what skills and equipment you need to do it, and why you find it interesting.

Write your **email**.

1 Will your email be formal or informal?

__________

2 How many activities do you need to choose?

__________

3 Can you choose an activity that you've never personally done?

__________

**4** **Make notes to complete the chart.**

| Activity: | What does it involve? | What skills/equipment do you need? | Why do you find it interesting? | Other information you'd like to include: |
|---|---|---|---|---|
| | | | | |

**5** **In pairs, tell each other what you're going to write about. Listen to your partner's advice**

**6** **Plan** **Make a paragraph plan.**

| Part | Purpose | Useful phrases | My notes |
|---|---|---|---|
| **First line** | greet the person you are writing to | *Dear ... ,*<br>*Hi ... !* | |
| **Paragraph 1** | thank the other person for their email and refer to a piece of news | *Thanks for your email.*<br>*It was great to hear from you.*<br>*I'm glad you had a good party*, etc. | |
| **Paragraph 2** | say what activity you like and explain what it is and what skills/ equipment you need | *You asked me about ...*<br>*I'd say that my favourite thing to do in the mountains is ...*<br>*You need ... to do it, and you have to be ...* | |
| **Paragraph 3** | explain why you like it | *I love it because ...*<br>*It's such a lot of fun when you ...* | |
| **Paragraph 4** | say you hope it helps and offer to help further | *Hope that helps!*<br>*Let me know if you need ...* | |
| **Closing expressions** | ask them to reply, express love, etc. | *Write soon!*<br>*Love, Lots of love,*<br>*Best wishes, (+ first name)* | |

**7** **Write** **Write your email in an appropriate style. Write 140–190 words.**

**8** **Check** **Before you hand in your email, complete this checklist.**

**Checklist ✓**

- ◯ I've used informal language.
- ◯ I've started and ended my email in the right way.
- ◯ I've referred to some news from Alex's email in the first paragraph.
- ◯ I've described and explained the activity in detail.
- ◯ I've written at least four main paragraphs.
- ◯ I've checked my spelling and grammar.

▶ **Writing reference,** page 171 ▶ **Workbook Unit 8**: Writing, page 66, exercises 1, 2, 3, 4 and Progress check 8, page 67

# PROGRESS CHECK UNITS 7–8

## GRAMMAR AND VOCABULARY

**1 Write a form of the word in capitals in each gap.**

**FRIENDS IN NEED**

We often go through our daily (1) ___________ without thinking about our health until something goes wrong. Then, the (2) ___________ we have with other people become important. Those we have a close (3) ___________ with will offer us love and (4) ___________, or so we hope. It is at times like these, when we are most in need of (5) ___________, that we discover who our friends really are, based on their (6) ___________. Each of our friends has a (7) ___________: to be there for us or not. Those who make the (8) ___________ to help us are our true friends.

**EXIST**
**RELATION**
**FRIEND**
**ENCOURAGE**
**ASSIST**
**BEHAVE**
**CHOOSE**
**DECIDE**

__/8

**2 Choose the correct word or phrase.**

1 The money for the tickets **is** / **are** in my backpack.
2 We haven't got **many** / **much** wood left for the camp fire.
3 I'm afraid the news **isn't** / **aren't** good.
4 A large **number** / **amount** of people were trapped on the mountain.
5 Only a **little** / **few** people have ever climbed this mountain.
6 Your advice **was** / **were** really helpful.
7 These trousers **is** / **are** really tight around the waist.
8 We've got **little** / **a little** water left, but not very much.
9 Those two pieces of information **is** / **are** extremely useful.
10 Of course that bridge is safe – it's made of **iron** / **an iron**.

__/10

**3 Write *a, an* or *the* in each gap where necessary. If an article is not necessary, put a dash (–).**

I had never tried (1) ___________ mountain-climbing before. When (2) ___________ friend suggested having (3) ___________ go, I thought it was (4) ___________ interesting idea. We went along to one of (5) ___________ local clubs and asked about having (6) ___________ lessons. (7) ___________ person in charge of the club was really friendly and explained what was involved. You spend some time on (8) ___________ ground, learning about different aspects of climbing, so that (9) ___________ accidents are less likely. The club has (10) ___________ climbing wall, and that's where you start to get experience. I can't wait to start on a real mountain!

__/10

**4 Match to make sentences. There is one ending you won't use.**

1 Eva says she's made ____
2 Teaching my friend how to climb took me ____
3 Our instructor hasn't said which mountain ____
4 Climbing can be hard when you fall ____
5 I don't know what's wrong ____
6 We had to take ____

**a)** up with the idea of climbing the mountain.
**b)** back to the time when I tried it myself for the first time.
**c)** shelter from the rain at one point.
**d)** a lot of friends since joining the climbing group.
**e)** out with the people you are on the mountain with.
**f)** with this torch but it's not working properly.
**g)** range we're going to next summer.

__/6

**5** **Put the verbs into the correct passive form.**

1 The three climbers will ______________ an award next week. (**give**)
2 Apparently, the mountain ______________ at last. (**just / climb**)
3 The railway ______________ in 1888. (**build**)
4 The ropes ______________ by a qualified instructor. (**always / check**)
5 I'll never forget ______________ and going to hospital in a helicopter. (**rescue**)
6 It was interesting for the kids ______________ a lecture about mountain-climbing. (**give**)

__/6

**6** **Complete the second sentence so it has a similar meaning to the first. Do not change the word given. Use two to five words, including the word given.**

1 Carrie Adams gave us the climbing equipment. **TO**
The climbing equipment ______________________ Carrie Adams.
2 We started climbing before 11 and we were still climbing at three! **CLIMBING**
By three o'clock, we ______________________ over four hours!
3 I told you not to take such an expensive watch to the beach. **AGAINST**
I ______________________ such an expensive watch to the beach.
4 Only people with enough experience are allowed to climb this mountain. **LACKING**
People who ______________________ aren't allowed to climb this mountain.
5 Do you think you'll solve the problem? **FIND**
Do you think you'll ______________________ the problem?

__/10

**Total score** __/50

## EXAM SKILLS

**Tick the statements that are true for you. Review the skills in the unit if you need more help.**

| **I can …** | **Unit/page** |
|---|---|
| ☐ understand linking words/phrases in a story | Unit 7 p70 |
| ☐ predict synonyms in short extracts | Unit 7 p74 |
| ☐ ask for clarification during a collaborative task | Unit 7 p76 |
| ☐ understand the form and function of different verbs and apply them in sentence transformations | Unit 7 p77 |
| ☐ use narrative tenses in a story | Unit 7 p78 |
| ☐ understand implication in blog posts | Unit 8 p80 |
| ☐ listen for words and phrases expressing opinions in a short talk | Unit 8 p84 |
| ☐ express and justify my opinions in a discussion | Unit 8 p86 |
| ☐ understand how nouns are formed and use them in word-formation exercises | Unit 8 p87 |
| ☐ explain things so other people can understand them in a letter / an email | Unit 8 p88 |

# 9 Music to my ears

## READING | Gapped text | A news article

**1 In pairs or groups, add more words to the lists below.**

| Musical instruments | Different genres of music |
|---|---|
| violin | pop |
| piano | classical |

**2 What genres of music do you like from Exercise 1? Number them in order of preference.**

**EXAM SKILL**

### Understanding text logic

- A well-written text has a logical order, where one idea links to another.
- Try to understand the main idea of each paragraph. Think about how the ideas in it are connected to each other.

**3 Read the article opposite then order these paragraph summaries, from 1 to 7.**

**a)** introduction _1_
**b)** general information about the violin ____
**c)** Ludlow's opinion of Ruisi ____
**d)** more similarities between Ludlow and Ruisi ____
**e)** first mention of similarities between Ludlow and Ruisi ____
**f)** Ruisi's opinion of Ludlow and the violin ____
**g)** Some biographical information about Ludlow ____

**4 Look at sentences A–G in Exercise 5, which have been removed from the article. For each one, choose the idea you think it refers to.**

**a)** a fact / an opinion
**b)** Ruisi's life / Ludlow's life
**c)** Ruisi's life / Ludlow's life
**d)** Ruisi's opinion / Ludlow's opinion
**e)** Ruisi's opinion / Ludlow's opinion
**f)** the violin / similarities between the people
**g)** a fact / an opinion

Search Comment

## Teenage violinist given £1m violin to take on tour

SHARE LIKE

**Teenage violinist Roberto Ruisi will take a £1 million violin on tour after a veteran musician spotted his talent and loaned it to him.**

By Hannah Furness, Arts Correspondent

A teenage violinist is to play a £1 million Stradivarius violin after a veteran musician spotted his talent and loaned him the rare instrument to take on tour. Roberto Ruisi, 18, has been entrusted with the prized Stradivarius violin for a series of high-profile performances, including the BBC Proms.

Veteran musician John Ludlow has loaned him the rare instrument after being touched by a series of remarkable similarities in their lives. Like Ruisi, he was the leader of the National Youth Orchestra of Great Britain (NYOGB). The 18-year-old became the youngest ever leader of the NYOGB four years ago. [ 1 ]

Professional musician Ludlow was the first leader of the orchestra back in 1948, retaining that position until 1950. [ 2 ]

His early life had numerous parallels with Ruisi's. [ 3 ] Ruisi will now go on to study at the Royal College of Music, where Ludlow was professor of violin for 27 years.

The instrument, dating from the 1680s, has travelled to concert venues all over Europe in the hands of previous owners, who include French composer Emile Suaret. [ 4 ]

Ruisi thanked John for his stories and advice, and for letting him play such a valuable violin. 'It's been amazing to play on such a remarkable instrument. [ 5 ] This is my last tour leading the NYOGB and being given this opportunity makes it such a fresh and incredible experience – it's a great way to end my National Youth Orchestra journey.'

Reflecting on the parallels between them, Ludlow – who bought the instrument in 1965 – said that Ruisi was already a more accomplished violinist than he had been at the same age. ' [ 6 ] What do you do when you find yourself outclassed? In this case, applaud it with enthusiasm. For this year's NYO concerts, the leader will be playing on the original leader's fiddle, an early Strad. It's a delightful way to span the 66 years of the NYO and a gesture of faith in Robbie's future.'

### OPTIMISE YOUR EXAM

### Gapped text

- Read the text quickly and decide on the main idea of each paragraph.
- Look for similar main ideas in the missing sentences.
- For example, if the sentences before and after a gap refer to key events in someone's early life, look for an option that fits logically with this.

**5** 3.01 **Read the text again. Choose which sentence A–G fits each gap 1–6. There is one extra sentence you do not need.**

**A** To me, the Strad is not just a violin, but is an extension of myself, allowing me to communicate all my musical ideas.

**B** He will perform with the Strad when he goes on tour with the ensemble over the coming days.

**C** After that, he went on to lead orchestras at the Royal Opera House, the English National Opera and the London Concert Orchestra.

**D** Robbie already plays the fiddle far better than I ever did, and has a really fine future ahead of him.

**E** Ruisi said that he had never seen a more expensive violin, and was unsure whether to accept Ludlow's offer.

**F** It will be played at the orchestra's performances at Birmingham's Symphony Hall and the BBC Proms at the Royal Albert Hall.

**G** As well as leading the NYOGB, they both come from Edgbaston in Birmingham and attended the same King Edward's School.

**6** **Find a word or phrase from the article to match each definition.**

1. visiting different places to perform (intro) ______________
2. very experienced (intro) ______________
3. important and talked about (para 1) ______________
4. places where events happen (para 4) ______________
5. a person who writes music (para 4) ______________
6. talented (para 6) ______________
7. celebrate, admire, clap (para 6) ______________
8. violin (often informal) (para 6) ______________

THINK | RESEARCH | CULTURE | LEARN | **ME**

How would you feel if someone gave or loaned you something very valuable? In pairs, discuss your ideas.

▶ **Workbook Unit 9:** Reading, page 68, exercises 1, 2, 3

# 9 GRAMMAR 1 | Reported speech

## Grammar in context

**Look at these sentences from the article on page 93 and choose the direct speech with the closest meaning.**

1 *Ruisi thanked John for his stories and advice, and for letting him play such a valuable violin.*

**a)** 'Thanks for his stories and advice and for letting him play such a valuable violin.'

**b)** 'Thanks for your stories and advice and for letting me play such a valuable violin.'

2 *Ludlow ... said that Ruisi was already a more accomplished violinist than he had been at the same age.*

**a)** 'Ruisi was already a more accomplished violinist than I had been at the same age.'

**b)** 'Ruisi is already a more accomplished violinist than I was at the same age.'

### REMEMBER

- We use reported speech when we are reporting, summarising or telling a story about what someone else said, without giving their exact words.
- Compared to direct speech, reported speech generally uses different tenses. For example: *'I'm **playing** the piano.'* → *Ed said he **was playing** the piano.* (present continuous → past continuous).
- Modal verbs are also used differently in reported speech. For example: *'I **can** play the piano.'* → *Ed said he **could** play the piano.*
- Some other words which refer to time and place are used differently in reported speech. For example: *'I'm playing the piano **tomorrow**.'* → *Ed said he was playing the piano **the following day**.*

▶ **See Grammar reference, Unit 9,** page 156

**1 Read the dialogue and complete the summary with the words in the box.**

**Henry:** Hi Lucy! Are you ready for the school concert this evening?
**Lucy:** I think so. I've been practising my solo for weeks now. I know it by heart.
**Henry:** Great! I'm really looking forward to it. Are your parents coming?
**Lucy:** My dad'll be there. My mum's working tonight, unfortunately, so she can't make it.
**Henry:** That's a shame. Still, I'll be there to cheer you on. Don't forget to come and find me afterwards.
**Lucy:** I won't! See you later!

| had | him (× 2) | night | not | that | thought | was | were | would (× 2) | wouldn't |
|---|---|---|---|---|---|---|---|---|---|

### Schoolmates – episode 6

Henry asked Lucy if she (**1**) ____________ ready for the school concert (**2**) ____________ evening. She said she (**3**) ____________ she was ready, because she (**4**) ____________ been practising her solo. Henry said he was really looking forward to it, and asked Lucy if her parents (**5**) ____________ coming. Lucy replied that her father (**6**) ____________ be there, but that unfortunately her mother was working that (**7**) ____________ . Henry pointed out to Lucy that he (**8**) ____________ be there to cheer her on. He also told her (**9**) ____________ to forget to come and find (**10**) ____________ afterwards. She said she (**11**) ____________ forget, and said she'd see (**12**) ____________ later.

**2 Complete each second sentence so that it means the same as the first sentence. Sometimes there is more than one answer.**

1 'Why don't we sit right at the front?' said Ron.
Ron suggested ____________________ .

2 'There's absolutely no way I'm playing a solo in the concert tomorrow,' said Paula.
Paula absolutely refused ____________________ .

3 'I didn't break the music stand!' said Sam.
Sam denied ____________________ .

**3 Write the direct speech. There is always more than one answer.**

1 Jim said that he'd never been to a better school concert than the one the night before.
____________________

2 Lucy asked Henry what he'd thought of the concert and whether he'd enjoyed it.
____________________

3 Lucy's mum told Lucy that she was really sorry she'd missed the concert and that she'd come to the next one.
____________________

## Idioms connected with *music*

**REMEMBER**

- Most languages, including English, have idioms – phrases that have a meaning which is different from that of the individual words.
- Idioms can often be grouped by a topic, such as music, which makes them easier to learn.
- All the idioms below are in the *Vocabulary reference*, page 166.

**1** 3.02 **Read the sentences (1–8) then match the phrases in bold with their synonyms (a–h). Listen and check.**

1 Jake's running a marathon next week. He's **as fit as a fiddle**. ____
2 Yes, the name Simon Cowell definitely **rings a bell**. ____
3 I need to **drum up some support for** the charity concert tonight. ____
4 It's time to **face the music** and tell Mum about my exam results. ____
5 I haven't got a plan for the meeting so let's just **play it by ear** and see what happens. ____
6 Mike didn't want to go to Spain last week but now he's really keen. He's **changed his tune**. ____
7 Fiona's always saying how good she is. She really **blows her own trumpet**. ____
8 Everyone needs to calm down and relax and not **make a song and dance about** it. ____

**a)** get people interested in
**b)** do something without preparation
**c)** healthy
**d)** accept the criticism or punishment
**e)** changed an opinion or attitude
**f)** is familiar
**g)** complain about something, make a fuss
**h)** boasts, talks proudly about oneself

**2** **In pairs, write your own example sentences for each of the phrases in Exercise 1.**

## Phrasal verbs

**3** 3.03 **Write one word in each gap. Use the words in italics to help you. Listen and check.**

1 Lily said she was thinking of *going* __________ *for* the school singing competition.
2 After that, Ludlow *went* __________ *to* lead orchestras at the Royal Opera House and the English National Opera.
3 Let's *put* __________ an end-of-term musical. It'll be great fun!
4 Charlotte had to *drop* __________ *of* the violin competition when she broke her arm.
5 Max entered a piano competition for teenagers but got *knocked* __________ in the first round.
6 Are you sure you want to organise the school concert? It's a huge amount of responsibility to *take* __________ .
7 The school talent show's *coming* __________ again soon. What shall we do this year?
8 I don't want to *give* __________ any secrets, but we've got a surprise guest performing at the concert tonight.

## Nouns with *-ant* / *-ist*

**4** 3.04 **Write *-ant* or *-ist* to complete these words for people. Listen and check.**

1 account__________
2 applic__________
3 assist__________
4 attend__________
5 consult__________
6 contest__________
7 cycl__________
8 guitar__________
9 journal__________
10 optim__________
11 particip__________
12 perfection__________
13 pian__________
14 serv__________
15 special__________
16 violin__________

**5** **Complete the sentences with words from Exercise 4.**

1 Our teacher knows an awful lot about music and is a __________ in 18th century instruments.
2 We left our jackets with the cloakroom __________ before going into the concert hall.
3 Nadia is passionate about newspapers and hopes to be a __________ one day.
4 I know I was the only __________ , but that's not why I got the job!
5 Can't you try to be more of a(n) __________ instead of always talking about problems.
6 Frazer has had to see a __________ because years of playing the drums have damaged his hearing.

**SAY IT RIGHT**

**Resource centre: Unit 9**
Pronunciation of *-ant* or *-ist*

▶ Vocabulary reference, page 166 ▶ **Workbook Unit 9:** Vocabulary, pages 70–71, exercises 1, 2, 3, 4

# 9 LISTENING | Sentence completion

**1** **In pairs or as a group, answer the questions.**

1 Do you watch TV singing contests?

2 Have you ever auditioned, or considered auditioning for a TV talent show like *Britain's got Talent*? If so, what happened? If not, would you ever consider auditioning in the future?

**EXAM SKILL**

**Taking notes**

- Taking notes while you listen can help you, whether you are listening for the main idea or specific information.
- Don't try to write every word. Just write down the most important information you hear.

**2** 3.05 **Listen to a boy called Josh talking about an audition. Choose the best set of notes.**

**A**
TV show – Pop Voice
Mum
online application (website)
6 mths later: email
Megaron Centre / 6 a.m. / next Saturday
surprised – heart racing

**B**
asked – short talk – event connected to music
watch TV with parents
better singer
not disagree
next series
surprised – heart racing

**3** **In pairs, discuss what makes one set of notes in Exercise 2 better than the other.**

**OPTIMISE YOUR EXAM**

**Sentence completion**

- You will hear the missing information in the order of the questions.
- Don't worry if you miss an answer. Answer the next question then focus on any missing answers the second time you listen.
- If you're not sure of the answer, make a sensible guess.

**4** 3.06 **Listen to the complete talk about auditioning for a singing contest. Complete the sentences with a word or short phrase.**

1 Josh received an email ______________ after the application.

2 He initially felt excited and ______________ .

3 He thought the song he chose was right for his ______________ .

4 They opened the doors to the venue at ______________ in the morning.

5 He described himself as funny, friendly and ______________ .

6 Auditions could be watched on ______________ in the hall.

7 Josh enjoyed watching the auditions, but mainly had a sense of ______________ .

8 Josh agrees with the judges that his singing was nervous, weak and ______________ .

**5** 3.06 **Listen again and check your answers.**

THINK | **RESEARCH** | CULTURE | LEARN | ME

Look online at auditions for a TV singing contest in English, if possible with the TV judges' comments included.

Choose your favourite and present it to the class.



▶ **Workbook Unit 9:** Listening, page 72, exercises 1, 2, 3

# GRAMMAR 2 | Indirect questions

## Grammar in context

**Look at these sentences from the audio in the listening lesson and answer the question.**

*Could you tell me your name and address?*

*I'd like you to give me three words that describe your character.*

**Why didn't the *Pop Voice* interviewer just say this?**

'Tell me your name and address.'

'Give me three words that describe your character.'

### REMEMBER

- Indirect questions are a way of being more polite when asking a question. We use a phrase to introduce the question.
- Some introductory phrases are like questions. *Could you tell me …?*, *Do you know …?*, etc., and end in a question mark.
- Some introductory phrases aren't like questions. *I'd be grateful if you could tell me …*, *I wonder if you know …*, etc., and don't end in a question mark.
- Remember that in indirect questions, we don't use question word order. *Do you know what time **the concert starts**?* (NOT *Do you know what time **does the concert start**?*)

▶ **See Grammar reference, Unit 9,** page 157

**1** **Complete the questions with the words in the box.**

| could | grateful | know | like | wonder |
|---|---|---|---|---|

1 Do you __________ where we can buy tickets?
2 I __________ if you could tell us why you chose that particular instrument.
3 I'd be __________ if you could tell us what you like and dislike about playing in public.
4 I'd __________ you to tell us how you rehearse.
5 __________ you tell us where the concert is?

**2** **Make indirect questions using the words in bold.**

1 When did you first start playing? **like**
__________
2 What do you like and dislike about being famous? **wonder**
__________
3 How do you travel around the country? **could**
__________
4 When is your next video coming out? **know**
__________
5 What are your plans for the future? **grateful**
__________

**3** **Choose the correct answers.**

**Zoe:** I'm delighted to welcome Lana Belfield to the studio. Now, Lana, I wonder (**1**) ____ tell us what you've been doing since your last album came out?

**Lana:** Well, Zoe, I've been touring the country with my band, and I've been back in the studio making a new album.

**Zoe:** Could you tell us what (**2**) ____ ?

**Lana:** It's a mix of my old, country style with a modern, urban rap sound.

**Zoe:** Sounds interesting. (**3**) ____ those two genres go together easily.

**Lana:** You'd be surprised! There are some old 'talking blues' numbers that are very like rap songs!

**Zoe:** Could you tell us (**4**) ____ making the album?

**Lana:** Oh, yes! It was a lot of fun.

**Zoe:** Finally, (**5**) ____ you could play us a track from the new album?

**Lana:** Sure. It would be my pleasure.

1 **a)** if you could **b)** you could **c)** could you
2 **a)** the album is like **b)** is the album like **c)** does the album like
3 **a)** I wonder that **b)** Do I wonder **c)** I wonder if
4 **a)** whether did you enjoy **b)** you enjoyed **c)** whether you enjoyed
5 **a)** do you think **b)** I wonder if **c)** do you wonder whether

**THINK** | RESEARCH | CULTURE | LEARN | ME

Imagine you could interview any musician or band – who would you choose and what would you ask?

Talk2Me — *I'm not really sure, but …*

Flipped classroom

**1** ▷ **Watch the *Talk2Me* video and for each person, note down their answers.**

- Who do you think the person is?
- What are they doing? Why?
- Why do you think they are wearing a mask?

**2** ▷ **Watch the video again and number the phrases from the *Phrase expert* box in the order you hear them.**

> **PHRASE EXPERT**
> He/She/They might be | I'm not really sure, but … | It's difficult to say, but … | It's not totally clear, but one possibility is that | Perhaps/Maybe | This is a photo of

**3** **In pairs or groups, answer the questions.**

- Do you ever see people playing music in the streets in your country? Why do they do it?
- What other kinds of street entertainers have you seen?

> **EXAM SKILL**
> **Expressing uncertainty and speculating**
> - In a speaking exam you may have to speculate if you're uncertain about something. Some useful phrases for this appear in Exercise 2.
> - It's fine to admit you are uncertain and is better than saying nothing, especially if you explain why you are uncertain.
> - Some exam tasks are specifically designed to allow you to use language of uncertainty and speculation.

**4** **Complete the sentences speculating about the picture in Exercise 1.**

1 It's not totally __________ , but perhaps he wants to hide his real identity.
2 It __________ be that he just wants to be anonymous …
3 __________ it's actually a famous musician under the mask.
4 I'm not really sure, but one __________ is that it's a publicity stunt.
5 Or he __________ be playing music for children.
6 It's __________ to say, but maybe I would go for a mixture of electronica, jazz and pop.

**5** **Look at these two photos and make notes to answer the questions.**

A

B

1 Who do you think the people are?
__________
2 What might the people be doing?
__________
3 Where do you think they are performing?
__________
4 How might they be feeling?
__________

> **OPTIMISE YOUR EXAM**
> **Photo task**
> - Remember to use the present continuous when describing an action in progress, e.g. *They are all singing.*
> - If you are not sure what you are describing, use phrases like those in the *Phrase expert* box or use the modal continuous, e.g. *They might be singing along at an outdoor concert.*

**6** **In pairs, take turns to do the exam task below.**

> **Student A:** Describe the photos, saying what you think the people are feeling. Talk for one minute.
>
> **Student B:** Listen and underline the phrases from the *Phrase expert* box that Student A uses, and listen to see if they use the present continuous when they describe. Which of the two situations would you prefer to be in? Why?

**7** **Give your partner feedback about the exam task in Exercise 6.**



▶ **Workbook Unit 9:** Speaking, pages 72–73, exercises 1, 2, 3

# USE OF ENGLISH | Multiple-choice cloze

**1** **In pairs or groups, answer the questions.**

1 What qualities do you think someone needs in order to become a successful singer?
2 Who is your favourite singer? Why do you like him/her?

**EXAM SKILL**

### Idioms

- The vocabulary lesson in this unit featured idioms connected to music. Remember that you can find all the idioms in this book in the *Vocabulary reference*, page 166.
- Learn idioms as a complete phrase along with their meanings.

**2** **Choose the correct answers. Use the words in italics to help you.**

1 I'm not sure if I've met him before, but *the name* ____ *a bell*.
a) plays b) rings c) pulls

2 I suppose it's time to *face the* ____ and tell the teacher we broke the window.
a) tunes b) songs c) music

3 I thought you liked online gaming, but it sounds as if you've ____ *your tune* and now you hate it!
a) lost b) moved c) changed

4 I've been ill, but now I feel *as* ____ *as a fiddle*!
a) well b) healthy c) fit

5 I can't read music, but I can *play* most things *by* ____ .
a) hand b) ear c) eye

6 During the audition, Oliver was *as cool as a* ____ .
a) snowman b) cucumber c) fridge

7 As she started to sing, I was *on the edge of my* ____ .
a) seat b) chair c) cushion

8 I was really nervous and *had* ____ *in my stomach*.
a) insects b) ants c) butterflies

**OPTIMISE YOUR EXAM**

### Multiple-choice cloze

- If a missing word is part of an idiom or set phrase, say the whole idiom or phrase to yourself to see if it sounds right.
- If you're still not sure, make a sensible guess.

**3** **Quickly read the text in Exercise 4. Which two gaps are testing your knowledge of idioms? Write the numbers.**

**4** **Choose the correct word to fill each gap.**

**Ella – we love you!**

Does the name Ella Henderson **(1)** __________ any bells? It might. Ella **(2)** __________ for the 9th series of The *X Factor* in the UK, and got through to the live shows. Although she got **(3)** __________ out in week seven and finished sixth, she's **(4)** __________ on to become one of the most successful and famous of the singers from that series. She's now recognised as a very **(5)** __________ singer and songwriter. She co-wrote her first single, *Ghost*, which went straight to Number 1 in the UK charts. A year later, she went on **(6)** __________ with the pop group Take That. Ella's quite shy and doesn't blow her own **(7)** __________ easily, but she has every right to – and we at *TeenPop* **(8)** __________ her!

1 **A** sound **B** buzz **C** ring **D** chime
2 **A** entered **B** practised **C** rehearsed **D** auditioned
3 **A** beaten **B** bashed **C** hit **D** knocked
4 **A** gone **B** passed **C** travelled **D** run
5 **A** managed **B** achieved **C** succeeded **D** accomplished
6 **A** route **B** tour **C** travel **D** round
7 **A** oboe **B** clarinet **C** trumpet **D** trombone
8 **A** approve **B** applaud **C** look up **D** wish

THINK | RESEARCH | **CULTURE** | LEARN | ME

Which of the people from *The X Factor* or shows like it in your country have become most successful?
Write a short paragraph about one of them, similar to the paragraph above.

# 9 WRITING | A review

**1 In pairs or groups, answer the questions.**

1. How do you decide what films to see?
2. Do you read reviews? If so, where do you get reviews from? If not, why not?
3. Can you think of any movies that got bad reviews but you liked or movies that got good reviews but you didn't like?

**2 Read this review and make notes to answer the questions.**

1. According to the writer, who should see this film?
2. Who shouldn't see this film?
3. What does the writer like about the film?
4. What different words and phrases does the writer use to recommend the film?

## Les Misérables: great songs and a great cast

Are you looking for an exciting film with loads of great songs and an incredible cast? If you are, then *Les Misérables* may be the perfect film for you.

*Les Misérables* came out, and was an instant hit. It isn't difficult to see why! Firstly, it's based on the award-winning stage musical of the same name. Secondly, the cast includes stars such as Hugh Jackman, Russell Crowe and Anne Hathaway.

The plot is complicated and difficult to explain, but it's set in Paris in the early 1800s, where a group of students start a rebellion. Hugh Jackman plays Jean Valjean, a prisoner who is released, and Russell Crowe is Javert, a prison guard. The songs and singing are fantastic, particularly when Anne Hathaway sings the most famous song from the musical, I Dreamed A Dream.

I would definitely recommend *Les Misérables* to older teenagers, but younger teenagers and children may find it a little boring, sad or even scary in places! Don't bother seeing it if you don't like musicals, but if you do, you won't be disappointed!

**EXAM SKILL**

### Making recommendations

- Some writing tasks have a particular target reader in mind and you should think about this audience when you write it.
- For example, if you are reviewing a film for young people, think about what interests them. Do they like films with young characters and lots of action or slower, more serious films?

**3 In pairs or as a group, discuss the questions.**

- Have you seen the film *Les Misérables*?
- If you have, do you agree with the review? Is it a good review of the film?
- If you haven't, does the review make you want to see the film?

**OPTIMISE YOUR EXAM**

### A review

- For this task, describe the key aspects of the film – plot, acting, music, special effects, etc.
- Try not to reveal too much – you don't want to ruin the film for the readers.
- Finish with your recommendation. Tell your readers whether they should or shouldn't see the film and briefly summarise your reasons why, using a phrase like *I would definitely (not) recommend …*, or *Young people will love/hate this film because …*.

## 4 Look at this writing task and make notes to answer the questions. Use your imagination if necessary.

You see this advert in an English-language magazine for young people.

> **REVIEWS WANTED!**
>
> **Films with great music**
>
> We're looking for reviews of films that have plenty of singing or great music in them. They may be musicals, but they don't have to be. Your review should include information about the plot, the cast, the music, and other relevant information. Would you recommend this film to other people your age?
>
> The best reviews will be published in next month's magazine.

Write your **review**.

1 What film are you going to review?

______________________________

2 What happens in the film? Describe the plot in one or two sentences.

______________________________

3 Who is in the film?

______________________________

4 What are you going to say about the singing?

______________________________

5 What other aspects of the film are you going to mention?

______________________________

6 Are you going to recommend the film? Why / Why not?

______________________________

## 5 Plan Complete the paragraph plan.

| Part | Purpose | Useful phrases | My notes |
|---|---|---|---|
| **Title** | briefly describe what the review is about – and make us want to read it! | | |
| **Paragraph 1** | introduce the film, and engage and interest the reader | *Are you looking for …*<br>*Have you ever seen …?*<br>*If you haven't, …* | |
| **Paragraphs 2/3** | over two paragraphs, describe the plot, the cast, the singing, and any other useful information | *it's based on …, it's set in …*<br>*it stars, X plays Y,*<br>*In my opinion, it makes you feel …* | |
| **Paragraph 4** | say if you recommend the film to other people your age, briefly explain why | *I would personally recommend it to …*<br>*It's perfect for …*<br>*I wouldn't recommend it to …* | |

## 6 Write Write your review in an appropriate style. Write 140–190 words.

## 7 Check Before you hand in your review, complete this checklist.

**Checklist**

- ◯ I've given my review a title.
- ◯ I've written at least four paragraphs.
- ◯ I've described the plot, the cast and the singing.
- ◯ I've given some other relevant information.
- ◯ I've said who should and/or shouldn't see the film.
- ◯ I've tried to interest and engage the reader.
- ◯ I've said whether I recommend the film or not.
- ◯ I've given my reasons.
- ◯ I've checked my spelling and grammar.

▶ Writing reference, page 170 ▶ **Workbook Unit 9:** Writing, page 74, exercises 1, 2, 3 and Progress check 9, page 75

# 10 Run till you drop

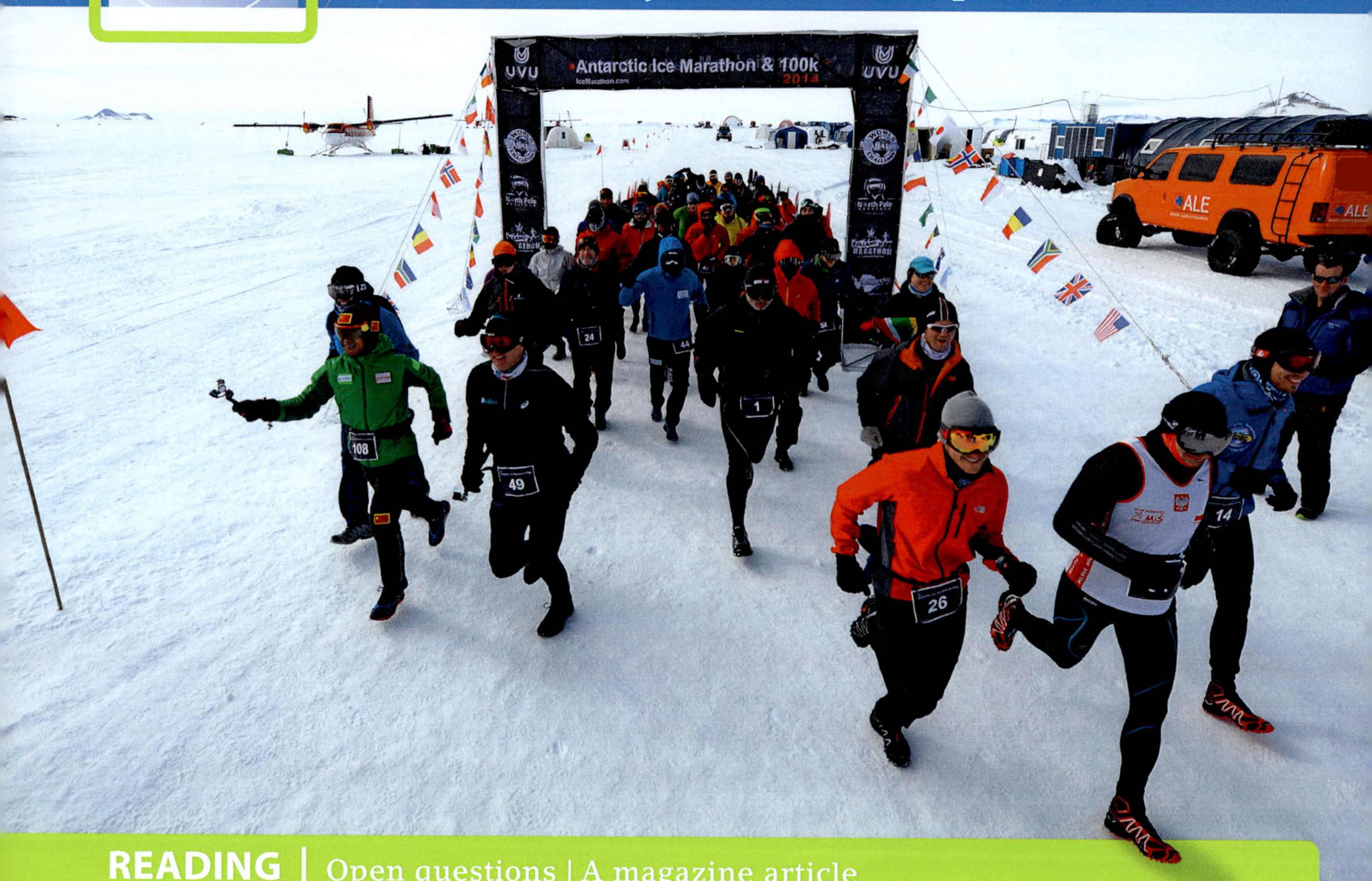


## READING | Open questions | A magazine article

**1 In pairs or groups, answer the questions.**

1 Can you name any famous runners from your country? What types of running are they famous for?

2 Do you like running? Do you think running should be a compulsory part of PE at school?

> **EXAM SKILL**
>
> **Identifying synonyms (1)**
>
> - In reading exam tasks, the questions often use different words from those in the text.
> - Before you read the text, identify and underline the key words/ideas in each question.
> - Looking for synonyms for these words/ideas in the text will help you answer the questions.

**2 Read the first two paragraphs of the article. For each question, find a synonym or close synonym in the article for the underlined word or phrase.**

**Example:** What's the weather like in a <u>standard</u> city marathon?

*normal*

1 What's the weather like in a standard <u>city</u> marathon?

______

2 Why is the AIM not a <u>conventional</u> marathon?

______

3 What are AIM entrants frequently <u>fighting</u> against?

______

4 What advice do <u>the people who run the event</u> give in terms of speed?

______

5 What won't you see on the <u>journey</u> round the course?

______

**3 In pairs or as a group, ask and answer the questions in Exercise 2.**

# The Antarctic Ice Marathon

Have you ever thought about running a marathon? At just over 26 miles, or 42 kilometres, it's too far for most people. And that's in normal urban conditions of mild temperature and hard road surfaces. But what about running on snow and ice at -20°C? Yes, people do this. For fun. Welcome to the annual Antarctic Ice Marathon (AIM)!

The AIM is held each year, usually in November, only a few hundred miles from the South Pole. As the only organised marathon in Antarctica, it provides a unique opportunity for participants to become members of an exclusive group: the 7 Continents Marathon Club. But it's far from a typical marathon, with runners often battling strong winds from the South Pole. As the organisers state, 'Don't expect to run your quickest time. Also, forget about penguins, or crowds cheering you along the route – no penguins live this far south.'

And what about running gear? In a standard marathon, people usually run in shorts and vests or T-shirts. It's so cold in Antarctica that you can't run wearing just that. The organisers recommend what they call a 'layering system'. In other words, it's best to wear a number of layers of clothing to stop your body from getting too hot or too cold. They suggest three layers for the upper body: a thermal layer, then a fleece layer underneath a windproof jacket. For the legs, they recommend a thermal layer and then windproof trousers on top. You'd also need gloves, sock liners and woollen socks, a balaclava, facemask, neck protection, hat and goggles. And a pair of high-end trail or off-road running shoes.

Before you start packing, remember that Antarctica is such a remote place that it's not cheap to get there. In fact, the entry fee is more than €10,000! This includes round-trip flights from Chile to Antarctica, all meals and accommodation while in Antarctica, and various other souvenirs, such as certificates and T-shirts. It doesn't include flights from where you live to Chile. The organisers are very aware that it's too expensive for most people, so they encourage potential entrants who haven't got enough money to approach companies and organisations for sponsorship. More than 50 runners take part each year, and several of them are usually running to raise money for charity.

If you like the idea but think that a full marathon is just too much for you, a half marathon is run on the same day. However, if you think 26.2 miles is a walk in the park, then you might be interested in the 100 km 'ultra race' held a couple of months later, in January. As the organisers say, 'this ultra-marathon challenge is reserved for only the toughest athletes. The 100 km (62.1 miles) distance will seem endless, run under a sun that never sets against the backdrop of hills, mountains and large expanses of ice.'

## OPTIMISE YOUR EXAM

### Open questions

- Identifying synonyms will help you answer questions 1, 2, and 4 in the exam task opposite.
- Remember to focus on the idea expressed in the question, not the specific words.
- When you've found the idea, write a word or short phrase to answer the question.

**4** **Look at the underlined words in Exercise 5, question 1 and find where this idea is expressed with synonyms in paragraph 2. Then answer question 1.**

**5** 3.07 **Write a short answer for each question. Use a maximum of four words.**

1. What often prevents <u>entrants</u> from <u>breaking their personal marathon time record</u>? __________
2. What people should runners not expect to see during the race? __________
3. What should a runner wear directly under their jacket? __________
4. What advice do the organisers give to runners who can't afford the fee? __________
5. How are the runners of the 100 km race described? __________

THINK | **RESEARCH** | CULTURE | LEARN | ME

Put 'Antarctic Ice Marathon' into a search engine or YouTube. Find five facts about the marathon not mentioned in the article.

# 10 GRAMMAR 1 | Result clauses: *so, such, too, enough*

## Grammar in context

**Complete the phrases and sentences with the words in the box. Then find them in the article on page 103 and check your answers.**

| enough \| much \| so \| such \| that \| too |
|---|

1 It's __________ cold in Antarctica that you can't run wearing just that.
2 … Antarctica is __________ a remote place __________ it's not cheap to get there.
3 The organisers are very aware that it's __________ expensive for most people …
4 … they encourage potential entrants who haven't got __________ money to approach companies …
5 If you … think that a full marathon is just too __________ for you, a half marathon is run on the same day.

**REMEMBER**

*So* and *such* are often followed by a *that* clause which explains the result. *Too* and *enough* are often followed by a full infinitive or *for* + person/noun.

*It's* ***so cold / such a cold day that*** *I can't go outside.*

*It's* ***too cold / not warm enough*** *to go outside.*

▶ **See Grammar reference, Unit 10,** page 158

### 1 Choose the correct word or phrase.

1 The wind was blowing **so / too** strongly that I nearly fell over.

2 I had **such a / so** fantastic time. I can't wait to do it again next year!

3 Twenty-six miles is **too / such** far for me to run in **too / such** difficult conditions, so I decided to do the half marathon instead.

4 You wear **so / too** many different things that you actually don't feel cold when you're running.

5 I don't have **enough / too much** money to do this every year unfortunately.

6 I'd done **so many / such a lot of** training beforehand in icy conditions that I knew what to expect.

7 All the runners are **so / such** interesting and friendly people that I can't wait to go back the following year.

8 A €10,000 entry fee is **too much / not enough** to pay unless you're very rich or have sponsors.

### 2 Write one word in each gap.

## THE MARATHON DES SABLES

If you want to run a marathon in extreme conditions but think that Antarctica might be just a little (1) __________ far away for you (2) __________ get to, or you haven't got (3) __________ money, then maybe you should consider the Marathon des Sables, or MdS. Held every year in the Sahara desert, the MdS is (4) __________ challenging it's been called 'the toughest footrace on Earth'. Competitors have to run the equivalent of five and half marathons over several days in the burning heat. It's (5) __________ hot (50°C) (6) __________ any sweat you produce evaporates instantly. According to the organisers' website, it's (7) __________ a difficult race (8) __________ 'your brain is screaming at you to stop' while you're running! They make sure there's (9) __________ water (10) __________ the runners to drink (more than 120,000 litres in total) throughout the route. Anything else you need, you have to carry with you in your backpack.

THINK | RESEARCH | CULTURE | LEARN | ME

If you had to compete in either the Antarctic Ice Marathon or the Marathon des Sables, which would you choose?

## People in sport

**1** 3.08 **Match the words in the box with the clues. Listen and check.**

| captain \| coach \| fundraiser \| leader<br>medic \| participant \| referee \| sponsor<br>supporters \| winner |
|---|

1 __________: a person who gives money to an event or a person taking part in an event
2 __________: a competitor, entrant, person taking part
3 __________: the people who watch a sporting event
4 __________: a person who gives medical help or treatment
5 __________: the person at the front of a race
6 __________: the person/team who comes first in a race or event
7 __________: the person in some sports who makes sure players obey the rules
8 __________: a person who organises an event to collect money for charity
9 __________: the player who is in charge of a sports team
10 __________: the person who trains a sports person or team

**2** **Look at the clues in Exercise 1. Underline more people in sport words.**

**SAY IT RIGHT**

**Resource centre: Unit 10**
Word stress

## Adjectives/nouns/verbs

**3** 3.09 **Complete the table. Listen and check.**

| adjective | noun | verb |
|---|---|---|
| deep | | |
| | | heighten |
| | largeness | |
| long | | |
| | lowness | |
| | strength | |
| wide | | |

**4** **Write a form of the word in capitals in each gap to complete the sentences.**

1 What's the __________ of the hill we have to run up today? **HIGH**
2 I need to __________ my leg muscles before I attempt a marathon. **STRONG**
3 If you __________ the photo a bit, we might be able to see which runner it is. **LARGE**
4 They've decided to increase the __________ of the route by 5 km. **LONG**

## Phrases connected with running

**5** 3.10 **Choose the correct word. Listen and check.**

1 Emma *ran a* ***mile*** */* ***kilometre*** when Bob asked her to help him with his homework!
2 Elaine *hit the* ***earth*** */* ***ground*** *running* when she moved to a new school and immediately made some friends.
3 We're so busy at work this week – I'm *run off my* ***legs*** */* ***feet***.
4 The car's been in the garage for months, so it'll be good to *get it* ***up*** */* ***out*** *and running again*.
5 We've been *running around in* ***rings*** */* ***circles*** trying to decide what to do the project on.
6 The first day of the course went well. In fact, I'd say we *got off to a running* ***beginning*** */* ***start***.
7 By not revising, you're really *running the* ***risk*** */* ***danger*** *of* failing the test.
8 Phil wants to record ten songs and hasn't even written one yet. He's *trying to run before he can* ***stand*** */* ***walk***!

**6** **In pairs, discuss the meanings of the phrases in Exercise 5.**

# 10 LISTENING | Multiple choice (single extract)

**1** **In pairs or as a group, look at the photo and answer the questions.**

1 What do you think the people in the photo are doing?
2 Why might they be doing that?
3 How do you think they feel?

**EXAM SKILL**

**Distractors (1)**

- With multiple-choice questions, you may hear words/phrases from all the options.
- Be careful. If you hear a word/phrase from an option, it doesn't necessarily mean that's the correct answer.

**2** **Look at question 1 in Exercise 5, then choose T (True) or F (False) for the sentences below.**

1 All of the answer options in the question will probably be mentioned in the interview. **T / F**
2 You should listen for the first idea to be mentioned and choose that as the answer. **T / F**
3 You should listen for the idea that is true for Aled at the relevant time. **T / F**

**3** 3.11 **Listen to the start of an interview with Aled Davies and complete each gap with a short phrase.**

**Aled:** Well, it actually all started about six months ago. I was (**1**) ______________ in the kitchen after school, and my dad was (**2**) ______________ in the living room. An item came on the local news about the park where my friends and I (**3**) ______________ after school.

**4** **Use the extract to help you choose the correct answer option for question 1 in Exercise 5.**

**OPTIMISE YOUR EXAM**

**Multiple choice (single extract)**

- Make sure you are clear about what the question is asking before you listen.
- Remember that the speakers may not use exactly the same words as in the answer options, so listen for synonyms.

**5** 3.12 **Listen to the complete interview about raising money and choose the best answers (A, B or C).**

1 What was Aled doing when he first heard about the council's plans?
**A** playing in the park
**B** watching a TV programme
**C** doing schoolwork

2 Who did Aled feel particularly worried about?
**A** his friends and family
**B** children younger than him
**C** older kids in the neighbourhood

3 What did Aled and his friends think about the council?
**A** They ought to install new playground equipment.
**B** They actually had more money than they admitted.
**C** They were wrong about how dangerous the park was.

4 What would affect how much money Aled's grandmother would give him?
**A** how far Aled ran
**B** how fast Aled ran
**C** what Aled wore

5 What does Aled say about the money they raised?
**A** They ended up with more than they had planned.
**B** It wasn't quite as much as they needed.
**C** All the runners contributed equally.

**6** 3.12 **Listen again and check your answers.**



▶ **Workbook Unit 10:** Listening, page 80, exercises 1, 2, 3, 4

## Grammar in Context

**Look at this sentence from the audio in the listening lesson and write *Yes* or *No* to answer the questions.**

*If we hadn't had the playground to play in, we would have been very bored.*

1 Did they have the playground to play in? ________

2 Were they very bored? ________

### REMEMBER

- The structure of the third conditional is: *if* + past perfect, *would have* + past participle.
- Both clauses in a third conditional sentence are hypothetical (i.e. they didn't really happen).
- Instead of *would*, we can also use *might* and *could* in the result clause.

▶ **See Grammar reference, Unit 10,** page 158

**1 Complete the sentences with the correct form of the verbs in brackets.**

1 If I ____________ (**train**) harder when I was on the track, I would probably ____________ (**improve**) on my personal best.

2 She ____________ (**finish**) second if she ____________ (**not fall**) over at the start.

3 The event ____________ (**cancel**) if there ____________ (**not be**) enough entrants.

4 They might ____________ (**participate**) if the entry fee ____________ (**cost**) less.

5 If the race ____________ (**not take place**) on a Saturday, I ____________ (**not take part**).

6 If she ____________ (**drink**) more water, she ____________ (**not be**) so dehydrated.

**2 Write a third conditional sentence for each of these situations.**

**Example:** She didn't check the time of the race so she went to the stadium on the wrong day.

*If she'd checked the time of the race, she wouldn't have gone to the stadium on the wrong day.*

1 Layla fell over during the race and hurt her leg.

________________________________

2 Oliver didn't win the race because he didn't enter.

________________________________

3 I didn't have my trainers so I didn't run.

________________________________

4 We had forgotten our tickets so we couldn't go in.

________________________________

5 I got fit quickly because I joined a gym.

________________________________

6 I lost my shoes so I was late getting to the starting line.

________________________________

**3 Read about Mo Farah. Write third conditional sentences using the prompts.**

**Bio:** Mo Farah

Mo Farah is the most successful British distance runner. He was born in 1983 in Somalia, where his twin brother still lives. His father, who is from England, met his mother there on holiday. Eight years later, Mo, who didn't speak much English, went to join his father in London.

Mo originally wanted to be a footballer, but his PE teacher recognised his talent and encouraged him to focus on running. In 1997, Mo won the first of five national schools titles and his first European Junior title followed in 2001, when he won the 5,000 metres.

From 2005 to 2008, Mo developed as an athlete, although he didn't reach the final of the 5,000 metres in the Beijing Olympics. In 2010, he took gold at both 5,000 metres and 10,000 metres in the European championships. He repeated this double at the 2012 Summer Olympics, the 2015 World Championships, and again at the 2016 Summer Olympics in Rio! Mo has won more awards than anyone else in British athletics.

1 Mo's father / meet / mother / on holiday / Mo / be born

________________________________

2 Mo / might not learn English / he / move / to England

________________________________

3 his teacher / recognise his talent / Mo / might not focus on running

________________________________

4 he / might not win a European title / he / not win / national titles first

________________________________

5 he / run faster / in the Beijing Olympics / he / might reach / the final

________________________________

**THINK** | RESEARCH | CULTURE | LEARN | ME

Think of three things that happened yesterday.

For each one, write a third conditional sentence.

I was late for school. *If I hadn't been late for school, I wouldn't have got into trouble.*

▶ **Workbook Unit 10:** Grammar 2, page 79, exercises 1, 2

# 10 SPEAKING | Interview

Talk 2 Me — *To be honest ...*

**Flipped classroom**

**1** **Watch the *Talk2Me* video and for each person, note down their responses.**

1 Have you ever run in a race such as a 5K, 10K or a half marathon?
2 Have you ever run in fancy dress? Would you like to?
3 Have you taken part in other sports competitions?

**2** **Watch the video again. Correct the mistake(s) in each of the underlined words or phrases.**

1 To see honest, if you asked …
______________________________
2 No, but it sounds as fun.
______________________________
3 It's funny you should speak that, because …
______________________________
4 Factually, we haven't. I prefer …
______________________________
5 Badly no. I'd love to go.
______________________________
6 I ran one race dressed as a giant banana, if this counts.
______________________________

**EXAM SKILL**

### Talking about experiences

- In speaking exams you sometimes have to talk about previous experiences you've had, and how you feel/felt about them.
- If you are asked a question beginning with *Have you ever …?* don't answer just *yes* or *no*, give a longer answer.

**3** **In pairs or groups, answer the questions.**

- Describe the photo.
- Have you ever won anything? How did you feel?

**OPTIMISE YOUR EXAM**

### Interview

- You may be asked questions about something you have never done or do not know much about.
- Avoid just saying *No* or phrases like *I don't know* and *I'm not sure*.
- Give an extended answer supported by examples, opinions or reasons.
- If you don't understand the question, ask the examiner to repeat it.

**4** **Make notes to answer each question in Exercise 5. Make sure your answers are extended and try to use phrases in the *Phrase expert* box.**

1 ______________________________
______________________________
2 ______________________________
______________________________
3 ______________________________
______________________________
4 ______________________________
______________________________

**PHRASE EXPERT**

actually | I'd love to though | if that counts | it's funny you should ask/say that | it sounds like | sadly | to be honest

**5** **In pairs, ask and answer the questions. Use your notes from Exercise 4 and the *Phrase expert* box.**

1 Have you ever been a member of a sports team?
2 Have you ever watched an athletics event, either on TV or in real life?
3 Have you ever taken part in a sports competition at school?
4 Have you ever met a famous sportsperson?

# USE OF ENGLISH | Sentence transformation

**1** **In pairs, imagine you took this photo. Describe it to your partner, saying where you took it, why you took it and how you feel about it.**

**EXAM SKILL**

## Conditionals

- Exam tasks often test your use of conditionals.
- Make sure you know the different types of conditional (zero, first, second, third), what they mean and how they are formed.

**2** **Label the conditionals below (*zero, first, second* or *third*).**

1 Your fitness would improve if you ran more often. ________
2 If you hadn't run so often, your fitness wouldn't have improved. ________
3 If we run more often, our fitness improves. ________
4 If she starts running often, her fitness will really improve. ________

**3** **Choose a sentence which means the same as each sentence in Exercise 2.**

**Sentence 1:** ____ **Sentence 2:** ____
**Sentence 3:** ____ **Sentence 4:** ____

**a)** Your fitness improved because you ran a lot.
**b)** It is a fact that running often improves fitness.
**c)** Starting to run often will help her get fit.
**d)** You don't run often which is why your fitness doesn't improve.

**4** **Look at the questions in Exercise 5. Which questions test your knowledge of conditionals?**

**OPTIMISE YOUR EXAM**

## Sentence transformation

- Check that your answers are grammatically correct and include all of the information from the first sentence.
- For example, for question 1 in Exercise 5, the answer 'WAS SUCH A SUCCESS' would not get full marks because a key piece of information (marathon) from the first sentence is missing.

**5** **Complete the second sentence so it has a similar meaning to the first. Do not change the word given. Use two to five words, including the word given.**

1 The marathon was so successful that we're going to do it again next year.
**SUCH**
It ________________ that we're going to do it again next year.

2 How deep is the snow that they run on?
**THE**
What ________________ the snow that they run on?

3 Joe didn't beat the record because he ran out of time.
**IF**
Jo would have beaten the record ________________ out of time.

4 I'd enter the Antarctic Ice Marathon but I'm not rich enough.
**MONEY**
If I had ________________ the Antarctic Ice Marathon, I would.

5 Without sunscreen, there's a chance you'll get sunburn while you train.
**RUN**
Without sunscreen, ________________ getting sunburn while you train.

6 We won because we were fitter than the other team.
**BEEN**
We wouldn't have won ________________ fitter than the other team.

THINK | **RESEARCH** | CULTURE | LEARN | ME

Find a song in English on YouTube with a form of the word 'run' in the title.

Present it to the class and say why you like/dislike it.

▶ **Workbook Unit 10:** Use of English, page 81, exercises 1, 2, 3, 4

# 10 WRITING | A story

**1 In pairs or as a group, answer the questions.**

1 What's your favourite book or film?
2 Describe the plot (in other words, the events) in one or two sentences and say why you like it.

**2 Read this story and make notes to answer the questions.**

*THE UNFINISHED RACE*

*Becky put on her goggles and checked she hadn't forgotten anything. She had her map, a mobile phone and several bottles of water. She was ready.*

*When Douglas blew the whistle, Becky, Alan, Greg and Polly ran off across the sand. All four of them thought the same thing: 'Why are we doing this stupid race?' Then they thought: 'I really want to win this!'*

*Becky had been running for over an hour when she suddenly heard something. She didn't want to stop, but something made her. She looked around, and finally saw Greg lying at the bottom of a sand dune. 'I've broken my leg!' he cried. 'Call someone to come and help me.'*

*Becky didn't like Greg very much, and part of her wanted to call and then continue the race. But she couldn't. She knew that if she'd had the accident, she'd want someone to stay with her until the medics came.*

*So, giving up all chance of beating the others, Becky ran down the sand dune. 'Don't worry, Greg. I'm here,' she said. She knew some things were more important than winning.*

1 Summarise the plot of the story in one sentence.

2 Is it a good short story? Give reasons.

3 For a story this length, should the plot be more complicated, simpler, or is it about right?

4 Many things in the story are unexplained. Make a list of all the things we don't know at the end:

**Example:** *why they decided to have a race*

5 Does it matter that many things in the story are unexplained? Does it make the story better or worse?

6 What do you think of the title? Is it appropriate? Can you think of a better title?

7 What do you think of the final sentence? Is it a good end to the story?

## EXAM SKILL

### Creating a good plot

- The 'plot' of a story is the events that happen in it.
- Successful plots in short stories are simple, with a few main characters and a few key events.
- Complicated plots with too many characters and too much action are not successful in short stories.

**3 In pairs or as a group, discuss your answers to the questions in Exercise 2.**

## OPTIMISE YOUR EXAM

### A story

- It's often a good idea to include some direct speech in a story, but make sure you do it correctly.
- Speech marks like this << >> are never used in English.
- Use single or double speech marks, e.g. *'Hi!' said Paul.* or *"Hi!" said Paul.*
- If you're writing a conversation, always start a new line for different speakers.

## 4 Look at this writing task and make notes to answer questions 1–7.

You have seen this announcement in an international magazine for schools.

### STORIES WANTED!

We are looking for stories for our new English-language magazine for teenagers. Your story must begin with this sentence:

*As he waited at the starting line, all Mike could think about was winning.*

Your story must include:

- a running race
- an unusual event

Write your **story**.

1 Why is Mike determined to win? *Is there a particular reason why this race is so important to Mike?*

______________________________

2 What kind of race is it? *How far do they have to run? Even if it's not all mentioned in the story, you need to know in your head.*

______________________________

3 Who is Mike racing against? *How many people? Do we know their names? Is one of them a rival of Mike's?*

______________________________

4 Why are they racing? *Is it explained in the story or not? Even if it's not, you need to know in your head why they're racing.*

______________________________

5 What's the unusual event? *An accident? Something outside of the race? Choose something interesting and/or exciting.*

______________________________

6 What happens at the end? *Don't finish with the same idea as in the model. Come up with your own idea!*

______________________________

7 Summarise the plot in one sentence.

______________________________

## 5 In pairs, provide feedback on each other's notes in Exercise 4.

## 6 Plan Complete the paragraph plan.

| Part | Purpose | My notes |
|---|---|---|
| **Title** | briefly describe what the story is about – and make us want to read it! | |
| **Paragraph 1** | copy the first sentence and set the scene – What kind of race was it? Who was Mike running against? | |
| **Middle paragraphs** | continue the story – What happened? (remember to include the actual race and the unusual event) | |
| **Final paragraph** | bring the story to a close – How did everyone feel? Did anything interesting happen afterwards? | |

## 7 Write Write your story in 140–190 words in an appropriate style.

## 8 Check Before you hand in your story, complete this checklist.

**Checklist**

- ◯ I've given my story a title.
- ◯ I've written between 140 and 190 words.
- ◯ I've created an appropriate and interesting plot.
- ◯ I've made sure my story mentions a race and an unusual event.
- ◯ I've written at least four main paragraphs.
- ◯ I've tried to include some direct speech.
- ◯ I've checked my spelling and my grammar.
- ◯ I've written a good ending.

# PROGRESS CHECK UNITS 9–10

## GRAMMAR AND VOCABULARY

**1 Write a form of the word in capitals in each gap.**

**JOINING AN ORCHESTRA**

As you might expect, any **(1)** ___________ wanting to join an orchestra needs to have the right musical talent and also needs to be a bit of a **(2)** ___________ . It isn't always easy to work hard for the **(3)** ___________ of time it takes to get good enough. Whether you are a **(4)** ___________ , a trumpeter or a **(5)** ___________ , the key thing is to realise that you are a small part of a large team. You need to **(6)** ___________ your experience in music and become a very **(7)** ___________ player. However, you also need to bear in mind that all the other musicians are experienced **(8)** ___________ too.

**APPLY**
**PERFECT**
**LONG**
**PIANO**
**VIOLIN**
**WIDE**
**ACCOMPLISH**
**SPECIALISE**

__/8

**2 Write one word in each gap.**

**1** Did you know the local theatre is putting ___________ a show for teenagers?
**2** If you lose this match, you'll be knocked ___________ of the competition!
**3** I've been run ___________ my feet at work this week!
**4** Jade decided to drop ___________ of college before finishing his course.
**5** You take ___________ a lot of responsibility when you get a dog.
**6** The end-of-year exams are coming ___________ again next month.
**7** After studying medicine, Lucas went ___________ to work in Australia.
**8** Don't give ___________ the name of the winner until tonight!

__/8

**3 Write a word or phrase from Units 9 and 10 to match each definition.**

**1** This describes someone who is very experienced. ___________
**2** This is a person who participates in something. ___________
**3** This is a person who writes music, especially for an orchestra. ___________
**4** This is another word for a violin. ___________
**5** This is a person who comes first in a race. ___________
**6** This is a judge in a sport such as football. ___________
**7** These are places where you go to see orchestras or other musicians perform. ___________
**8** This is the person or company who pays for a sporting event. ___________
**9** This is what members of an audience do when they like a performance. ___________
**10** This is a person who provides medical assistance. ___________

__/10

**4 Write each verb in the correct tense to form third conditionals.**

**1** If I ___________ (**know**) you could play guitar, I would ___________ (**invite**) you to join us.
**2** What instrument would you ___________ (**learn**) if you ___________ (**have**) the chance when you were young?
**3** If I ___________ (**train**) harder, then perhaps I could ___________ (**do**) better in the race.
**4** It might ___________ (**be**) a more interesting competition if more people ___________ (**take**) part.

__/8

## 5 Underline the mistake in each sentence and correct it.

1 Could you let me knowing when your train arrives? ______________________
2 I wonder if you could tell me where is the nearest police station. ______________________
3 Do you think you tell me who I need to get permission from? ______________________
4 I like to know how much tickets for tonight's performance are. ______________________
5 Can you tell me where can I park the car? ______________________
6 I'd be grateful you could tell me what time the concert starts. ______________________

__/6

## 6 Complete the second sentence so it has a similar meaning to the first. Do not change the word given. Use two to five words, including the word given.

1 You look really healthy since you went on holiday. **FIDDLE**
You look ______________________ since you went on holiday.
2 You didn't tell me about the concert so I didn't come. **HAVE**
I ______________________ the concert if you had told me about it.
3 I might enter the Young Musician of the Year competition. **GO**
I might ______________________ the Young Musician of the Year competition.
4 'I didn't break your tablet, Ed,' said Liam. **BREAKING**
Liam ______________________ tablet.
5 I remember his face but I can't quite remember his name. **BELL**
His face ______________________ but I can't quite remember his name.

__/10

**Total score** __/50

## EXAM SKILLS

Tick the statements that are true for you. Review the skills in the unit if you need more help.

| I can ... | Unit/page |
|---|---|
| ☐ understand text logic in a news article | Unit 9 p92 |
| ☐ take notes while listening to a short talk | Unit 9 p96 |
| ☐ express uncertainty and speculate in a photo task | Unit 9 p98 |
| ☐ recognise some idioms and complete them in a multiple-choice cloze exercise | Unit 9 p99 |
| ☐ make recommendations for a target audience in a review | Unit 9 p100 |
| ☐ identify synonyms in a magazine article | Unit 10 p102 |
| ☐ listen for distractors in an interview | Unit 10 p106 |
| ☐ talk about my experiences in an interview | Unit 10 p108 |
| ☐ understand and form conditionals and use them in sentence transformations | Unit 10 p109 |
| ☐ create a good plot in a story | Unit 10 p110 |

# 11 All in a day's work

## READING | Multiple matching | Blog posts

**1** **In pairs or groups, answer the questions.**

1. Have you ever had a part-time job? If so, what was/is it?
2. What are the pros and cons of teenagers having part-time jobs?
3. What are the most appropriate jobs for teenagers who want to work part-time?

**EXAM SKILL**

### Identifying synonyms (2)

- In Unit 10 we saw the importance of looking in the text for synonyms of key words in the questions.
- Sometimes you may need to find a synonym for a complete idea.
- For example, *I was working there for the summer* might match a reference to *a temporary job*.

**2** **Look at the eight statements in Exercise 5. In pairs or as a group, suggest different ways these ideas could be expressed.**

*I made an error that cost the company a lot of money.*

**3** **Read paragraph A of the text opposite and find close synonyms for these words and phrases. Use a dictionary if necessary.**

1. after leaving school ________
2. collect ________
3. very small ________
4. pay (noun) ________
5. extremely upset ________
6. happiness ________

**4** **Read paragraph B. For each word or phrase, put a cross if there isn't a close synonym in the paragraph. Write the synonym if there is.**

1. most important ________
2. rushing (= doing something quickly) ________
3. to fire (= make someone leave their job because of a serious mistake) ________
4. to make redundant (= make someone leave their job because they are no longer needed) ________
5. to earn ________
6. very soon ________

# Bad Job!

**We all make mistakes sometimes.**

**What's the most embarrassing thing you've ever done at work?**

726 people like this

39 comments

21 shares

A

**Jon**
14 April – 7.32pm

My embarrassing incident happened while I was working in my dad's garage for the summer just before university. It was my job to drive a car out so the owner could pick it up. I can't have been paying attention because I reversed it straight into another car that was parked outside! I immediately jumped out to see the damage. The car I was driving had a slight scratch on the bumper but the other car had a really bad dent. It was awful! At that point, Dad rushed over, looked at both cars, and told me it was going to cost me my whole wages that summer. I couldn't believe it – I was devastated. A few minutes later, he admitted that the bad dent was already there – that was why they'd brought the car in. You can't imagine my relief!

B

**Daisy**
14 April – 7.33pm

It's funny looking back at it now, but it wasn't funny at the time because my mistake cost me my job. It was actually my very first job, too. I was working as an admin assistant in a busy office. One day, my manager asked me to send some important documents to one of our biggest clients. I got everything together, but I must have been in a hurry because I stupidly printed out the wrong address label and sent it to the client's main competitor instead! It was such an easy mistake to make, but one with really serious consequences. I didn't realise until about a week later, when my manager called me in and told me what had happened. She said it had cost the company a large amount of money and they had to sack me. Thankfully, I got another job shortly afterwards.

C

**Rod**
14 April – 7.35pm

Well, my story happened before I'd even started work. I'd been looking for a Saturday job for ages, so I was pleased when I finally got a letter inviting me for an interview. I read the letter so many times ... I really don't know how I confused Tuesday for Thursday, but I did. So, there I was, waiting to see the manager, wearing my smart clothes, only to be told by the receptionist that I might have missed my chance as I was two days late! I felt so embarrassed! I should have read the letter more carefully. Amazingly, I did get the job. But when he told me the hours – eight until six every Saturday and two till four on Sundays, he made me repeat them to him twice, just to be sure I'd got it right!

D

**Liz**
14 April – 7.39pm

I still have nightmares over this. It was about ten years ago, and our company was sponsoring a group of local people raising money for charity. They were going to hold a 48-hour karaoke party. We'd paid for the venue, and I was responsible for getting T-shirts made for all of them. The T-shirt company sent me an email with the wording, but I should have checked it more carefully because when they opened the box just before the event, they realised the shirts said 'Signing for charity!' and not 'Singing'. Luckily, they saw the funny side and didn't make a fuss. I don't think it affected how much money they raised, but I kept calling them to tell them how sorry I was. I'll never make a mistake like that again. At least, I hope I won't!

## OPTIMISE YOUR EXAM

### Multiple matching

- The key reading skills for this task are skimming (Unit 4) and scanning (Unit 3).
- Remember to choose each person at least once.

**5** 3.13 **For each question, choose from the people A–D. The people may be chosen more than once.**

**Which person**

1 made an error which was very expensive for their employer? [1 ______]

2 apologised many times for their mistake? [2 ______]

3 was threatened with a financial punishment for the mistake? [3 ______]

4 says they were doing a temporary job when they made their mistake? [4 ______]

5 was asked to repeat basic information to their employer? [5 ______]

6 caused someone to see something meant for someone else? [6 ______]

7 says they carefully checked the information beforehand? [7 ______]

8 suggests that these days they often think about their mistake? [8 ______]

**THINK** | RESEARCH | CULTURE | LEARN | ME

Which mistake in the text do you think is the most/least serious?

How would you feel if you'd made each of the mistakes?

How would you feel if you were one of the other people in each story?

# GRAMMAR 1 | Modals (3): modal perfect

## Grammar in context

**Without looking back at the text on page 115, write one word in each gap. Then check your answers by finding the phrases and sentences in the text.**

1 I __________ have been paying attention …
2 I __________ have been in a hurry …
3 I __________ have missed my chance as I was two days late!
4 I __________ have read the letter more carefully.

### REMEMBER

- The modal perfect is formed using modal + *have* + past participle.
- We use it for making deductions about the past. We can show that we are certain (*must, can't, couldn't*), or that we think something is possible (*may, might, could*) or probable (*should, ought to*).
- We can also use it to criticise past behaviour (*should/shouldn't/ ought to)* or show that a past action was unnecessary (*needn't*).
- In Unit 10 we saw modal perfect used for the third conditional (*would/could/might*).

▶ **See Grammar reference, Unit 11,** page 159

**1** **Look back at *Grammar in context*. For the four sentences, think of another modal you could use without changing the meaning. Which sentence can't be changed?** ___

**2** **Read the sentences in italics and write *yes* or *no* to answer each question.**

*Maddy must have finished the report by now.*
1 Is this expressing a command? __________
2 Is this expressing certainty about the past? __________

*Maddy can't have finished the report yet.*
3 Does the speaker think Maddy's finished the report? __________
4 Can *can't* be replaced by *couldn't* here without changing the meaning? __________

*Maddy should have finished the report by now.*
5 Can this be followed logically by *I wonder why she hasn't.*? __________
6 Can it be followed logically by *I'll go and see if she has.*? __________
7 Can *should* be replaced by *ought to* here without changing the meaning? __________

*Maddy would have finished the report by now.*
8 Is this describing a hypothetical past situation? __________

**3** **Rephrase the words in italics using the modal perfect so that the meaning stays the same. Use the verbs in brackets to help you.**

1 I went to the office on Saturday morning but it turned out *I wasn't needed*. (**need**)
I ______________________________.
2 *I'm sure you didn't see Sophie yesterday* because she's in Spain on a business trip. (**can**)
You ______________________________.
3 *I expect Sophie's come back from her business trip* to Spain by now. (**ought to**)
Sophie ______________________________.
4 *There's a small chance they made some people redundant* today but I doubt it. (**might**)
They ______________________________.
5 *Adam didn't ask for help*. If he had done, the company wouldn't be in trouble now. (**should**)
Adam ______________________________.
6 It's possible that *they were interviewing job applicants* that morning. (**may**)
They ______________________________.
7 *There was a chance that the boss would fire Amelia*. (**can / fire**)
The boss ______________________________.
8 *I didn't call the office* to let them know I was off sick and now I'm in trouble. (**ought to / call**)
I ______________________________.

### SAY IT RIGHT

**Resource centre: Unit 11**
Pronunciation of *have*

THINK | RESEARCH | CULTURE | LEARN | ME

In pairs, talk about things you should/could have done recently but didn't, and things you would have done recently if you'd had the chance.


▶ **Workbook Unit 11:** Grammar 1, page 86, exercises 1, 2, 3

## Nouns with *-er* / *-or*

**1** 3.14 **Complete the words in the box then write them in the correct column. Be careful! One of the words goes in both columns. Listen and check.**

~~act*r~~ | administrat*r | advis*r | ~~build*r~~ | commentat*r | conduct*r | counsell*r | direct*r | edit*r | inspect*r | invent*r | lectur*r | manag*r | newsread*r | operat*r | present*r | produc*r | report*r | sail*r | supervis*r

| with *-er* | with *-or* |
|---|---|
| *builder* | *actor* |

**2** **Complete the sentences with words from Exercise 1.**

1 There's a new history ___________ at college and now the students are enjoying the subject much more.
2 I know you're playing the drums, but who's the ___________ for your school concert.
3 The problem in the factory was caused by a machine ___________ in one of the workshops making a mistake.
4 I loved the film – in fact, I love every film with that ___________ in.
5 Has the ___________ who's repairing your roof finished the job yet?

## Phrasal verbs

**3** 3.15 **Choose the correct word. Use the words in italics to help you. Listen and check.**

1 Our local bookshop was recently *taken* **over / up** by a large chain.
2 Mr Hedges is ill so he's asked me to *stand* **out / in for** him at tomorrow's meeting.
3 Hello, could you *put me* **through / about** to whoever's responsible for customer complaints?
4 I find it impossible to *get* **in / through** the working day without some chocolate!
5 It's very hard to *get* **by / down** on such low wages.
6 Dan, a problem's *come* **up / over** with a customer and I need to talk to you about it.
7 Our manager asked us to *put* **up / forward** any ideas or suggestions we had.
8 She didn't like my idea at first but apparently she's *coming* **round / across to** it now.

**4** **In pairs or as a group, discuss the meaning of each of the phrasal verbs in Exercise 3.**

## Words connected with *work*

**5** 3.16 **Read the text about Frazer and then match the words in bold with the definitions (1–12). Listen and check.**

Frazer was an excellent accountant, but last year he **was made redundant**. There weren't many **vacancies** and he was **unemployed** for six months. Eventually, he found a **part-time** job in a factory working night **shifts**. His weekly **wages** were quite low but it was a **temporary** job. He sometimes worked extra hours to earn more but all the **overtime** made him tired and one night he fell asleep at work. His boss found out and **gave** him **the sack**.

Frazer went to the park and sat down and cried. Soon, a man stopped and asked him what the problem was. Frazer explained he had just lost his job. The man told Frazer that he had just started a new company and was looking for someone to help him with the finances. They met the next day and the man offered Frazer a **full-time** job with a **permanent** contract. Frazer was delighted and accepted the job straight away. The man looked surprised and asked Frazer, 'Are you sure you're an accountant?'

'Why do you ask?' replied Frazer nervously.

'Well,' he laughed, 'your job is looking after money, and I haven't even told you your annual **salary** yet!'

1 told to leave a job: ___________
2 for a limited period of time: ___________
3 money paid for work, usually based on hours/days worked: ___________
4 jobs available: ___________
5 periods of work time: ___________
6 without a job: ___________
7 regular amount of money paid for work, usually paid monthly: ___________
8 be without a job because the job didn't exist anymore: ___________
9 about 35 hours a week or more: ___________
10 continuing without stopping or happening for a long time: ___________
11 less than about 35 hours a week: ___________
12 extra hours worked: ___________

▶ **Vocabulary reference,** page 167 ▶ **Workbook Unit 11:** Vocabulary, pages 86–87, exercises 1, 2, 3

# 11 LISTENING | Multiple matching

**1** **In pairs or as a group, make a list of different problems that people sometimes face at work.**

**EXAM SKILL**

## Identifying attitude (3)

- Sometimes to identify someone's attitudes or feelings, you need to focus on how they react to a situation.
- For example, if a speaker says, *I started crying* or *I stormed out of the room*, they are probably upset or angry about something.

**2** **Choose an attitude/feeling from the box to match each action/reaction.**

| angry | confident | delighted |
|---|---|---|
| guilty | stressed | |

1 When I heard I'd got the job, I laughed and punched the air. ________
2 I didn't get much sleep because I was thinking about the interview the next day. ________
3 I couldn't believe the boss had done something so thoughtless and selfish. ________
4 I wish I could change what I said to my manager. ________
5 I felt sure that I would get the job. ________

**3** **In pairs or groups, play the game.**

- **Student A:** Choose one of the statements A–H in Exercise 4 and imagine it refers to you. Say one or two sentences so your partner can guess your situation. Do not use any of the key words (nouns, verbs, adjectives, adverbs) in the statement.
  **Example:** I'm feeling ignored by the boss.
  *My manager doesn't listen to what I say and that makes me sad.*
- **Student B:** Guess which statement in Exercise 4 Student A is describing.
- When a statement's been guessed correctly, swap roles.

**OPTIMISE YOUR EXAM**

## Multiple matching

- This type of task has distractors – extra options, which are partly related to something you hear in the audio, but don't match it exactly.
- For example, an option may mention being jealous of a work colleague and one of the speakers mentions being jealous, but not about a colleague.
- Remember that the whole option must match what you hear.

**4** 3.17 **You will hear five extracts about problems at work. Choose from A–H what each speaker says about it. There are three extra letters you do not need.**

**A** I'm feeling financially undervalued.
**B** I'm feeling ignored by the boss.
**C** I think that our boss is keeping a big secret from us.
**D** I need to get someone to stop lying and being nasty.
**E** I'm lacking in confidence.
**F** I'm jealous of a colleague.
**G** I'm very upset about some information I've learnt.

**Speaker 1:** ☐
**Speaker 2:** ☐
**Speaker 3:** ☐
**Speaker 4:** ☐
**Speaker 5:** ☐

**5** 3.17 **Listen again and check your answers.**

**THINK** | RESEARCH | CULTURE | LEARN | ME

**Student A:** Imagine you have a problem at work. Briefly describe it.

**Student B:** Give Student A some advice, starting with *If I were you, I'd …*

# GRAMMAR 2 | The causative

## Grammar in context

**Look at this sentence from the audio in the listening lesson and choose T (True) or F (False) for each question.**

*I had my hair cut and got my suit dry-cleaned ...*

1 The speaker cut their own hair and dry-cleaned their own suit. **T / F**

2 The grammatical structure in this sentence is *have/had* + object + past participle. **T / F**

### REMEMBER

- We can use the causative (*have or get* + object + past participle) for situations when someone else performs an action or service for us, such as *have/get my computer repaired.*
- We can also use it to talk about things that happen to us, such as things being stolen, broken, etc. We don't usually use *get* with this meaning. *Hans had his mobile phone stolen last week.*
- We can use *by* to show who or what 'does' the action. *I've had my office decorated* ***by*** *a local firm.*

▶ **See Grammar reference, Unit 11,** page 159

**1** **If a sentence is correct, put a tick. If it is incorrect, underline the mistake and correct it.**

1 My mum likes having her car professionally cleaned. ________

2 My little sister has had her face painted and she looks like a tiger! ________

3 I want to have decorated my room all in black, but my parents won't let me. ________

4 Did you know Jake's had his tablet taken? He has no idea who did it. ________

5 I didn't know you'd had your bike stole! That's terrible! ________

6 Let's get our nails do them before the party! ________

7 Teenagers often don't like having their lives controlled by their parents. ________

8 I have to stay home because I'm having delivered something tomorrow. ________

**2** **Use the nouns and the verbs to make sentences about things someone can have done, as in the example. Sometimes there is more than one answer.**

| Nouns | Verbs |
|---|---|
| car | break into |
| house | clean |
| living room | decorate |
| nose | install |
| photograph | pierce |
| program | repair |
| windows | take |

**Example:** *I need to have a photograph taken for my passport.*

THINK | RESEARCH | CULTURE | LEARN | **ME**

Think of something you or your family have had done recently. Explain what happened.

*My mum and dad have had our car repaired. There was a problem and ...*

**3** **Complete the text with the causative form. Use the correct form of the words in brackets and add other words if necessary.**

How to GET THAT Dream JOB!

» So, you've seen an advertisement for your dream job.

» And now you're going to apply for it.

» How can you give yourself the best chance of getting it?

HERE'S OUR ADVICE.

**First of all, there's your CV.** Think about (1) ________ (**it / check**) someone you trust. Ask them for suggestions about how to make it better. Consider (2) ________ (**photo / take**) and adding that to your CV as well. And why not (3) ________ (**it / print**) a professional printer? It's all about making the right impression!

**Make sure you've prepared well** for the interview by reading about the company you're hoping to work for. Why not (4) ________ (**a friend / give**) you a 'mock' interview by asking you some possible questions, to see how well you can answer them. Maybe you could even (5) ________ (**someone / video**) the mock interview so you can watch it back and see how you did.

**Think about your appearance.** It's not necessary to spend money (6) ________ (**hair / do**). But take a bit of time over your appearance so that you look good and feel confident at the interview.

Good luck!

Talk2Me
My first observation is …

Flipped classroom

**1** ▷ **Look at the photos and read the exam task. Then watch the *Talk2Me* video and answer the questions.**

I'd like you to compare these photographs and say what you think the people enjoy about doing their jobs.

**Which speaker …**

- doesn't talk about the similarities?
- only says what one of the people enjoys about their job?
- doesn't compare the pictures at all?
- answers the question completely?

**2** ▷ **Watch the video again. Which phrases from the *Phrase expert* box do the people use to compare the pictures (C) and which do they use to organise their responses (O)?**

**PHRASE EXPERT**

A final observation is that … | And not forgetting the question | And now in answer to the question | Looking more closely… | My first observation is that … | The key difference/similarity between the photos is … | The two photos differ in so far as … | They have more things in common than differences. | To begin with …

**3** **In pairs or groups, answer the questions.**

- Which of the jobs in the photos on this page would you most/least like to do? Explain why.
- What qualities do you think you need for each job?

**EXAM SKILL**

**Organising your ideas**

- Try to approach the exam task in a relaxed and organised way.
- In some tasks you may have to do more than one thing, so be clear about what you have to do before you start speaking.
- Try not to include irrelevant information.

**4** **Read the three sentences and number them in order.**

**A** The key difference between the photos is that one shows a manual worker. ☐

**B** And now in answer to the question, I would definitely prefer to work as a chef. ☐

**C** My first observation is that the two photos both show people at work. ☐

**OPTIMISE YOUR EXAM**

**Photo task**

- Remember that for this task you need to compare two photographs AND answer a question.
- First focus on the similarities and differences, and then answer the question with reference to both photos.
- It's not easy to do all this in one minute, so do practice exam tasks at home and time yourself.

**5** **Look at these photos and the exam task, and answer the questions.**

**Compare the photos and say what you think the people find most difficult about their jobs.**

1 What are the main similarities between the jobs in the photos?

______________________________

2 What are the main differences between the jobs?

______________________________

3 What are the difficult things about doing the job in Photo A?

______________________________

4 What are the difficult things about doing the job in Photo B?

______________________________

**6** **In pairs, take turns to practise the exam task in Exercise 5. Student A does the task and Student B times them and gives feedback. Then swap roles.**

 ▶ **Workbook Unit 11:** Speaking, pages 88–89, exercises 1, 2

# USE OF ENGLISH | Multiple-choice cloze

**1** **In pairs or groups, answer the questions.**

1 What do you think it would be like to work as a writer? Would you like it?

2 What's your favourite book? What do you like about it?

**EXAM SKILL**

## Phrasal verbs

- Exam tasks often test phrasal verbs.
- Remember that they can have a very different meaning from the individual words they use (e.g. *take up = start something new*)
- It will help you to remember phrasal verbs if you learn them with words that remind you of their meaning (e.g. *take up a new hobby / golf*, etc.) and with example sentences.

**2** **Choose the correct word.**

1 The manager refused to **come** / **get** / **put** up with us being late any longer.

2 I'm so busy at work that I don't know how I **get** / **put** / **take** through the day sometimes.

3 We got lost and ended **on** / **out** / **up** in the wrong meeting room!

4 Mum's going to be late home – something's **come** / **gone** / **taken** up at the office.

5 I applied for three jobs and finally decided to go **at** / **for** / **into** the one in Berlin.

6 We **get** / **put** / **take** by on my salary, although it's not very much.

7 I used to love my job, but I've gone **off** / **out** / **to** it recently for some reason.

8 Josh is under a lot of pressure because he's **come** / **put** / **taken** on so much work.

**OPTIMISE YOUR EXAM**

## Multiple-choice cloze

- In this exam task (Exercise 4), you may need to choose a correct verb or particle to complete a phrasal verb.
- Try each option in the gap, thinking about the meaning of the phrasal verb.
- Check the words before and after the gap and the general meaning of the text.

**3** **Quickly read the text in Exercise 4. Which four gaps are testing your knowledge of phrasal verbs? Write the numbers.**

___ ___ ___ ___

**4** **Choose the correct word or phrase to fill each gap.**

### Who is it?

This person had a **(1)** ___ job as a researcher when she came **(2)** ___ with the idea of writing a novel. So, she secretly began to write at work until a problem **(3)** ___ up – she got caught and was given **(4)** ___ . For a while, life was difficult and she found it hard to get **(5)** ___ every day. She was **(6)** ___ and looking after a baby. It was difficult to **(7)** ___ by on very little money, but she was determined to find **(8)** ___ to publish her work. The rest is history … she's now one of the most famous female writers in the world.

| | | | | |
|---|---|---|---|---|
| **1** | **A** overtime | **B** vacancy | **C** full-time | **D** extra time |
| **2** | **A** through | **B** round | **C** up | **D** down |
| **3** | **A** did | **B** came | **C** woke | **D** set |
| **4** | **A** the sack | **B** the bag | **C** the rejection | **D** the target |
| **5** | **A** through | **B** round | **C** up | **D** down |
| **6** | **A** permanent | **B** unemployed | **C** temporary | **D** salary |
| **7** | **A** get | **B** make | **C** take | **D** put |
| **8** | **A** a counsellor | **B** an editor | **C** a newsreader | **D** an administrator |

**THINK** | RESEARCH | CULTURE | LEARN | ME

What lesson do you think people might learn from the life of the writer in Exercise 4?

▶ Vocabulary reference, page 167 ▶ Workbook Unit 11: Use of English, page 89, exercises 1, 2, 3

# 11 WRITING | A letter / An email

**1 In pairs or as a group, answer the questions.**

1 Do you ever write emails? If so, who do you write them to?

2 Have you ever written a letter? If so, who was it to?

**2 Read this letter and choose the best words or phrases to complete the report below.**

*Dear Mr Langton,*

*I am writing with regard to your request for suggestions about local people with particularly interesting skills or abilities who you could invite to give a lecture at school. I believe I know the perfect person.*

*Lucas Martin, who lives in the town, is a professional magician. He performs regularly at parties and events and is an extremely interesting and friendly person. I know him well because we used to live next door to him. He would often show me tricks, and he even taught me a few.*

*I have little doubt that if you invited him, he would be happy to give a lecture. He would probably perform some tricks, and tell some fascinating stories about how he became a magician and the people he has met in his career.*

*Please let me know if you would like me to give you his contact details, or if you would prefer me to contact him first myself.*

*I look forward to hearing from you.*

*Yours sincerely,*
*Deborah Clarkson*
*Year 11*

This is a letter from a (**1**) **teacher** / **student** to a teacher or school principal. Because of their teacher-student relationship, and perhaps because the writer knows that the teacher (**2**) **doesn't care about** / **expects and values** good-quality writing, the writer has used (**3**) **a formal** / **an informal** tone. In other words, it sounds more (**4**) **polite** / **friendly** and (**5**) **lighthearted** / **serious** than a letter or email to a friend or close relative. For example, the writer says, 'I am writing with regard to' rather than, 'I'm writing about'. The writer (**6**) **has** / **hasn't** carefully and successfully separated the letter into paragraphs, and uses some (**7**) **appropriate** / **inappropriate** letter expressions, such as *Yours sincerely*, for a person whose name they (**8**) **don't know** / **know** but is not a close friend or relative.

**EXAM SKILL**

## Using formal and informal language

- Always think about what your relationship is with the person you're writing to, so you know if your style should be formal or informal.
- Informal texts are chatty, friendly and conversational, for friends, close family members or young people.
- Formal texts are serious or respectful rather than friendly, for (older) people in authority and people you don't know well.

**3 Read this email and write examples for each category below.**

To: Sam
Subject: part-time job

Hi Sam,

Thanks for your email yesterday. It was great to hear from you! That tablet you got for your birthday sounds really cool. I hope I get one for my birthday next month!

You said you're thinking of looking for a part-time job. I think that's a great idea! I love my job working in a café every Sunday. I know you don't want to work as a waiter so the question is – what should you do?

If I were you, I'd do something connected to something you enjoy. You love sport, so maybe you could look for a job in a sports shop or a sports centre. You also like music and acting, don't you? Perhaps you could find something in a local theatre or concert venue. And don't wait for them to advertise. Write to them or send them an email asking if they're looking for anyone and saying you're available and interested. Lots of people get jobs that way!

Anyway, let me know how it goes. Good luck!

Bye for now!
Dave

Find two or three examples of informal …

1 letter/email expressions. ______________________

______________________

2 vocabulary. ______________________

______________________

3 grammar/punctuation. ______________________

______________________

OPTIMISE YOUR **EXAM**

## A letter / An email

- Formal letters/emails: avoid exclamation marks and contractions (*he'd, can't*, etc.), and use formal phrases, such as *I look forward to hearing from you.*
- Informal letters/emails: you can use exclamation marks, contractions and informal vocabulary and phrases, such as *cool* and *Bye for now!*

**4 Look at these writing tasks. Tick the statements that are true for each one.**

**Task A**

You have received this letter from your school principal, Mrs Holt. Read this part of the letter and then write your letter to Mrs Holt.

> The school is planning to organise a series of lectures by local people who can teach students new skills. Do you know anyone appropriate locally who we could invite? Please give me a little information about how you know them and what makes them interesting.

Write your **letter**.

**Task B**

You have received this email from your English-speaking friend, Alex.

> **From:** Alex
> **Subject:** I need your advice
> I'm thinking of taking a part-time job, working in a sports shop on Saturdays. It'll be good experience for me, and I'll earn some extra money, but it will mean giving up karate lessons. Do you think it's a good idea?
> What should I do?
> Alex

Write your **email**.

| | Task A | Task B |
|---|---|---|
| 1 Your letter/email will be informal. | | |
| 2 You know the name of the person you are writing to. | | |
| 3 You only have to write one paragraph. | | |
| 4 You should recommend a person, explaining why. | | |
| 5 You should give advice, expressing your opinion. | | |
| 6 You will need to use your imagination to come up with ideas. | | |

**5 Plan** Make a paragraph plan for each writing task in Exercise 4.

**6 Write** Write your letter and your email in an appropriate style. Write 140–190 words each time.

**7 Check** Before you hand in your letter and email, complete this checklist.

**Checklist**

| Task A | Task B | |
|---|---|---|
| ○ | ○ | I've used the right level of formality. |
| ○ | ○ | I've followed the notes in my paragraph plan. |
| ○ | ○ | I've included all the information I need to include. |
| ○ | ○ | I've started and ended my letter/email the right way. |
| ○ | ○ | I've checked my grammar and spelling. |

# 12 My hero!

## READING | True/false with explanation | A magazine article

**1** **Write a definition for *hero*.**

**Hero (n)** /ˈhɪərəʊ/ ..............................................................

..............................................................................................

..............................................................................................

**2** **Think of heroes for the categories below.**

figures from history

______________________________

characters in a film/book

______________________________

**EXAM SKILL**

### Identifying examples

- When a writer wants to explain a point, they often use examples to help the reader understand. (See Writing, Unit 4.)
- Writers often use specific phrases, e.g. *for instance*, to introduce examples, so look for these in a text.

**3** **Quickly read the article. Find and underline places where the writer gives examples of the following things.**

1 people we often consider to be heroes
2 a system that gives honours to people in that country
3 people we are not surprised to see getting an award
4 people we might be surprised to see getting an award
5 honours given out in Britain
6 someone honoured for running a charity

**4** **Write a word from the article to complete these phrases used to introduce examples.**

1 They might __________ …
2 For __________ , …
3 … public figures __________ …
4 … such __________ …
5 One __________ of …

**OPTIMISE YOUR EXAM**

### True/false with explanation

- Underline the key words in the questions and use them to find the part of the text that contains the answer.
- Read this part carefully to decide if the statement is true/false and identify the key sentence which tells you this.
- Only choose 'true' if everything in the statement is true.

# HONOURING EVERYDAY HEROES

**This June, like every June and January, over a thousand people will be celebrating their new honours. Ed Francis explains.**

We all have people we look up to or admire: our heroes. They might include famous people from the worlds of sport and entertainment who we see as role models. We might also admire the achievements of great leaders or figures from history. We think of them as special people, different from ourselves. But what about people who aren't well-known? Can they be considered to be heroes? And what does it take to be a hero, or a heroine?

One way to think about what we value in our heroes is to look at the people we give awards to. For instance, in Britain, the state awards honours to people twice each year, at New Year and on the monarch's (king or queen's) official birthday. A list is announced of people from all walks of life, ranging from politicians to lollipop ladies. You might expect that public figures like MPs would appear on the Honours List, and indeed they do. It's a little more surprising, perhaps, to see charity workers and volunteers also being honoured.

The honours system works like this. If you believe someone deserves an honour, you nominate them to a special committee, which considers the nomination. They decide whether the person deserves an honour or not. They also decide what kind of honour to give the person. The person may receive an honour, such as an MBE (Member of the British Empire), an OBE (Order of the British Empire) or a knighthood, an honour that allows them to use the title 'Sir'. The equivalent honour for women allows them to use the title 'Dame'.

One example of an everyday hero honoured recently is Gbolahan Bright, a volunteer maths teacher. He and his wife were originally from Nigeria. By the end of this year, they will have been living in Britain for over 25 years. During that time, Gbolahan has been running the Bright Academy maths club, offering free maths for underprivileged primary school pupils who struggle with the subject. He recently received an MBE for services to education.

Another is Maria Hanson, who recently received an MBE for her charity work. Since 2006, she has run a charity which enables seriously ill people and their families to have a holiday. Her charity provides accommodation in caravans by the sea so that families can spend time together and create lasting memories. In poor health herself, by the time she retires, she will have helped well over a thousand families.

Maria and Gbolahan are typical of the kind of ordinary person that the honours system aims to celebrate. They are people who give their time and energy to their community and to those less fortunate than themselves. They truly are everyday heroes.

**5** 3.18 **Choose T (true) or F (false) for each statement. Write the first four words of the sentence in the text which supports each answer.**

1 We usually consider our heroes as exceptional and not like us.
T / F ______________________

2 Many different types of people are on the Honours List.
T / F ______________________

3 People suggest themselves to be considered for an honour.
T / F ______________________

4 Both men and women may receive a knighthood and a new title.
T / F ______________________

5 Maria Hanson's charity tries to cure people who are very ill.
T / F ______________________

6 The two people mentioned are unusual examples of people on the Honours List.
T / F ______________________

**6 Complete the summary with highlighted words/phrases from the text in the correct form, and explain the meanings.**

We often consider famous people to be heroes (or perhaps **(1)** ________ if they are women). We look up to them and think of them as **(2)** ________ . We also celebrate people who make significant **(3)** ________ , but what about **(4)** ________ heroes? The British honours system rewards people **(5)** from ________ , rich and poor, famous and unknown. The honours system is simple. Anyone can **(6)** ________ someone for an honour. A committee then decides which people **(7)** ________ the award. Honours are given for voluntary work, charity work and other forms of service to your local **(8)** ________ .

**SAY IT RIGHT**

**Resource centre: Unit 12**
Silent and non-silent initial *h*-

THINK | RESEARCH | **CULTURE** | LEARN | ME

What system does your country have for honouring people? Is it a good idea to honour ordinary people in this way?

# GRAMMAR 1 | The future (2): continuous, perfect simple and continuous

## Grammar in context

**Look at these sentences from the text on page 125 and match them with what they describe.**

1 This June, like every June and January, over a thousand people will be celebrating their new honours. ____

2 By the end of this year, they will have been living in Britain for over 25 years. ____

3 In poor health herself, by the time she retires, she will have helped well over a thousand families. ____

**This sentence describes:**

**a)** an action completed between now and a point in the future.

**b)** an action in progress at a point in the future.

**c)** an action continuing up to a point in the future.

### REMEMBER

- The form for the future continuous is *will/won't* + *be* + *-ing* (*will be working, won't be travelling,* etc.). It's used to talk about actions happening (in progress) at a point in the future.
- The form for the future perfect simple is *will/ won't* + *have* + past participle (*will have finished, won't have started,* etc.). It's used to talk about actions completed at some time between now and a point in the future.
- The form for the future perfect continuous is *will/won't* + *have been* + *-ing* (*will have been living, won't have been working,* etc.). It's used to talk about actions happening up to a point in the future.

▶ **See Grammar reference, Unit 12,** page 160

**1 Choose the correct phrase.**

1 This time tomorrow, I **will be travelling / will have been travelling** to London to get my award!

2 At the end of the month, Kay **will be working / will have been working** as a firefighter for two years.

3 I don't think we **will have been leaving / will have left** the office by five o'clock.

4 Tomorrow morning, I **will be going / will have been going** to Buckingham Palace to get my honour!

5 **Will you have finished / Will you have been finishing** your work by the time I get home?

6 What **will you be doing / will you have done** at midday tomorrow?

**2 Complete the second sentence so it has a similar meaning to the first. Do not change the word given. Use two to five words, including the word given.**

1 I started doing voluntary work a year ago next Friday. **WILL**
Next Friday, I ______________________ voluntary work for a year.

2 I should finish writing this email before half past three. **HAVE**
I ______________________ writing this email by half past three.

3 They will announce the names of the people getting honours during the next hour. **BEEN**
The names of the people getting honours ______________________ in an hour's time.

4 We started waiting at six and now it's five to ten! **FOR**
In five minutes, we ______________________ four hours!

5 I won't be awake if you call at five in the morning, so don't bother! **SLEEPING**
If you call at five in the morning, I ______________________, so don't bother!

6 I'm sure that Oliver will go out before you get here. **GONE**
Oliver ______________________ by the time you get here.

**3 Complete the text with the correct form of the verbs in brackets.**

## A year of helping out

Can you believe that next Monday I (**1**) __________ (**help**) out at this food bank for a year? That's crazy! I worked out that by the end of my first year I (**2**) __________ (**hand**) out something like a thousand food parcels! It's great to give something back to my community. I wonder what I (**3**) __________ (**do**) this time next year. I might still be here, but I think I'll move on to something else. I hope that I (**4**) __________ (**travel**) the world by the time I'm 21, and to do that, I'm thinking of volunteering in other countries. Just think – I've always lived at home. I love my parents, but on my next birthday I (**5**) __________ (**live**) with them for 17 years! That's long enough! So, maybe this time next year I (**6**) __________ (**explore**) another part of the world. But for now, people closer to home still need my help.

▶ **Workbook Unit 12:** Grammar 1, page 94, exercises 1, 2, 3

## Nouns with *-ism*

**1** 3.19 **Most of these words have noun forms that end in *-ism*. Cross out the one which doesn't and check that you know what the noun forms for the other words are. Listen and check.**

| capital | critic | favourite | friend | hero | ideal | race | tour | vegetarian |

**2 Write a word formed from one of the words in Exercise 1 in each gap. You won't use all the words.**

1 When you do something very brave, it might be described as an act of ___________ .
2 When you think you are better than people from other countries or cultures, you may be accused of ___________ .
3 If you believe in ___________ , you choose not to eat meat.
4 If you help only your friends and family and not everyone, you may be accused of ___________ .
5 The business of providing services for people who are on holiday is known as ___________ .
6 Negative comments about other people and their behaviour may be described as ___________ .

**3 Here are some more words that end in *-ism*. Using a dictionary or the internet, find out what they mean and write a short definition.**

1 egotism ___________
2 sexism ___________
3 magnetism ___________
4 escapism ___________

## Collocations with *do* and *make*

**4** 3.20 **Complete the phrases in italics with *do* or *make* in the correct form. Listen and check.**

1 When Oscar got an OBE, it really ___________ him *proud* of his achievements.
2 We should all ___________ *our duty* and help those less fortunate than ourselves.
3 Local heroes can really ___________ *a difference* to their community.
4 You should try to ___________ *good* in the world and not worry about the rewards.
5 Stop ___________ *excuses* and start trying to follow your role models.
6 Helping others ___________ *sense* because one day you might need help too.
7 It certainly won't ___________ you any *harm* to volunteer at the food bank from time to time.
8 Lily believes she's ___________ *the right thing* by supporting her local charity.

**5 Explain what each phrase in Exercise 4 means.**

## Words connected with *describing people*

**6** 3.21 **Write the words in the correct gaps. Listen and check.**

1 Someone who is ___________ has lots of friends. Someone who is ___________ is well-known and may appear on TV, etc.
**popular / famous**
2 Someone who is ___________ is not a famous person. Someone who is ___________ is well-known for a negative reason.
**unknown / infamous**
3 Someone who is ___________ is good at listening to and understanding other people's problems. Someone who is ___________ has an attractive personality.
**sympathetic / likeable**
4 Someone who is ___________ uses language that shows respect, such as 'please' and 'thank you'. Someone who is ___________ does nice things to help other people.
**kind / polite**
5 Someone who is ___________ is an everyday person, not unusual in any way. Someone who is ___________ of a sort of person is a good example of that sort of person.
**typical / ordinary**
6 Someone who is ___________ is kind, helpful and sympathetic. Someone who is ___________ thinks about what they are doing to avoid making mistakes.
**careful / caring**
7 Someone who is ___________ does things in a reasonable and practical way. Someone who is ___________ does things in a caring way that is considerate of others.
**sensitive / sensible**

# 12 LISTENING | Multiple choice (single extract)

**1** **In pairs or as a group, discuss the questions.**

1 What local charities do you know?
2 Do you or anyone you know do charity work? If so, explain what you do. If not, would you like to do charity work?

**EXAM SKILL**

## Distractors (2)

- Remember that in multiple-choice tasks you may hear words/phrases on the audio that appear in one of the answer options, but that does not mean that answer option is the correct one. The words might be there as distractors.
- One strategy is to avoid looking at the answer options until after you listen. Formulate your own idea of what the answer is, then decide which option best matches it.

**2** 3.22 **Look at the first two questions in Exercise 3. You will hear someone saying three different sentences for each question. Decide which option (A, B or C) matches the meaning of each sentence.**

| Question 1 | Question 2 |
|---|---|
| Sentence 1 ____ | Sentence 1 ____ |
| Sentence 2 ____ | Sentence 2 ____ |
| Sentence 3 ____ | Sentence 3 ____ |

**OPTIMISE YOUR EXAM**

## Multiple choice (single extract)

- If you can't decide which option is correct, make a sensible guess.
- Answer every question – you don't lose marks for a wrong answer.

**3** 3.23 **Listen to a radio interview with teenager Amelie Richardson. As you listen, choose the best answer (A, B or C).**

1 Before her nomination, what was Amelie's view of awards?
  **A** They only went to people like firefighters.
  **B** They were for people who helped their local community.
  **C** They were for people facing difficulties in their lives.
2 What does Amelie find most challenging about the work?
  **A** working long hours
  **B** not getting paid for the work
  **C** dealing with members of the public
3 Amelie first heard about the charity from someone she
  **A** met who had been homeless.
  **B** knew who worked for the charity.
  **C** emailed for information about the charity.
4 Amelie says the key qualities of a hero include
  **A** the ability never to give up.
  **B** being sympathetic to other people.
  **C** becoming well-known for caring.
5 Amelie advises young people interested in charity work to
  **A** research different areas before making a choice.
  **B** choose something that they care about.
  **C** find a charity that needs their skills.

**4** 3.23 **Listen again and check your answers.**

THINK | **RESEARCH** | CULTURE | LEARN | ME

Go online and find out about a local charity.

Make notes on what volunteers at that charity do and tell the class what you learnt.

Say how you would feel about volunteering for that charity.

## Grammar in context

**Choose the correct word or phrase to complete each extract from the audio in the listening lesson.**

1 *It's time I **introduce** / **introduced** my first guest of the afternoon, Amelie Richardson.*
2 *If only there **are** / **were** more hours in a day!*
3 *Supposing other young people listening **wanted** / **will want** to do the same kind of thing as you, what would you say to them?*

### REMEMBER

We sometimes use the past simple and continuous to describe the present, the future, or general situations (usually hypothetical), as follows:

- second conditionals: *If he **had** a home, he wouldn't be on the streets all day.*
- phrases using *suppose, supposing, what if, imagine (if)*: *Imagine (if) if you **were** homeless.*
- phrases with *wish, if only: I wish I **had** more time to help.*
- phrases with *would rather: I'd rather they **gave** the award to someone else.*
- with the phrase *It's (high/about) time: It's high time the government **did** something about the problem.*
- in polite questions, requests, offers, hopes, etc.: *I **thought** you might need some help collecting money.*

▶ **See Grammar reference, Unit 12,** page 160

**1 Complete the sentences with the words in the box.**

| about | did | imagine | rather |
|---|---|---|---|
| suppose | unless | what | wish |

1 No-one would get a Local Hero Award ________ they deserved it.
2 ________ you won a lot of money. Would you give some of it to charity?
3 ________ if you were the Prime Minister. What would you do to help poor people?
4 ________ if we only had to work two days a week?
5 It's ________ time the government helped the unemployed find jobs.
6 I ________ there was a local charity shop round here.
7 'I'd ________ you helped hand out blankets than pack boxes,' said Julie to Jo.
8 Excuse me, Mrs Sugden. ________ you want to see me about something?

**2 Complete each second sentence so it has a similar meaning to the first sentence.**

1 They should give Mrs Jennings an award.
It's high ________________ .
2 I really want to help, but I can't.
I wish ________________ .
3 Can you come on Thursday rather than Friday this week?
I'd rather you ________________ .
4 Will you sponsor me for the charity bike ride?
I was wondering ________________ .
5 You haven't been to the local animal rescue centre so you don't know about the great work they do.
If you ________________ .

**3 Put the verbs into the correct tense.**

### Mildon Animal Rescue Centre

**Lizzie:** We've got so many animals now! It's time we **(1)** ________ **(think)** about getting someone to help us.

**Zach:** I'd rather we **(2)** ________ **(not take)** someone on full-time, though. I don't think we can afford it.

**Lizzie:** I wish we **(3)** ________ **(have)** enough money but I agree – we don't. What if we **(4)** ________ **(find)** a volunteer to work here for free for a few hours on Saturdays? That would help us a lot.

**Zach:** Yes, it would. If only I **(5)** ________ **(know)** where to find someone who'd do that for free. They'd have to love animals, and be very trustworthy!

**Lizzie:** Oh yes, we couldn't take anyone on unless we totally **(6)** ________ **(trust)** them. Let's put up an advert on the noticeboard.

**Zach:** Good idea! However, I'd rather you **(7)** ________ **(do)** that. You're better at making posters than I am.

# 12 SPEAKING | Collaborative task

Talk2Me

*Shall we move on to …?*

**Flipped classroom**

**1** **Watch the *Talk2Me* video and answer the questions.**

- Which heroes are mentioned?
- Are they mostly famous people or everyday heroes?
- What qualities do the people think a hero should have?

**2** **Choose the correct word. Then watch the next part of the video to check your answers.**

1 **Shall** / **Will** we start with this one?
2 Do you think we should go **for** / **on** …?
3 Shall we move **in** / **on** to …?
4 **Should** / **Would** we consider …?
5 Do you agree that our first **choice** / **decision** should be …?
6 It looks as **if** / **like** we agree that we should choose …
7 I suggest our **end** / **final** choice should(n't) be …

**3** **In pairs, ask and answer the questions.**

- Who are your personal heroes?
- Why do you consider them to be a hero?
- What qualities should a hero have?
- Do famous people make better heroes? Why / Why not?

**EXAM SKILL**

## Reaching a decision

- In speaking exams, you often have to discuss a question with a number of options (see Exercise 4) and then reach a decision (see Exercise 5).
- Some useful phrases for reaching a decision appear in Exercise 2 and in the *Phrase expert* box.

**OPTIMISE YOUR EXAM**

## Collaborative task

- It doesn't matter if you don't agree with your partner. The important thing in this task is how you collaborate with them.
- When reaching a decision, take turns to briefly cover each point, saying why you would/wouldn't choose something.
- Don't get stuck on a point if you don't agree. Move on to the next one.

**PHRASE EXPERT**

Do you agree that our first choice should be …? | Do you think we should go for …? | How/What about …? | It looks as if we agree that we should | Shall we move on to …? | Shall we start with this one? | So, do we agree on …? | What do you think?

**4** **Talk in pairs for two minutes. Follow the instructions.**

Here are some qualities that could be important in a hero. Talk to each other about why you think these qualities may or may not be important in heroes.

What qualities are important in a hero?

- being a good role model
- helping those less fortunate
- physical strength
- bravery
- fame

**5** **You have about a minute to decide together which two qualities are most important in a hero. Write your choices below.**

1 ______________________

2 ______________________

# USE OF ENGLISH | Open cloze

**1 In pairs or as a group, discuss the questions.**

1 The person in the photo is performing something called 'CPR'. Is it important to know how to do this?
2 Would you know what to do in an emergency if someone stopped breathing?

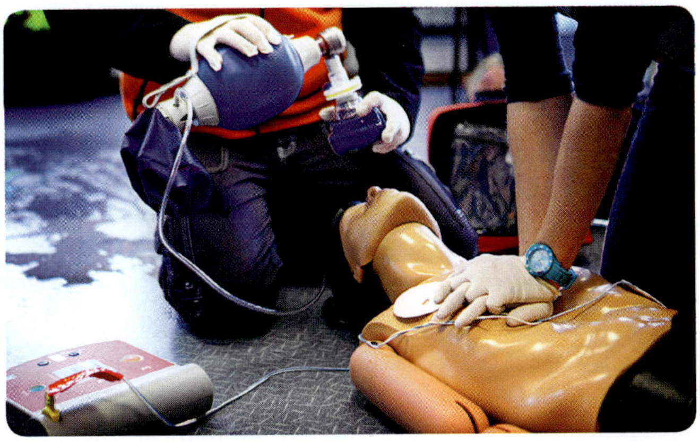

**EXAM SKILL**

## Verbs (3)

- Different verb forms are tested in exams (e.g. see the Use of English lessons in Units 2, 7 and 11).
- Auxiliary verbs are grammar words needed to form certain tenses, such as the present perfect (*She <u>has</u> won an award.*), the passive (*He <u>was</u> given an award.*), questions (*<u>Did</u> you win the award?*), etc.
- Main verbs carry the main meaning and can include past participles (*He was <u>awarded</u> a certificate.*) and <u>*-ing*</u> forms (*She has been <u>collecting</u> money.*).

**2 Write a form of *be*, *have* or *do* in each gap to complete the sentences.**

1 Most of the actors ________ standing around backstage when Nigel collapsed.
2 Dr Peters ________ ________ watching the play for about an hour when someone rushed onto the stage.
3 Excuse me, ________ anyone in the audience know how to do CPR?
4 Excuse me, ________ there anyone here who knows how to do CPR?
5 The good news is that he ________ definitely not suffered a heart attack.
6 The well-known actor ________ taken to hospital for further tests and is said to ________ doing well.

**3 Complete the sentences with one word in each gap, then decide if the underlined word is a main verb (M) or an auxiliary verb (A).**

1 Think of someone who <u>has</u> ____ a real difference to your life. **M / A**
2 Debbie <u>has</u> ____ real difference of opinion with Greg about giving money to charity. **M / A**
3 You <u>are</u> ____ of the volunteers, aren't you? **M / A**
4 You <u>are</u> ____ the most of being a volunteer, aren't you? **M / A**
5 Does ____ <u>do</u> charity work every weekend? **M / A**
6 Her help <u>does</u> ____ a huge difference to people's lives. **M / A**

**OPTIMISE YOUR EXAM**

## Open cloze

- Some of the gaps in open-cloze tasks will test verbs.
- Complete the easy gaps first and leave the more difficult ones until last.
- Always make a sensible guess, even if you're not 100% sure of the answer.

**4 Quickly read the text in Exercise 5 for 30 seconds. All the gaps require either a main verb or an auxiliary except one. Which one?**

**5 Write one word in each gap.**

**MY HERO**

One of the people I most admire because they have **(1)** ________ a real difference to other people's lives is my dad. When he was younger, he **(2)** ________ planning to become an architect, and then he learnt about people in the developing world who live in terrible conditions. He decided he **(3)** ________ set up a charity to build proper houses for these people. By the end of this year, he will have **(4)** ________ working for the charity for 20 years, and he's helped hundreds of families move into decent houses.

I've decided that I want to be involved too. Next week, I will **(5)** ________ travelling with my dad to India to see what conditions are like there. We **(6)** ________ going to travel around the country, but we've decided to stay in the Delhi area instead. After a couple of weeks, we should **(7)** ________ got a good idea of the problems and then we can start thinking about solutions. Sometimes heroes are people who just quietly do **(8)** ________ duty and help others.

**THINK** | RESEARCH | CULTURE | LEARN | ME

What's your view on whether or not the writer's dad is a hero?
How do you imagine the people who he helps feel?

# WRITING | An essay

**1** **In pairs or as a group, answer the questions.**

1 Do you think guide dogs are heroes?
2 Do you think the people who train the dogs are heroes?

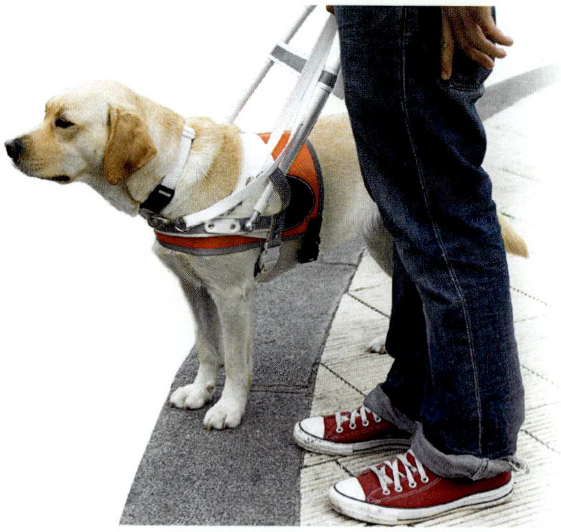

**EXAM SKILL**

## Drawing conclusions

- For any piece of writing where you present an argument or discuss ideas, you will probably need to come to a conclusion.
- Give a logical conclusion that summarises the arguments you have presented, or explain your opinion(s).

**2** **Complete the essay with the words in the box. Sometimes there is more than one answer.**

| because \| consequently |
|---|
| reason \| so \| therefore |

Every day, people such as firefighters and police officers help people who are in trouble, sometimes putting their own lives at risk. For this (1) ________ , we admire them and many people say they are heroes.

They are heroes, and do an extremely dangerous and brave job. However, it is important to remember that you do not have to do something dangerous to be a hero. Some people spend hours every week doing charity work. They give up their free time to help other people. (2) ________ of this, I believe we should consider them heroes too.

Doctors save people's lives every day. Teachers help us in many different ways. People who train guide dogs for the blind – and the dogs themselves – improve people's lives and make the world better. (3) ________ , I believe they are as admirable as firefighters.

In conclusion, I believe that the most important quality is being selfless rather than selfish. This might involve putting your life at risk. However, it might just involve being kind in your daily life, (4) ________ anyone who helps an old person across the street is a hero to me.

**3** **Look again at the essay in Exercise 2 and make notes to answer the questions.**

**Paragraph 1:** Why do we 'admire them and call them heroes'?

________

**Paragraph 2:** Why does the writer believe 'we should consider them heroes too'?

________

**Paragraph 3:** Why does the writer believe doctors are 'as admirable as firefighters'?

________

**Paragraph 4:** Why does the writer think that helping an old person across the street is heroic?

________

**OPTIMISE YOUR EXAM**

## An essay

- Essay questions often ask you to include certain points in your answer.
- In this task, you are given two qualities to talk about AND you must add another quality of your own.
- If you don't include these points, you will lose marks.

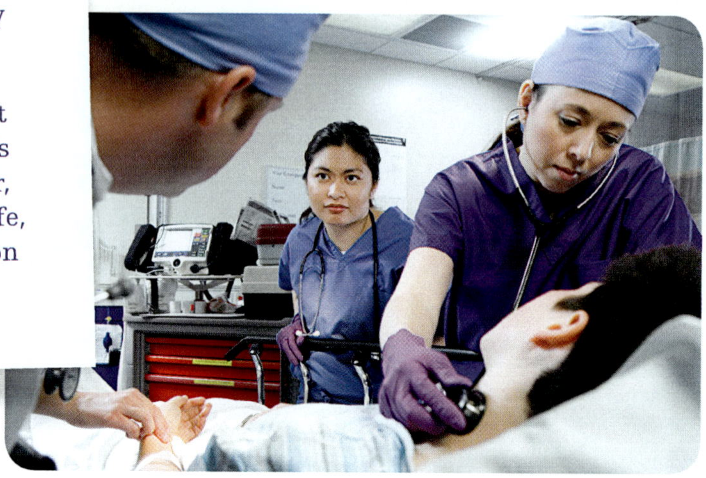

## 4 Look at this writing task and make notes to answer the questions below.

In your English class, you have been talking about heroes. Now, your English teacher has asked you to write an essay for homework. Write an essay using **all** the notes and give reasons for your point of view.

**What qualities do all heroes share?**

**Notes**
Write about:

1 being brave
2 doing something dangerous
3 ........................... (your own idea)

Write your **essay**.

| | |
|---|---|
| 1 Do you think all heroes are brave? Why / Why not? Provide at least one example. | |
| 2 Do you think all heroes have done something dangerous? Why / Why not? Provide at least one example. | |
| 3 In your opinion, what quality or qualities do all heroes share? Why? Provide at least one example. | |
| 4 In one or two sentences, summarise your opinion. | *I personally believe that all heroes ...* |

## 5 Plan Make a paragraph plan.

| Part | Purpose | Useful phrases | My notes |
|---|---|---|---|
| **Paragraph 1** | introduce the subject | *Many people say …*<br>*Some people believe …* | |
| **Paragraph 2** | explore the ideas of bravery and danger | *One aspect we should consider is …*<br>*There is also the question of …* | |
| **Paragraph 3** | write about your own idea | *Another aspect to be considered is …*<br>*We should also take into account …*<br>*Personally, I believe …* | |
| **Paragraph 4** | conclude with a summary of your opinion | *In conclusion,*<br>*In summary,*<br>*I tend to think that …,*<br>*I believe that …* | |

## 6 Write Write your essay in an appropriate style. Write 140–190 words.

## 7 Check Before you hand in your essay, complete this checklist

**Checklist**

- ◯ I've talked about the two notes in the question.
- ◯ I've come up with my own idea for a third point.
- ◯ I've expressed my personal opinion, and given reasons for it.
- ◯ I've given examples where necessary.
- ◯ I've written at least four main paragraphs.
- ◯ I've used an appropriate style for an essay.
- ◯ I've checked my spelling and grammar.

▶ **Writing reference,** page 174 ▶ **Workbook Unit 12:** Writing, page 98, exercises 1, 2, 3 and Progress check 12, page 99

# PROGRESS CHECK UNITS 11–12

## GRAMMAR AND VOCABULARY

**1 Write a form of the word in capitals in each gap.**

**JOBS IN THE TRAVEL INDUSTRY**

If you want to work in (**1**) ___________ , there are a huge number of different jobs to choose from. These range from being the (**2**) ___________ of or a writer for a travel magazine (with the possibility, of course, for lots of free trips), to being the (**3**) ___________ of a hotel or resort. If you're interested in (**4**) ___________ (positive and negative), you might enjoy being a resort (**5**) ___________ , the person who's responsible for checking that standards are kept. If you've got a more (**6**) ___________ personality, you might prefer to work as a (**7**) ___________ at a summer camp, helping teenagers with their problems. If you prefer office work, then you could always be an (**8**) ___________ for a travel agency.

**TOUR**
**EDIT**
**MANAGE**
**CRITICISE**
**INSPECT**
**SYMPATHY**
**COUNSEL**
**ADMINISTRATE**

__/8

**2 Write one word in each gap.**

1 Hello, could you put me ___________ to the managing director, please?
2 Orla, can I talk to you about a problem that's just come ___________ ?
3 I don't know how I'm going to get ___________ the day without my mobile phone!
4 Harry, I have to go to the dentist now so could you stand ___________ for me at the meeting this afternoon?
5 Well done, everyone! You've all put ___________ some really great suggestions today.

__/5

**3 Write a form of *do* or *make* in each gap.**

1 Stop ___________ excuses. You messed up. Admit it!
2 Thanks, Jack. Your help really ___________ a difference to the project.
3 Is it possible to run a business and ___________ good for the local community at the same time?
4 Your son winning that award for bravery must ___________ you very proud.
5 We all need to ___________ our duty and help people who are less fortunate than ourselves.

__/5

**4 Put the verbs into the correct form.**

1 It's high time you ___________ responsibility for your actions. (**take**)
2 I'd rather you ___________ gum in class, Alison. (**not / chew**)
3 I wouldn't buy a big house even if I ___________ a million euros. (**have**)
4 If only nobody ___________ in poverty. (**live**)
5 Imagine if no-one ___________ to work. What would we do all day? (**have**)
6 Suppose someone famous ___________ on your door. How would you react? (**knock**)
7 I ___________ if you'd like to go to the cinema with me sometime. (**wonder**)
8 Supposing something ___________ wrong, how do you think you'd cope? (**go**)
9 If Rosie ___________ you to work on Saturday, what would you say to her? (**ask**)
10 I wouldn't put myself in danger unless it ___________ absolutely necessary. (**be**)

__/10

## 5 Match the sentences to the summaries.

1 Mrs Fisher should have come back from lunch by now, so I expect she's in her office. ____
2 Mrs Fisher should have come back from lunch by now, so she'll be in trouble when she gets back. ____
3 Mr Baker must have gone to a meeting. ____
4 I would have asked you for help but you seemed busy. ____
5 Adam needn't have taken all that work home with him. ____
6 Lily might have been promoted. ____

**a)** I'm almost certain.
**b)** This is probably true.
**c)** This is possibly true.
**d)** This is totally hypothetical.
**e)** This is criticising someone's behaviour.
**f)** This wasn't necessary.

__/6

## 6 Write the verbs in the correct form.

1 This time tomorrow, ______________ (**he** / **drive**) to Brighton.
2 ______________ (**we** / **finish**) dinner by seven o'clock so I'll call you then.
3 This time next year, ______________ (**she** / **not** / **work**) here for ten years, but for 11 years.
4 ______________ (**no-one** / **be**) in the factory this time next Tuesday as it's a holiday.
5 In two months, ______________ (**they** / **sell**) toys in Manchester for exactly 100 years.
6 By this evening, ______________ (**I** / **put**) more than a thousand stamps on envelopes.

__/6

## 7 Complete the second sentence so it has a similar meaning to the first. Do not change the word given. Use two to five words, including the word given.

1 Asking Freddy to do those repairs was a mistake. **SHOULD**
We ______________________ Freddy to do those repairs.
2 I decided to ask my assistant to write the report. **TYPED**
I ______________________ my assistant.
3 I know you're upset but please don't cause any trouble, Don. **FUSS**
I know you're upset but please don't ______________________ , Don.
4 Many teenagers benefit from getting a part-time job. **SENSE**
Getting a part-time job ______________________ many teenagers.
5 She's finding it difficult to survive on such a low salary. **BY**
She's not finding it ______________________ on such a low salary.

__/10

**Total score** __/50

## EXAM SKILLS

**Tick the statements that are true for you. Review the skills in the unit if you need more help.**

| I can ... | Unit/page |
|---|---|
| ☐ identify synonyms in blog posts | U11 p114 |
| ☐ identify speakers' attitudes from their actions or reactions in short extracts | U11 p118 |
| ☐ organise my ideas before doing a photo task | U11 p120 |
| ☐ understand some phrasal verbs and use them in a multiple-choice cloze exercise | U11 p121 |
| ☐ use formal and informal language correctly in a letter / an email | U11 p122 |
| ☐ identify examples in a magazine article | U12 p124 |
| ☐ recognise distractors in multiple-choice answer options when listening to a radio interview | U12 p128 |
| ☐ reach a decision in a collaborative task | U12 p130 |
| ☐ understand the form and function of auxiliary verbs and apply them in an open-cloze exercise | U12 p131 |
| ☐ draw conclusions at the end of an essay | U12 p132 |

# OPTIMISE YOUR EXAMS | Reading

**OPTIMISE** Make sure you know what an exam task or question is asking you to do. Always read the instructions carefully.

**OPTIMISE** It´s important to decide how you will read each text in order to answer the questions. Individual tasks require you to look for different information and to approach them in a specific way so you can successfully answer the questions.

**1 Match each exam question (1–3) with a description (a–c). Then find units in the book that practise this reading task.**

**1 Question type:** ____
**Units** ___________

You're going to read an extract from a novel about a teenager called Eddie, who is on a school trip abroad. For questions **1–6**, choose the answer (**A**, **B**, **C** or **D**) which you think fits best according to the text.

**2 Question type:** ____
**Units** ___________

You're going to read an article about a teenager whose life suddenly changed. Six sentences have been removed from the article. Choose from the sentences **A–G** the one which fits each gap (**1–6**). There is one extra sentence which you do not need to use.

**3 Question type:** ____
**Units** ___________

You're going to read an article about four teenagers who started their own business projects. For questions **1–10**, choose from the teenagers (**A–D**). The teenagers may be chosen more than once.

**You have to …**

**a)** match each question with a person or text.
**b)** answer multiple-choice questions.
**c)** decide where missing sentences go in the text.

**2 Decide which of the following strategies are useful for each exam question type in Exercise 1. Write 1, 2 or 3 next to each sentence. There may be more than one possible answer.**

**a)** Quickly read the complete text first to get a general idea. This can help you locate information more quickly when you answer the questions. *1, 2, 3*
**b)** Read the removed sentences carefully and underline any reference words (pronouns, linking words, etc.) that may help you decide which part of the text they belong to. ___________
**c)** Look carefully at the questions and underline any key words/phrases that you need to scan for. ___________
**d)** Look at the sentences before and after the gap in the text and focus on reference words (people, pronouns, linking words, etc.) that may connect to one of the missing sentences. ___________
**e)** Remember that the information you are scanning for may be expressed in a different way in the text from how it is expressed in the question. ___________
**f)** Check the completed text is logical before you choose the final answers. ___________
**g)** Read and check you understand the main part of the question or sentence before focusing on the possible answer options. ___________
**h)** When you need to decide what a word or phrase means or refers to, form an idea in your mind by reading the sentences before and after it. Then see which option matches your idea. ___________
**i)** Thinking about the purpose or function of the text or of individual paragraphs can help you answer some questions. ___________
**j)** Beware of words or phrases in the questions that appear in the same or similar forms in the text. They may not answer the complete question! ___________

**3 A student has underlined the key words in the first question and the answer options for exam question type 1. Do the same for question 2.**

1 How did Eddie say he felt about the experience at first?
**A** He was shocked by the differences in eating hours.
**B** He was relieved to be away from home.
**C** He really missed his family and friends.
**D** He didn´t think the trip was appropriate for the age group.

2 What do we learn about Eddie in the final paragraph?
**A** He felt the experience was positive, despite the problems.
**B** He was looking forward to going on another trip soon.
**C** He didn´t think the trip had taught him anything new.
**D** He wishes he had taken more advantage of the whole experience.

**4** **Read part of a text for exam question type 2. Decide which two options below (A–F) fill the gaps. Find words in the options you chose and in the text to justify your answers.**

Jane Park from Edinburgh was only 17 years old when she won a million pounds on the UK lottery and consequently became one of the youngest lottery winners ever. It was during the summer of 2013 when Jane decided to stop off at a local shop near where she lived after seeing a lottery sign outside. At that moment, Jane wasn´t even sure that she was old enough to buy a lottery ticket. 1 ____ But that wasn´t the case and she won the big prize! Jane was sharing a room with her sister in a small home in south-east Edinburgh and working in an office as an assistant administrator. Like most girls of her age, she enjoyed going out and having a good time at weekends. For someone so young, a sudden windfall was bound to have a huge impact on her life. Most lottery winners prefer to remain anonymous and avoid public interest. 2 ____ She let everyone know about her win by posting it on social media. And none of her friends believed it at first.

**A** She was going to be 18 next month.
**B** So, Jane decided to do the same thing.
**C** She assumed she had to be 18.
**D** She had never played the lottery before.
**E** However, Jane immediately went public.
**F** And Jane understood how they felt.

**5** **Read one extract from exam question type 3. Decide which statements (1–5) match the person.**

**B Jarek Bukowski**

Jarek set up his own sports training business as soon as he was 18 years old. 'I had been warned that it would be pretty tough and that I lacked the experience initially to get it off the ground, but I felt confident and was ready to have a go.' Jarek took no notice of any negative advice and still let people give him tips. As a result, he applied for and received funding to start up a project to work with disabled children interested in sport. 'In the beginning it was tricky managing all the administrative work, but with a bit of help from friends I managed it.' Last month his company was given a prize for being one of the most adventurous and imaginative new projects started by young people. 'That really means everything to me, after all the effort.'

**Which young entrepreneur …**

1 recognised they lacked experience to set up a business?
2 didn´t take notice of any advice they were given?
3 was given financial help to start their business?
4 still finds doing administrative work difficult?
5 got an award in recognition of their work?

**6** **Which words in the text and questions in Exercise 5 help you justify your answers? Why are the other questions wrong?**

**OPTIMISE**

Make sure you know the regulations of the exam you are sitting so you are clear what you can and can't do, how much time you have, and how to use it effectively.

**7** **Alexandra has a reading exam tomorrow and she´s a bit nervous. Can you answer her questions? Discuss in pairs or as a group.**

1 How much time should I spend on each reading task?

2 What do I do if I don´t understand a word or phrase in the text?

3 What do I do if I get stuck and can´t find the answer to one specific question?

4 Can I make any notes when I´m reading?

5 Do I write on the exam paper or is there a separate answer sheet where I write my answers?

# OPTIMISE YOUR EXAMS | Listening

> **OPTIMISE**
> In most listening exams you have some time (between 30 seconds and one minute) before you start listening. Use this time carefully to check you understand what you have to do and to read through the questions.

**1** **Match each exam task (1–4) with an example question (A–D).**

**1** ______

You will hear people talking in eight different situations. For questions **1–8**, choose the best answer (**A**, **B or C**).

**2** ______

You will hear a student called Adrian Glossop talking about his recent trip to the Isles of Scilly to study sea birds called puffins. For questions **1–10**, complete the sentences with a word or short phrase.

**3** ______

You will hear five short extracts in which teenagers are talking about free-time activities. For questions **1–5**, choose from the list (**A–H**) what each speaker says about it. Use the letters only once. There are three extra letters which you do not need to use.

**4** ______

You will hear an interview with a teenager called Jenny Carter, who is talking about starting a school website. For questions **1–7**, choose the best answer (**A**, **B or C**).

**A**

What surprised her when she suggested an adventure blog section?

**A** how unenthusiastic most people were about it
**B** how helpful her close friends were with ideas
**C** how supportive her teachers were about the concept

**B**

You hear a girl telling a friend about climbing a mountain with her mother.

What does she remember most clearly about reaching the summit?

**A** being glad she'd followed her mother's advice
**B** feeling quite a lot of physical pain
**C** enjoying the beautiful scenery around her

**C**

**G** Doing it once a week helps me meet many different people.

**D**

He agrees that adult birds make a noise that is similar to a (**3**) .............

**2** **Choose an exam strategy which helps you do the different exam tasks (1–4) in Exercise 1. Write 1, 2, 3 or 4 next to the sentences (A–I). There may be more than one possible answer.**

**A** Look at words before and after each gap and predict the kind of words or information you expect to hear. __2__

**B** Read the statements/questions and underline any key words or phrases. ____

**C** Be careful when a question asks if speakers agree or disagree. They may express this in different ways, e.g. *I know what you mean, Definitely*, etc. ____

**D** Don´t write too much or re-phrase what you hear. The answer should be no more than three words long and you will hear the exact words you need to complete the sentence. ____

**E** The words used in the audio will often be different from those used in the questions, so listen for the ideas expressed in the options rather than the exact words. ____

**F** During the first listening, cross any statement off the list when you are sure you have identified the speaker. This reduces the number of options to choose from during the second listening. ____

**G** Check your answers make sense and are grammatically correct. ____

**H** If you realise you have missed an answer, don't panic. Continue listening and try to answer the other questions. Answer any 'missed' questions the second time you listen. ____

**I** Never leave a question unanswered. If you aren't sure, make your best guess. You do not lose marks for a wrong answer. ____

**3** 3.24 **You will hear a teenager talking about mountains. Read the multiple-choice exam question below and some notes a student made. The answer is wrong. Listen to the extract and choose the correct answer.**

> **OPTIMISE**
> Remember, you may hear the exact or very similar words you read in the question, but they may not always help you choose the right answer.

**What does Sandra say about giving a definition of a mountain?** — *there isn't one definition of a mountain*

**A** It's impossible to give one definition of a mountain.
**B** Some geologists think a mountain has to be 600 metres above sea level. — *argue other factors*
**C** She believes it doesn't matter if the definition isn't exact. — *call it a mountain ... it's a mountain*
**D** How steep and how high a mountain are very important factors. — *steepness, much higher*

**4** 3.24 **Listen again and answer the questions.**

1 Did exactly the same words help you get the right answer?
2 Did you hear the answer at the beginning, middle or end?

**5** 3.25 **A student has written some ideas to fill the missing gaps. Make other suggestions of your own. Then listen to the extract and write the correct answers.**

> **OPTIMISE**
> For sentence-completion tasks, it's a good idea to try to predict what sort of words or phrases might fit before you listen.

**You will hear a boy talking about an audition for a talent show.**
**For questions 1–5, complete the sentences with a word or short phrase.**

1 The boy says there were ______________ other people at the audition. — *number ... 100? 1 word or 2?*
2 The studio opened the doors at 6.45 am but they all had to stand ______________ until 10 am. — *up? around? 2 words?*
3 While they were waiting, people were singing, dancing and ______________ . — *verb ... playing games?*
4 The boy was interviewed and a woman filled out his ______________ . — *noun: I.D? form?*
5 The woman asked him to use three words to describe his ______________ . — *noun: personality, talent?*

**6** **You will hear an extract in which a speaker talks about using social media. Look at the key words a student has underlined for statements A and B, and some notes they made. Do the same for the statements C and D.**

*big? huge? fans? viewers? hate? not fun?*
**A** I have a large online audience but I don't enjoy editing the videos.

*worried? nervous? play? live? public?*
**B** I get anxious if I have to perform in front of a real audience.

**C** I perform my own songs but also work with other artists online.

**D** I'm less shy when I use the camera and it improves my performance.

> **OPTIMISE**
> Remember, in a multiple-matching task, it's a good idea to find key words in the statements and try to think of other ways a speaker might express them..

**7** 3.26 **Now listen to the extract and decide which two statements fit the speaker. Did your notes help you?**

**8** **Yuri has a listening exam tomorrow and he's a bit nervous. Can you answer his questions? Discuss in pairs or as a group.**

1 How many times do I hear each part of the listening exam?
2 Is spelling important in a gap-filling listening exercise?
3 Do I have to write exactly the same words in a gap-filling exercise?
4 Do I have time at the end of the exam to check my answers?
5 What should I do if I don't understand a question?

# OPTIMISE YOUR EXAMS | Speaking

OPTIMISE

- In the first part of a speaking exam you will answer some questions about yourself and your experiences (people, studies, free time, interests, travel, places).
- Practise asking for and giving personal information with other students.
- Don´t memorise answers. You won´t sound natural!
- Try to extend your answers to more than one sentence.

**1** **Read questions 1–10 and write the topic each one asks about (e.g. people, studies, free time, interests, travel, places). More than one answer may be possible.**

1 Do you have a best friend? What do you like about him/her? *people*
2 Tell us about the things you like doing in the evening. ______
3 If you could choose to visit anywhere in the world, where would you go? ______
4 Do you enjoy using the internet in your free time? ______
5 Have you done anything interesting recently with your family? ______
6 Where would you like to go for your next holiday? ______
7 Which part of the day do you like best? ______
8 Tell us about the area where you live. ______
9 Who do you usually spend time with at the weekends? ______
10 Is there something new you´d like to learn in the future? ______

**2** **Watch two students answering questions about themselves. Complete the information about each student. Make some notes.**

| | **Which questions from Exercise 1 do they answer?** | **Do they extend their answers?** (Note down reasons, explanations or examples given) | **What interesting language do they use?** (Note down structures, tenses, expressions or linking words used) |
|---|---|---|---|
| **Student A** | | | |
| **Student B** | | | |

OPTIMISE

- In some Speaking exams you get a mark for your pronunciation.
- Your accent doesn´t have to be perfect, but you should try to speak clearly so that your partner and the examiners can hear you.

**3** **Watch again and complete the table. Is there anything the students could improve?**

| | **Does the student speak clearly?** | **Does the student stress the right words and parts of sentences?** | **Does the student use intonation correctly?** |
|---|---|---|---|
| **Student A** | Yes, all the time. ☐<br>Yes, most of the time. ☐<br>No, not very often. ☐<br>No, not at all. ☐ | Yes, all the time. ☐<br>Yes, most of the time. ☐<br>No, not very often. ☐<br>No, not at all. ☐ | Yes, all the time. ☐<br>Yes, most of the time. ☐<br>No, not very often. ☐<br>No, not at all. ☐ |
| **Student B** | Yes, all the time. ☐<br>Yes, most of the time. ☐<br>No, not very often. ☐<br>No, not at all. ☐ | Yes, all the time. ☐<br>Yes, most of the time. ☐<br>No, not very often. ☐<br>No, not at all. ☐ | Yes, all the time. ☐<br>Yes, most of the time. ☐<br>No, not very often. ☐<br>No, not at all. ☐ |

**4** ▷ **Watch an examiner giving instructions for the photo task in a Speaking exam. Circle T (True) or F (False) for the statements below.**

> **OPTIMISE**
> Remember it´s important to listen carefully to the instructions the examiner gives you in each part of the test. Make sure you understand what you have to do.

1 The exam candidates talk together about two photographs. **T / F**
2 You only have to describe what you can see in the two photographs. **T / F**
3 You have about a minute to talk about the photographs. **T / F**
4 There is a question to help you but you don´t need to answer it. **T / F**
5 Both candidates talk about a different pair of photos. **T / F**
6 After each of the candidates has talked about their photo(s), the other candidate must answer a question about them. **T / F**

**5** **Work in pairs. Student A looks at the photographs in Set 1. Student B looks at the photographs in Set 2. Spend two minutes making a list of words and expressions related to your photos. Show your ideas to your partner and add more to your lists.**

> **OPTIMISE**
> - When you talk about photographs remember you need to **compare** them, not describe them individually.
> - Try to find two or three similarities or differences between the photos first.
> - Then answer the question at the top of the page above the photos.

What are people enjoying about eating in these places? **1**

How difficult might it be to play well in these situations? **2**

**6** **In pairs, find two or three similarities or differences between the photos in Set 1. Then find similarities and differences between the photos in Set 2.**

*In the first photo it looks like the students are eating in a canteen, whereas the second photo shows some friends cooking and eating together outside.*

> **OPTIMISE**
> - In Speaking exams, you usually get marks for how well you use grammar structures, and for the range of vocabulary you use.
> - Think about what you have to do in each task, and what grammar structures and vocabulary you need in order to do the task well.

**7** Watch two students doing a speaking photo task. Complete the table for each student. Is there anything students could improve?

| | Does the student compare the photographs describing similarities and differences? Give examples. | Does the student use a range of grammar structures, vocabulary and expressions, and linking words? Give examples. | Does the student talk for one minute? Does the student answer the question about the photographs? |
|---|---|---|---|
| Student A | | | |
| Student B | | | |

**8** Look at the exam task and sentences in Exercise 9. Then watch two students and choose the correct options in sentences 1–8.

**9** Work in pairs to check your answers.

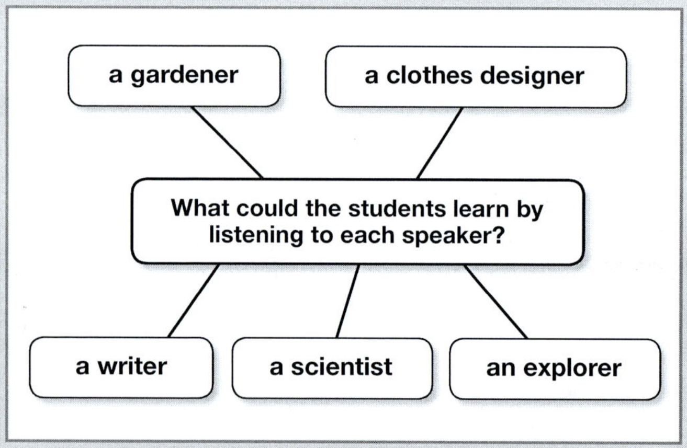


1 You talk ***together*** / ***individually*** about the question and different points.
2 First, you talk for about ***two*** / ***three*** minutes.
3 You ***don't have any time*** / ***have some time*** to look at the question first.
4 You should ***discuss the points together*** / ***take individual turns on each point***.
5 You have ***30 seconds*** / ***a minute*** to decide on the best options at the end.
6 You ***should try to agree*** / ***must agree*** with your partner at the end.
7 You ***must*** / ***don't have to*** talk about all the different options to do the task well.
8 The examiner ***will*** / ***won't*** time you and tell you when to start and stop each part of this exam task.

**10** In pairs, look at the *Skills for Speaking exams* section. Tick which points are useful for this part of the exam. Write down any examples of useful language you could use for each point.

**Making suggestions:**
*What about ...? Why don't we ...?*

**Skills for Speaking exams**

| | | |
|---|---|---|
| A | talking about habits | ☐ |
| B | comparing | ☐ |
| C | making suggestions | ☐ |
| D | agreeing and disagreeing | ☐ |
| E | talking about hopes and ambitions | ☐ |
| F | expressing preferences | ☐ |
| G | asking for clarification | ☐ |
| H | expressing and justifying opinions | ☐ |
| I | expressing uncertainty and speculating | ☐ |
| J | talking about experiences | ☐ |
| K | organising your ideas clearly | ☐ |
| L | reaching a decision | ☐ |

> **OPTIMISE**
> - In most Speaking exams, you get a mark for how well you interact with your partner and the examiner.
> - It´s important to listen to your partner. You may need to answer their questions or develop more ideas based on what they say. Try not to repeat your partner's ideas.
> - Try to organise your ideas in the discussion. Remember you need to start off, move on, keep going and try to come to a conclusion, but you don´t have to agree.

**11** **Watch again. Make notes about the students by answering the questions 1–8.**

**Do the students ...**

1. organise the discussion, e.g. start off, move on, finish up? How?
2. listen to each other and answer questions in a logical way?
3. talk about all the options? If not, how many and which ones?
4. invite each other to talk? How?
5. ask for and give opinions? How?
6. agree or disagree? How?
7. add and develop new ideas during the discussion? How?
8. reach a final agreement?

> **OPTIMISE**
> - In some Speaking exams, the examiner may ask you to develop discussions further.
> - The examiner may ask you questions individually, or they may ask you to discuss questions with your partner.
> - During the discussion, try to expand on your answers by explaining what you mean, giving examples, explaining reasons and sharing opinions.

**12** **Look at the exam task on page 142 again. In pairs, write six questions you think the examiner might ask in relation to the topic, e.g. work, school and studies.**

**Example:** *How useful is it for students to listen to different speakers talk about their jobs? (Why / Why not?)*

**13** **Watch students doing an exam discussion task and write down the examiner's questions. Then compare them to your questions.**

> **OPTIMISE**
> - In Speaking exams, you usually get a mark for discourse management. This relates to what you say and how you say it.
> - Make sure you express your ideas clearly and they are relevant. Try to speak fluently.
> - Try to link your ideas with connecting words and expressions.
> - Try not to repeat yourself or the same ideas as your partner, but develop new ideas and arguments.

**14** **Match the examiner's questions 1–3 to the answers A–C. In pairs, discuss how you could improve the answers.**

1. Do schools prepare students well for the future world of work? ____
2. What is more important, being happy in your job or earning a lot of money? ____
3. If you could choose any job to do, what would it be? Why? ____

**A** I think money. You can´t live without it. Most people don´t really like their jobs. But I guess doing a job you like is important. In the end, money is most important.

**B** A pilot. You can travel a lot. You work with many different people. It´s exciting. But you work long hours and it´s tiring.

**C** I don´t think so. We don´t get much careers advice at school. It´s difficult to know what job to choose. We need to do more practical studies. We should study about team work, managing different situations, problem solving ...

**15** **Watch again. Choose <u>one</u> of the students to focus on. Make notes about them by answering questions 1–6. Compare your notes with a partner.**

**Does the student ...**

1. organise their ideas clearly? If so, how?
2. speak fluently or hesitate?
3. use words and expressions to connect their ideas? If so, which ones?
4. give examples and reasons for their ideas? If so, how?
5. invite their partner to discuss the question? If so, how?
6. add and develop new ideas during the discussion? If so, how?

**OPTIMISE**
Make sure you are clear about what each question is testing you on, e.g. is it grammatical structures, vocabulary or both?

**1 Look at the three sentences below from multiple-choice gap-filling texts and answer the questions.**

It generally .................. a long time to learn a skill such as painting.

1 The key words to focus on here are ***a long time*** / ***learn a skill***.
2 Which of these words do we use in a phrase with the key words in the sentence?
**A** does **B** takes **C** makes **D** has

It's important to be able to .................. out any problems you have with people at work.

3 The key word to focus on here is ***able*** / ***out***.
4 Which of these words forms a phrasal verb with the key word and is used with 'problems'?
**A** take **B** run **C** sort **D** make

Later in his career, Smith was accused by a large number of people .................. copying the work of others.

5 The key word to focus on here is ***accused*** / ***people***.
6 Which preposition goes after the key word and before an *-ing* form?
**A** in **B** with **C** for **D** of

**OPTIMISE**
When the missing word in a gap-filling exercise is a verb, always make sure it agrees with the subject of the sentence.

**2 Read the text and decide what each gap is testing.**

**A success story**
Li Ka Shing, said to be the richest man in Asia, was born in China in 1928. Not long after, Li's family moved to Hong Kong, **(1)** ___________ sadly his father died when Li was a young boy. At the age of 12, Li dropped **(2)** ___________ of school and by the time he was 14, he **(3)** ___________ started working full-time to support his family. In 1950 Li set **(4)** ___________ his own plastic manufacturing company. His big breakthrough came **(5)** ___________ he decided to produce artificial flowers. Buyers were **(6)** ___________ impressed with the quality that they placed massive orders, making Li a highly successful businessman. His success continued as he **(7)** ___________ on to develop new businesses. If Li's father was alive today he **(8)** ___________ be very proud of his son.

1 Gap 1 is testing ***an auxiliary verb*** / ***an idiom*** / ***a relative pronoun***.
2 Gap 2 is testing ***a phrasal verb*** / ***a relative pronoun*** / ***an auxiliary verb***.
3 Gap 3 is testing ***an auxiliary verb*** / ***a collocation*** / ***the passive voice***.
4 Gap 4 is testing ***an auxiliary verb*** / ***a collocation*** / ***a phrasal verb***.
5 Gap 5 is testing ***an idiom*** / ***an adjective*** / ***a relative pronoun***.
6 Gap 6 is testing ***a grammar structure*** / ***a collocation*** / ***a phrasal verb***.
7 Gap 7 is testing ***a phrasal verb*** / ***an auxiliary verb*** / ***an idiom***.
8 Gap 8 is testing ***an adverb*** / ***an auxiliary verb*** / ***a relative pronoun***.

**3 Write one word in each gap in Exercise 2 to complete the text.**

**4 Look at the word formation task in Exercise 5 and answer the questions.**

1 Which gaps need a noun
____ ____ ____ ____ ____
2 Which gaps needs an adjective?
____ ____
3 Which gap needs an adverb?
____

**5** **Complete the gaps using the correct form of the word given.**

**Becoming a chess master**

| | |
|---|---|
| Chess is a game which has a lot of **(1)** __________ . So how does anyone | **COMPLEX** |
| become good at it? It's important to start **(2)** __________ and learn the | **GRADUAL** |
| basics first. Once you've done that, it's time to get more **(3)** __________ . | **CREATE** |
| Study other players' **(4)** __________ and learn from the best. Listen to | **PERFORM** |
| other players' **(5)** __________ of your own games and think about where | **CRITIC** |
| you went wrong when you lose. With the **(6)** __________ of experienced | **ASSIST** |
| players, you'll eventually learn which moves are **(7)** __________ in a | **SENSE** |
| game and which are not! Work on each **(8)** __________ as a player, and you'll | **WEAK** |
| soon become a chess master. | |

**OPTIMISE**

Remember to check your spelling after you have completed each gap and read through the complete text again to check it makes sense.

**6** **Read the sentences in Exercise 7 and decide which question is testing ...**

**A** a phrasal verb that means have an argument? __________
**B** a phrase that means laugh at someone in an unkind way? __________
**C** a word pattern with a preposition and followed by *-ing* form? __________
**D** the causative (have something done)? __________
**E** a phrasal verb that means avoid or escape something? __________
**F** an idiomatic expression which means very busy? __________

**7** **Complete the second sentence so that it has a similar meaning to the first sentence, using the word given. Do not change the word given. You must use between two and five words, including the word given.**

**1** I heard the company managed to land a vehicle on the moon successfully. **IN**
I heard the company ______________ a vehicle on the moon.

**2** Have you and Toby had an argument? **OUT**
Have you and Toby ______________ each other?

**3** I can't help you because I'm really busy with work right now. **NECK**
I can't help you because I'm ______________ in work right now.

**4** Uma was upset when her friends laughed at her new hairstyle. **FUN**
Uma was upset when her friends ______________ her new hairstyle.

**5** The driver was only slightly injured in the accident. **AWAY**
The driver ______________ slight injuries in the accident.

**6** The face painter painted my little sister's face at the fair. **HAD**
My little sister ______________ at the fair.

**OPTIMISE**

Remember that if you write contractions, they count as two words, e.g. *he'd* = *he had/would*.

**8** **Read the advice in 1–10 and match it with the Use of English tasks in A–D. There may be more than one possible answer.**

**a)** multiple-choice gap-filling **b)** open gap-filling
**c)** word formation **d)** sentence transformations

**1** Read the text quickly before you begin in order to get the general meaning. ____
**2** Use the word given without making any changes to it. ____
**3** Think carefully about whether the word you need should be positive or negative. ____
**4** If you're not sure, try all the options in the gap and see which sounds best. ____
**5** Read the text quickly when you have finished to check it makes sense. ____
**6** If you aren't sure of the answer, try putting different prefixes (*un-/in- imaginative*) or suffixes (*help -ful/-ness*) with the main word to see if it sounds right. ____
**7** Think about phrases and idioms that might include the word given. ____
**8** This exam task often tests prepositions, relative pronouns and auxiliary verbs. ____
**9** You should underline the information in the first sentence that is missing from the second sentence to help you. ____
**10** Always try to fill in a gap or answer a question. You may get it right even if you aren't 100% sure! ____

**OPTIMISE**

You can often use similar exam strategies in different Use of English exam tasks.

# OPTIMISE YOUR EXAMS | Writing

**1 For each writing skill, choose the TWO exam text types where that skill is relevant.**

| | | | |
|---|---|---|---|
| **1** advising | **a)** essay | **b)** letter/email | **c)** review |
| **2** agreeing and disagreeing | **a)** letter/email | **b)** essay | **c)** story |
| **3** drawing conclusions | **a)** article | **b)** story | **c)** essay |
| **4** using good descriptions | **a)** story | **b)** essay | **c)** review |

Learn the **OPTIMISE** characteristics of the different text types in exam questions and make sure you are clear on their purpose as well as relevant language and skills.

**2 Match each description to an exam text type.**

**In this type of text ...**

**1** you explain your ideas about an issue, give your opinion, and give reasons and examples to explain your ideas. ____

**2** you describe the good and bad points about a product, place, film, etc. and give your opinion. You may make a recommendation. ____

**3** you describe imaginary events and characters in order to entertain your readers. ____

**4** you write to one person, e.g. a friend, a teacher, a magazine editor, about a specific topic, e.g. a problem, to ask for some information about something, The style can be formal or informal. ____

**5** you write about a topic, often for a magazine, and the readers are usually a similar age to you. You need to try and make the readers interested in the topic. You can also give your opinion. ____

**a)** article
**b)** essay
**c)** letter/email
**d)** review
**e)** story

Many writing tasks ask you to include different **OPTIMISE** pieces of information. Make sure you include all the information in your answer. You may lose marks if you don´t.

**3 Match students' comments to each exam task, A, B or C.**

**1** The style can be informal. ____

**2** I´m writing for an adult not a friend or classmate. ____

**3** I must include a specific sentence in the piece of writing. ____

**4** I have to write about personal information and something about my culture. ____

**5** I must include three main points and give my opinion with reasons why. ____

**6** I have to use my imagination but also include some specific text and ideas. ____

**A** In your English class you have been talking about the environment. Now your teacher has asked you to write an essay for homework.

Write your essay using **all** the notes and giving reasons for your point of view.

**'Young people are under more pressure than ever before.' Do you agree?**

**Notes**

Write about:

**1** school
**2** friends
**3** .................. (your own idea)

**B** You have received this email from your English-speaking friend, Oscar.

> **From:** Oscar
> **Subject:** School project
>
> I'm doing a school project on food around the world. Could you tell me what you and your family eat at home and what you eat when you go out? What dishes are typical of your country and how do you feel about them?
>
> Thanks!
>
> Oscar

Write your **email**.

**C** You have seen this announcement in a magazine:

> Write a story for us! Your story must **begin** with this sentence:
>
> **Hannah read the text message again and quickly found a taxi.**
>
> Your story must include:
> - a surprise
> - a family event

Write your **story**.

**OPTIMISE**

How you organise your writing is important in an exam. It´s a good idea to make a clear plan before you begin. This will help you make your piece of writing logical and structured, and ensure that what you write actually answers the requirements of the task.

**4** **Choose the best plan (1 or 2) for Task A in Exercise 3. Explain why it is better.**

1
- brief introduction
- describe exam pressure and other pressures at school, compare to the past
- describe peer pressure, compare to the past
- describe pressure to keep up with fashion, compare to the past
- brief conclusion

2
- brief introduction
- describe pressure I'm under from school
- talk about school generally and how hard it is
- talk about pressure I get from my friends
- suggest ways of dealing with pressure

**5** **Choose the best plot (1 or 2) for Task C in Exercise 3. Explain why it is better.**

1 The text is from Hannah's friend and it says that her dog is missing. Hannah goes to her friend's house and they both search for the dog. Hannah's friend becomes upset, but then to their surprise they find the dog in a neighbour's garden.

2 The text is from Hannah's mother and it tells her to go home straight away. On the journey, Hannah is worried that something has happened. When she gets there, her mum and dad have arranged a surprise party to celebrate her exam results.

**6** **You have 40 minutes for each writing task. Look at the following possible stages of writing. Tick the ones you think you should do and say how much time you should spend on them.**

- Make a paragraph plan and notes ☐
  Time: ____________
- Write first draft and final draft ☐
  Time: ____________
- Count number of words ☐
  Time: ____________
- Check for mistakes ☐
  Time: ____________

**7** **In pairs or small groups, compare and explain your answers to Exercise 6.**

# GRAMMAR REFERENCE

## GRAMMAR REFERENCE | Unit 1 | Tense review: present simple and continuous, stative verbs

### Present simple

**FORM:** *I/You/We/They* ***live*** */* ***don't live*** *…*
*He/She/It* ***lives*** */* ***doesn't live*** *…*

***Do*** *I/you/we/they* ***live*** *…?* ***Does*** *he/she/it* ***live*** *…?*

**!** We form the emphatic present simple with *do/does*:
*Yes, it's true! Sophie* ***does have*** *a dog!*

**USE:** to talk about: **1** general truths and facts, **2** current habits, **3** how often things happen, **4** permanent situations, and **5** states:

| | |
|---|---|
| 1 | *The Moon* ***goes*** *round the Earth.* |
| 2 | *I* ***drive*** *to work.* |
| 3 | *Jen* ***goes*** *on holiday twice a year.* |
| 4 | *We* ***live*** *in Portugal.* |
| 5 | *I* ***love*** *your hair!* |

### Present continuous

**FORM:** *I* ***am*** */* ***'m not working*** *… You/We/They* ***are/ aren't working*** *… He/She/It* ***is/isn't working*** *…*

***Am*** *I* ***working*** *…?* ***Are*** *you/we/they* ***working*** *…?*
***Is*** *he/she/it* ***working*** *…?*

**USE:** to talk about: **1** actions happening now, **2** temporary situations, **3** changing and developing situations, **4** temporary series of actions, and **5** annoying habits (+ *always*):

| | |
|---|---|
| 1 | ***I'm not enjoying*** *this show.* |
| 2 | *Where* ***are*** *you* ***living*** *at the moment?* |
| 3 | *Technology* ***is becoming*** *more important.* |
| 4 | ***I'm driving*** *Harry to work this week.* |
| 5 | *You****'re always interrupting*** *me!* |

### Stative verbs

**USE:** to refer to states rather than actions. Stative verbs include verbs about thinking (*believe, know, think*, etc.), existence (*be, exist*, etc.), emotions (*love, like, hate*, etc.), human senses (*hear, see, smell*, etc.), appearance (*appear, look, seem*, etc.) and possession or relationships between things (*belong to, have, include*, etc.).

**!** Some verbs can refer to either states or actions, but their meaning changes (e.g. *feel, have, imagine, look, see, smell, think* and *taste*).

*Can you* ***see*** *that plane over there?* (state)
***Are*** *you* ***seeing*** *Lucas this weekend?* (action)

## GRAMMAR REFERENCE | Unit 1 | *-ing* and infinitives

### Verbs/phrases usually followed by the full infinitive (+ *to*)

*be able, agree, appear, arrange, ask, attempt, choose, decide, hope, manage, offer, plan, prepare, pretend, promise, refuse, seem, tend, want, would like*

**!** Some of these verbs/phrases can be followed by an object before the full infinitive.

*My parents want* ***me*** *to study medicine.*

### Verbs/phrases usually followed by the *-ing form*

*admit, appreciate, avoid, can't, deny, discuss, dislike, enjoy, fancy, feel like, mention, mind, miss, practise, put off, risk, succeed, suggest, understand*

**!** Some of these verbs/phrases can be followed by a possessive form or object before the *-ing* form.

*Do you mind* ***me/my*** *using your tablet?*

**!** Verbs and phrases with prepositions can often be followed by the *-ing* form.

*I'm* ***interested in buying*** *a new laptop.*

***Thanks for helping*** *me install that new software.*

### Verbs/phrases usually followed by an object + bare infinitive

*feel, hear, let, make, notice, see, watch*

### Verbs/phrases followed by the full infinitive or *-ing* form with little or no change in meaning

*begin, continue, hate, intend, love, start*

### Verbs/phrases followed by the full infinitive or *-ing* form with a change in meaning

*forget, go on, like, mean, regret, remember, stop, try*

*Oh! I've* ***forgotten to upload*** *the photos.* /
*I'll never* ***forget getting*** *my first smartphone.*

### *prefer, would prefer, would rather* and *had better*

**FORM:**

| | |
|---|---|
| *prefer* (+object) + *-ing* | I prefer reading on an e-reader. |
| *prefer* (+ object) + full infinitive | I prefer to read books rather than play games. |
| *prefer* + noun | I prefer books to games. |
| *would prefer* (+ object) + full infinitive | I would prefer to go to Russia on holiday this year. |
| *would prefer* + noun | I would prefer a holiday in Russia. |
| *would rather* (+ object) + bare infinitive | I would rather not go out this evening. |
| *would rather* (+ object) + past tense | I would rather you didn't use my laptop. |
| *had better* (+ bare infinitive) | We had better finish the project before tomorrow! |

! We use *prefer* to talk about general preferences. We use *would prefer* to talk about specific preferences.

*I **prefer** coffee to tea. / **I'd prefer** to watch a film this evening rather than go out.*

! The negative form of *I prefer* to is *I prefer not to*.

✔ *I **prefer not to** go out during the week.*
✘ ***I don't prefer to** go out during the week.*

! The phrase *had better* can be confused with *would rather*, but is not used to talk about preferences. It means *should* and is followed by the bare infinitive.

***I'd better** leave now or I'll be late.*

## GRAMMAR REFERENCE | Unit 2 | Tense review: past simple and past continuous

### Past simple

**FORM:** Regular verbs in the past simple end in *-ed* (*explained, tried, wanted,* etc.); irregular verbs don't follow a pattern (*get, have, said, taught, went,* etc.). You need to learn the past simple of irregular verbs.

**USE:** to talk about: **1** single completed actions in the past, **2** main events in a story, **3** habits and repeated actions in the past, **4** permanent situations in the past, and **5** general truths and facts about the past:

| | |
|---|---|
| 1 | *Freddie **drove** to Brighton at the weekend.* |
| 2 | *Emma **sat down**, **went** online and **began** to look for information.* |
| 3 | *She always **read** her emails before breakfast.* |
| 4 | *He **was** always the cleverest in the class.* |
| 5 | *The Ancient Greeks **developed** many of the sciences we study today.* |

! We form the emphatic past simple with *did*:

*I **did** understand what you said!*

! When we repeat a verb in the past simple, we usually just use the auxiliary verb. We don't repeat the main verb:

✔ *Dan didn't understand but I **did**.*
✘ *Dan didn't understand but I **understood**.*

### Past continuous

**FORM:** *I **was/wasn't running** ... You **were/weren't running** ... He/She/It **was/wasn't running** ...*

***Was** I **running** ...? / **Were** you **running** ...? **Was** he/she/it **running** ...?*

**USE:** to talk about: **1** an action in progress at a specific time in the past, **2** background information or description in a story, **3** an action in progress in the past when another thing happened (possibly interrupting it or stopping it), **4** two situations in progress at the same time, **5** temporary situations in the past, **6** changing/developing situations in the past, and **7** annoying or unexpected habits (usually + *always*):

| | |
|---|---|
| 1 | *At four o'clock yesterday afternoon, I **was downloading** music.* |
| 2 | *Dylan opened the curtains. Snow **was falling** heavily outside.* |
| 3 | *They **were riding** through town on their bikes when Ellie got a puncture.* |
| 4 | *When I arrived Connor **was reading** and Eva **was playing** the guitar.* |
| 5 | *I **was using** my friend's mobile because mine had no credit.* |
| 6 | *At that time, more and more people **were learning** how to abseil.* |
| 7 | *When I was at school, my teachers **were** always **telling** me to work harder.* |

! The past continuous is not used to talk about repeated actions in the past:

✔ *I **fed** the cat three times yesterday.*
✘ *I **was feeding** the cat three times yesterday.*

! When we repeat a verb in the past continuous, we usually just use the auxiliary verb. We don't repeat the main verb:

✔ *Jan wasn't playing but I **was**.*
✘ *Jan wasn't playing but I **was playing**.*

## GRAMMAR REFERENCE | Unit 2 | *would, used to, be used to*

### *would / used to*

**FORM:** *would / used to* + bare infinitive

*As a boy, I **would** always **walk** to school. As a boy, I always **used to walk** to school.*

**USE:** to talk about past habits (particularly the distant past).

! We can't use *would* to talk about past states.

✔ *I **used to** have long hair when I was young.*
✘ *I **would** have long hair when I was young.*

### *used to*

**FORM:** *used to* + bare infinitive

*I **used to** like playing the piano, but I'm not so keen now.*

**USE:** to talk about past states (particularly the distant past).

### *be used to*

**FORM:** *be used to* + *-ing* form / noun

***I'm used to writing** emails so they don't take me long.*

*She**'s used to cold water** so swimming in winter doesn't bother her.*

**USE:** to talk about something that is familiar or no longer strange.

**!** We can use this form to talk about the past:

*I **was used to writing** emails ... / She **was used to cold water** so swimming ...*

### *used to / be used to* – negative

**FORM:** *never used to / didn't use to*

*I **never used to / didn't use to** enjoy camping but these days I love it.*

**USE:** to talk about negative situations.

### *used to / be used to* – questions

**FORM:** ***Did** you/he/etc. **use to** ...? / **Are** you **used to** ...? / **Is** he/she/etc. **used to** ...?*

***Did** they **use to** live next door to you? **Are** you **used to** singing in front of people?*

**USE:** to ask questions.

## GRAMMAR REFERENCE | Unit 3 | Modals (1): review

**FORM:** Modals have only one form and are followed by the bare infinitive:

*I/He/They **can** come on Monday.*
*You **must** study harder!*

**USE:** some modals (*can, could, may, might, must, should*) and semi-modals (*have to, ought to*) can express the following:

ability, possibility, probability, advice or criticism, obligation and permission

We can use the modals *shall, will* and *would* to talk about the future, to make offers and to talk about hypothetical situations.

### Ability – *can/could*

To talk about ability now or generally.

*I **can** drive a car.*

To make a decision now about future ability.

*I **can** see you next Friday.*

To talk about ability in the past.
*I **could** use a video camera when I was four.*

To talk about hypothetical situations.

*If only I **could** be a famous actor.*

**!** To talk about ability in the future, use *will be able to*.

*I **will be able to** finish my book when I'm on holiday.*

**!** We don't use *can* as an infinitive. We use *be able to*.

✔ *I'd love **to be able to** sing.*
✘ *I'd love **to can** sing.*

### Possibility – *can/could*

To talk about possibility now or generally.

*It **can** be difficult making videos everyone enjoys.*

To talk about general possibility in the past.

*Winters **could** be very cold when I was a child.*

### Possibility – *may/might/could*

To talk about possibilities in the present, the future and generally.

*You **may/might/could** make money from vlogging.*

### Probability – *should / ought to*

To talk about what is probably true.

*Their latest video **should** / **ought to** be available now.*

### Advice or criticism

To ask for / give advice, or to criticise someone, now, in the future, or generally.

*You **ought to** speak to Ben about the problem.*
*You **shouldn't** let Jess tell you what to do.*

**!** *Should* is much more common in spoken and written English than *ought to*.

### Obligation – *must/have / has to*

To talk about personal obligation now, in the future, or generally.

*I **must** tell Olivia about the online discussion this weekend.*

To talk about external obligation now, in the future, generally or in the past:

*I **have to** see the headteacher in the morning.*
*Jack **had to** work until midnight last night.*

**!** In official contexts, such as notices and rules, *must* is sometimes used for external obligation.
*All passengers **must** show their passports.*

**!** *Mustn't* and *don't have to* mean different things.

*You **mustn't** do that!* = Don't do that!

*You **don't have to** do that.* = You can do that if you want to but it's not necessary.

**!** *Must* cannot be used as an infinitive. Use *to have to*.

✔ *I'd hate **to have to** work on Sundays.*
✘ *I'd hate **to must** work on Sundays.*

### Permission – *can/could/may*

To talk about permission now, in the future, or generally:

***Can/Could/May** I borrow your pen for a moment?*

**!** *May* and *could* are more polite than *can*.

**!** To talk about permission in the past, we don't usually use a modal.

✔ *I **was allowed to** stay up late.*
✘ *I **could** stay up late.*

**!** *Could* might refer to permission in the past, in reported speech.

*Dad said I **could** borrow the car.*

## GRAMMAR REFERENCE | Unit 3 | Modals (2): deductions about the present

**USE:** When we make deductions, we use different modals to show how sure we are about something.

### *must*

If we are certain that something is true or is the case, we use *must*.

*Jo* ***must*** *be here. Her coat is hanging up behind the door.*

### *can't*

If we are certain that something is not true or is not the case, we use *can't*.

*Harry* ***can't*** *be here. His car isn't in the car park.*

### *could/may/might*

If we think something is possibly true or may be the case, we use *could*, *may* or *might*.

*Keisha* ***could/may/might*** *be here. I'm not sure because I haven't seen her yet.*

## GRAMMAR REFERENCE | Unit 4 | Tense review: present perfect simple and continuous

### Present perfect simple

**FORM:** *I/You/We/They****'ve lived*** */* ***haven't lived*** *…*
*He/She/It****'s lived*** */* ***hasn't lived*** *…*

***Have*** *I/you/we/they* ***lived*** *…?* ***Has*** *he/she/it* ***lived*** *…?*

**USE:** to talk about the following situations: **1** situations that started in the past and are still true, **2** completed actions at a time in the past which is not mentioned, **3** completed actions where the important thing is the present result, and **4** a series of actions continuing up to now:

| | |
|---|---|
| **1** | *She****'s lived*** *in London all her life.* |
| **2** | *I****'ve seen*** *this documentary before.* |
| **3** | *He****'s*** *just* ***bought*** *a flat in the city centre.* |
| **4** | *So far this summer, we****'ve visited*** *Milan and Turin.* |

We can also use the present perfect simple: **5** to refer to the future, in time clauses (*when*, *as soon as*, *once*, etc.), **6** with words/phrases like *already*, *ever*, *for*, *just*, *never*, *since*, *so far*, *up to now*, *yet*, **7** with superlatives, and **8** with ordinal numbers:

| | |
|---|---|
| **5** | *I'll call you* ***as soon as*** *I****'ve arrived*** *at the airport.* |
| **6** | *I****'ve already bought*** *a new bike for my holiday.* |
| **7** | *That's the* ***biggest*** *city I****'ve*** *ever* ***been*** *to!* |
| **8** | *It's only the* ***second*** *time I****'ve*** *ever* ***been*** *to London.* |

**!** We use *for* + a period of time, and *since* + the moment when it started:

*We've had this flat* ***for three years / since 2014****.*

### Present perfect continuous

**FORM:** *I/You/We/They****'ve been*** */* ***haven't been sleeping*** *… He/She/It's been / hasn't been* ***sleeping*** *…*

***Have*** *I/you/we/they* ***been sleeping*** *…?*

***Has*** *he/she/it* ***been sleeping*** *…?*

**USE:** to talk about: **1** actions and situations (often temporary ones) continuing up to now, and **2** actions and situations (often temporary ones) that ended recently:

| | |
|---|---|
| **1** | *I****'ve*** *only* ***been living*** *here for a couple of weeks so I don't know my way around yet.* |
| **2** | *She****'s been travelling*** *all summer and we haven't seen her since she got back.* |

**!** Phrases used with the present perfect continuous include: *all day/week/morning/*etc., *for*, *just* and *since*.

## GRAMMAR REFERENCE | Unit 4 | Question review: question tags and question forms

### Question tags

**FORM:** When the verb *be* is a main verb, we form the question tag with *be*:

*It****'s*** *a big city,* ***isn't*** *it?*

When *be*, *have* or *do* are used as auxiliary verbs, we form the question tag with the auxiliary:

*It* ***doesn't*** *look very nice,* ***does*** *it?*

With other main verbs that don't have an auxiliary verb, we form the question tag with *do*:

*She* ***lives*** *in a big flat,* ***doesn't*** *she?*
*She* ***has*** *a big flat,* ***doesn't*** *she?*

With modals, we form the question tag using the modal:

*It* ***can't*** *be easy to live there,* ***can*** *it?*

With *there*, we repeat *there* in the question tag:

***There****'s no better hotel in this city, is* ***there****?*

With *let's*, we form the question tag with *shall we*:

***Let's*** *go to Paris again soon,* ***shall we****?*

With a positive imperative, we form the question tag using *will*, *would* or *could*: ***Hand*** *me the guidebook,* ***will/would/could*** *you?*

With a negative imperative, we form the question tag using *will*: ***Don't forget*** *to bring the guidebook,* ***will*** *you?*

**USE:** to ask questions: **1** when we expect someone to agree with our opinion, **2** to express surprise or doubt about something, **3** to suggest doing something (+ *Let's*), and **4** when we want someone to do something for us (+ an imperative).

| | | |
|---|---|---|
| **1** | *That's a beautiful building, **isn't it?*** | Our voice goes down at the end of the sentence. |
| **2** | *You just said Mia's from Belfast but she's from Dublin, **isn't she?*** | Our voice goes up at the end of the sentence. |
| **3** | *Let's go sightseeing, **shall we?*** | |
| **4** | *Hand me the guidebook, **would you?*** | |

**!** With words like *never, little, no, hardly, nobody,* etc., we use a positive question tag: ***Nobody lives** there, **do** they?*

### Question forms:

### Questions without question words

**FORM:** We use the question form of the verb in the correct tense.

***Have** you **been** to Beijing? **Did** Alec **fly** to Perth?*

### Questions with question words

**FORM:** We begin the question with a question word (*who, what, where, why, when, which, how*) or a question phrase:

- *how come / what for*

  These both mean *why* but the verb form differs:

  ***Why did you choose / How come you chose** to visit Berlin?*

  ***Why did you do** that? / **What did you do** that **for**?*

- *How about / What about*

  These are used for making suggestions:

  ***How about / What about** going to Paris this weekend?*

## GRAMMAR REFERENCE | Unit 5 | The future (1): *will, be going to*, present simple and continuous

### Predictions

For a prediction saying what we think or guess will happen, we often use *will*.

*Do you think Toby **will** pass all of his exams? Yes. I'm sure he **will**.*

For a prediction based on evidence seen at the time of speaking, we often use *be going to*.

*Look at that man! I think he's going to fall!*

**!** Sometimes *will* and *be going to* are both correct. In general, *be going to* is more informal and is common in speech.

*Lily and Mason **will** be at the wedding. / Lily and Mason **are going to** be at the wedding.*

For a prediction when we are not certain what will happen, we can also use *may/might* (possibility) or *should* (probability).

*Do you think Ollie will pass his exams?*

*I'm not sure. He **might** do. / He **should** do. He's studied hard.*

### Intentions and arrangements

To talk about intentions (something planned but not yet arranged), we often use *be going to*.

*Mum said we can have a puppy! We**'re going to** get it next week!*

To talk about arrangements (something agreed and arranged), we often use the present continuous.

*Dad**'s taking** us to the pet shop tomorrow!*

**!** Sometimes the present continuous and *be going to* are both correct.

*We**'re getting** a puppy! Dad**'s going to** take us to the pet shop tomorrow!*

### Instant decisions

For decisions made at the moment of speaking, we often use *will*.

*I know! **I'll** ask Mum to help me!*

### Timetabled future events

To talk about things that happen according to a schedule, we often use the present simple.

*Our bus **leaves** in five minutes.*

**!** Words/phrases used with the present simple include: *as soon as, before, once, the moment that, unless, until, when.*

### Offers, requests, promises, suggestions, refusals

To make offers or requests, we use *will* or *shall*. *Shall* is quite rare except in questions.

***I'll** drive you home if you like. **Will** you drive me home, please? **Shall** I drive you home?*

**!** We don't use *will* in questions to make offers.

✗ ***Will** I drive you home?*

**!** To make or ask about promises, we use *will*.

*I **won't** tell anyone your secret. Do you promise you**'ll** be there on Saturday?*

**!** To make suggestions and offers (for *I* and *we* only), we use *shall*.

***Shall** I speak to Poppy about the party? Let's go out this evening, **shall** we?*

## GRAMMAR REFERENCE | Unit 5 | Comparatives and superlatives

**FORM:**

| Type of adjective | Normal | Comparative | Superlative |
|---|---|---|---|
| Regular adjective (one syllable) | *old* | + *-er older* | + *-est oldest* |
| Regular adjective (one/two syllables) ending in *-e* | *wide* | + *-r wider* | + *-st widest* |
| Regular adjective (one syllable) ending in a vowel + consonant | *big* | double the final letter + *-er* *bigger* | double the final letter + *-est* *biggest* |
| Regular adjective (two syllables) ending in *-y* | *silly* | replace *-y* with *-ier sillier* | replace *-y* with *-iest silliest* |
| Other regular adjective (two or more syllables) | *difficult* | *more* + adjective *more difficult* | *most* + adjective *most difficult* |
| Irregular adjective | *good*<br>*bad*<br>*far*<br>*little*<br>*many/much* | *better*<br>*worse*<br>*farther/further*<br>*less*<br>*more* | *best*<br>*worst*<br>*farthest/furthest*<br>*least*<br>*most* |

| Regular adverb | Comparative | Superlative |
|---|---|---|
| *quickly* | *more/less quickly* | *most/least quickly* |
| **Irregular adverb** | **Comparative** | **Superlative** |
| *hard* | *harder* | *hardest* |
| *early* | *earlier* | *earliest* |
| *well* | *better* | *best* |
| *badly* | *worse* | *worst* |
| *far* | *farther/further* | *farthest/furthest* |
| *fast* (run fast) | *faster* | *fastest* |
| *late* | *later* | *latest* |
| *often* | *more/less often* | *most/least often* |

**USE:** We use **comparative** adjectives and adverbs to show that things or people are different or separate from each other:

*Aiden is a **better** photographer **than** me.*

*Aiden sees photo opportunities **better than** everyone else in the club.*

We use **superlative** adjectives and adverbs to show that one member of a group is at the top or bottom of the group:

*Aiden is **the best photographer** in the club. Aiden did **the best** in the photography competition.*

**!** We don't always use *than* with comparatives:

*This is my **older** brother.* (the comparative describes the noun)

*In the north, the weather is usually **worse**.* (= worse than it is in other places)

**!** We don't always use *the* with superlatives:

*This skyline is **my best photo** so far.*

**!** We can use *even* and *much* with comparatives:

*My photo is good, but Aiden's photo is **even/much** better!*

**!** To talk about the result of something increasing, we can use *the* + comparative, *the* + comparative:
*The **more** photos you take, the **better** you get.*

**Other ways of comparing**

| | | |
|---|---|---|
| *as* + adjective + *as* | To describe how things are the same in some way | *I am **as clever as** Owen (is).* |
| *not as/so* + adjective + *as* | To describe how things are different | *I didn't work **as hard as** Owen (did).* |

## GRAMMAR REFERENCE | Unit 6 | Conditionals (1): zero, first and second conditionals

### Zero conditional

**FORM:** *If* + present simple, present simple

**USE:** general truths, scientific facts:

*If you **eat** fish regularly, your brain **stays** strong.*

*Your brain **stays** strong if you **eat** fish regularly.*

**!** We can also use other present tenses in the *if* clause, depending on the meaning:

*If you**'re eating** fish, be careful of the bones!*

### First conditional

**FORM:** *If* + present simple, *will/won't* + bare infinitive

**USE:** possible or likely situations now, generally, or in the future:

*If you **eat** fish tonight, it **will help** you in your exams.*

*It **will help** you in your exams if you **eat** fish tonight.*

**!** We can also use other present tenses in the *if* clause, depending on the meaning:

*If you've eaten fish recently, you'll do well in the test tomorrow.*

**!** We can also use other modals in the result clause, depending on the meaning:

*If you eat fish tonight, it **might/may/could/should** help you in your test tomorrow!*

**!** We can also use the imperative for commands, instructions and advice:

*If you eat fish tonight, **make** sure there aren't any bones in it.*

### Second conditional

**FORM:** *If* + past simple, *would/wouldn't* + bare infinitive

**USE:** impossible, unlikely or hypothetical situations now, generally, or in the future:

*If you **lived** at the North Pole, you **would** probably **eat** a lot of fish.*

*You **would** probably **eat** a lot of fish if you **lived** at the North Pole.*

**!** We can also use past continuous in the *if* clause, depending on the meaning:

*If you **were living** at the North Pole, you **would** probably **eat** a lot of fish.*

**!** We can also use other modals in the result clause, depending on the meaning:

*If you **lived** at the North Pole, you **could** go fishing every day.* (= would be able to)

**!** With the verb *to be*, there are two forms with the second conditional:

*If I **were** a doctor, I'd* ... more formal and often used in writing.

*If I **was** a doctor, I'd* ... more informal and often used in speech.

### *Unless, as long as, in case*

***unless*** (= 'except if', and replaces *if not*).

***If you don't go / Unless you go** and see a doctor, you won't get better.*

***as long as*** (= 'if the following situation is true or happens', or 'on condition that', and replaces *if*).

***If / As long as** you're careful, swimming after eating is fine.*

***in case*** (= 'because the following might happen').

*Take an umbrella with you **in case** it rains.*

## GRAMMAR REFERENCE | Unit 6 | Relative clauses

**USE:** to tell us exactly who or what we are talking about (defining relative clause) or give us extra information about who or what we are talking about (non-defining relative clause). Relative clauses are often introduced by relative pronouns.

### Relative pronouns

*who* – for people (and sometimes animals):
*The coach **who** trains us is from Spain.*

*which* – for things (and sometimes animals):
*Jogging, **which** is good for you, is easy to do.*

*that* – for people and things; in defining relative clauses only:
*Is that the man **that** you were telling me about?*

*where* – for places:
*This is the place **where** the hospital will be built.*

*when* – for time:
*The day **when** I met her was the happiest day of my life.*

*why* – used after *reason*:
*Do you know the reason **why** she's decided to become a vegetarian?*

*whose* – possessive:
*Will the person **whose** car is blocking the entrance please move it?*

*whom* – people as the object of the relative clause and after prepositions (very formal):
*The people with **whom** you will be training are very fit.*

### Defining relative clause

**FORM:** In defining relative clauses we:

- don't use a comma.
  *The man **who I met** was called Simon.*
- can use *that* instead of *who* or *which*.
  *The man **that I met** was called Simon.*
- often leave out the relative pronoun when it is the object of the clause.
  *The man **I met** was called Simon.*

### Non-defining relative clauses

**FORM:** In non-defining relative clauses we:

- separate the relative clause with commas.
  *My brother, who lives with me, is a doctor.*
- can't use *that* as a relative pronoun.

✗ *My brother, that lives with me, is a doctor.*

- can't leave out the relative pronoun.

✗ *My brother, lives with me, is a doctor.*

### Relative pronouns and prepositions

We can use a preposition + *which* instead of *where*.

*The village **where / in which** we stayed was very remote.*

We can also put the preposition at the end of the clause. This is less formal and we can replace *which* with *that*.

*The village **which/that** we stayed **in** was very remote.*

## GRAMMAR REFERENCE | Unit 7 | Tense review: past perfect simple and continuous

### Past perfect simple

**FORM: regular verbs**

*had* + past participle

*I/you/he/she/it/we/they* ***had ('d) walked*** *far.*

*I/you/he/she/it/we/they* ***had not (hadn't) walked*** *far.*

***Had*** *I/you/he/she/it/we/they* ***walked*** *far?*

*Yes, I/you/he/she/*etc. ***had***. *No, I/you/he/she/*etc. ***hadn't***.

**irregular verbs**

You need to learn the past participle of irregular verbs. See the Irregular verbs reference, page 175.

**USE:** to talk about: **1** completed actions before a moment in the past, **2** situations and states before the past, and **3** completed actions where the important thing is the result at a moment in the past:

| | |
|---|---|
| **1** | *He* ***had finished*** *his homework by the time I arrived.* |
| **2** | *I* ***had known*** *Richie for two years before we became friends.* |
| **3** | *I didn't want to go out to eat because I'****d*** *just* ***had*** *a snack.* |

**!** Phrases such as *It was the first/second/*etc. *time …* are followed by the past perfect simple.

*It was the first time I* ***had met*** *someone called Addison.*

### Past perfect continuous

**FORM: all verbs**

*had been* + *-ing*

*I/you/he/she/it/we/they* ***had ('d) been working***.

*I/you/he/she/it/we/they* ***had not (hadn't) been working***.

***Had*** *I/you/he/she/it/we/they* ***been working***?

*Yes, I/you/he/she/it/we/they* ***had***. *No, I/you/he/she/it/we/they* ***hadn't***.

**USE:** to talk about: **1** actions continuing up to a moment in the past, and **2** actions stopping just before a moment in the past:

| | |
|---|---|
| **1** | *By midnight, I* ***had been working*** *for six hours.* |
| **2** | *I was tired because I* ***had been working***. |

## GRAMMAR REFERENCE | Unit 7 | Connectors of contrast

**USE:** *although, even though, in spite of, despite* and *however* are used to contrast one idea with another:

| | |
|---|---|
| *although / even though* + clause, clause | ***Although / Even though*** *he's a bit shy, he's my best friend.* |
| *in spite of / despite* + *-ing*, clause | ***In spite of / Despite*** *being a bit shy, he's my best friend.* |
| *in spite of / despite* + the fact that + clause, clause | ***In spite of / Despite*** *the fact that he's a bit shy, he's my best friend.* |
| *in spite of / despite* + noun, clause | ***In spite of / Despite*** *the fact that he's a bit shy, he's my best friend.* |
| *However*, clause | *He's shy.* ***However***, *he's my best friend.* |

**!** With *although, even though, in spite of* and *despite*, the clauses can come in a different order:

*He's my best friend* ***although / even though*** *he's a bit shy.*
*He's my best friend* ***in spite of / despite*** *being a bit shy.*

**!** *However* can also come at the end or in the middle of a sentence.

*He's a bit shy. He's my best friend,* ***however***.
*He's a bit shy. He is,* ***however***, *my best friend.*

## GRAMMAR REFERENCE | Unit 8 | The passive

**FORM:** *be* + past participle (+ *by/with/of*)

We don't use the passive in the present perfect continuous or past perfect continuous.

We can use it in all other tenses, plus with modals, *-ing* forms and infinitives:

*They* ***should be given*** *a medal for their work.*

*I loved* ***being asked*** *to be team leader.*

*It was nice* ***to be told*** *I was good for a beginner.*

**!** Some verbs are not usually used in the passive. These include intransitive verbs (verbs which don't take objects), such as *appear* and *seem* and some transitive verbs, such as *have* and *let*.

**USE:** We often use the passive: **1** when we don't know who 'does' the action: **2** when it's not important who 'does' the action, **3** when it's obvious who 'does' the action, and **4** for emphasis, or to sound more formal:

| | |
|---|---|
| **1** | *My mountain bike* ***has been stolen***. |
| **2** | *The snow* ***is cleared*** *every afternoon.* |
| **3** | *We'****ve been given*** *a geography project.* |
| **4** | *The school trip* ***has been cancelled***. |

We use *by* to show who or what does the action:
*They were rescued* ***by*** *the Mountain Rescue Team.*

We can use *with* for tools and equipment: *They were rescued* ***with*** *a long rope.*

We can use *of* for materials: *The harness is made* ***of*** *nylon and metal.*

We often don't use *by* if we don't know who does the action, if it's not important or if it's obvious:
*My mountain bike has been stolen ~~by someone~~.*
*She was taken to hospital ~~by an ambulance driver driving an ambulance~~.*
*The snow is cleared every afternoon ~~by people with machines~~.*

# GRAMMAR REFERENCE | Unit 8 | Countable/uncountable nouns, articles and quantifiers

## Countable and uncountable nouns

**Countable nouns** can be counted and have a singular and plural form.

**Uncountable nouns** are often abstract ideas (*truth, information,* etc.), materials (*iron, glass, water, wood,* etc.) and collections (*furniture, luggage, baggage, money,* etc.). Nouns like these are followed by a verb in the singular, even if they're describing more than one object:

*All the information **was** helpful.*
*Lots of money **isn't** the solution to the problem.*

**!** To talk about one object in a collection, we can use *piece of, sheet of, item of,* etc. and we can use plural verbs where appropriate:

*Could you give me a **sheet of** paper? Two pieces of furniture **are** enough.*

**!** Some nouns are both countable and uncountable. Often, this is because the word refers to a substance/ material or a thing that's made of that substance:

- material/substance – uncountable: *glass, chocolate, coffee, paper,* etc.
- a thing containing that material/substance – countable: *a glass* (to drink from), *a chocolate* (one from a box), *a coffee* (a drink), *a paper* (a newspaper), etc.

## Quantifiers

**USE:** with countable and uncountable nouns (*a lot of, lots of, some, the*).

with countable nouns (*a, an, one/two/*etc. *a number of, a few, few, many, how many*).

with singular uncountable nouns (*a piece of, an amount of, a little, little, much, how much*).

## Articles

- **indefinite article (*a(n)*)**

**USE:** with singular countable nouns (when we are not being specific or when we mention something for the first time): *I saw **an** interesting article yesterday.*

**!** Whether we use *a* or *an* depends on the sound, not the spelling:

*He gave me **a euro**. It's an honour to be here.*

- **definite article (*the*)**

**USE:** with singular countable nouns (specific or general): ***The** computer has changed our lives.*
*That's **the** game I want.*

plural countable nouns (when we are being specific): ***The** books you lent me are on the desk.*

uncountable nouns (when we are being specific): ***The** information he gave me was incorrect.*

**!** We usually use *the* when there is only one of something: ***the** sun, **the** sky, **the** internet,* etc.

- **no article**

**USE:** with plural countable nouns (when we are talking generally): *Children learn a lot from using tablets.*

uncountable nouns (when we are talking generally): *It's very easy to give advice.*

**!** Notice how we use articles in these phrases:

**time:** *in **the** 2000s, in **the** morning, in June, on Friday, at night*

**people and work:** *work as **a** ..., have **a** job, go to work, **the** Queen, **the** Chinese*

**places:** ***the** Alps, **the** USA, **the** UK, Madrid, Russia*

**entertainment:** ***the** media, on **the** radio, on TV, go to **the** cinema*

**organisations:** ***the** army, **the** police, **the** fire brigade*

**travel:** *on **the** bus, catch **a/the** bus, take **a** taxi*

# GRAMMAR REFERENCE | Unit 9 | Reported speech

**FORM:** In reported speech, we don't use all the words and tenses of direct speech.
Be careful with tenses and time/place words.

| Direct speech | Reported speech |
|---|---|
| present simple<br>*'I play the piano.'* | past simple<br>*Ed said (that) he **played** the piano.* |
| present continuous<br>*'I'm playing the piano.'* | past continuous<br>*Ed said (that) he **was playing** the piano.* |
| past simple / present perfect simple / past perfect simple<br>*'I played / have played / had played the piano.'* | past perfect simple<br>*Ed said (that) he **had played** the piano.* |
| past continuous / present perfect continuous / past perfect continuous<br>*'I was / have been / had been playing the piano.'* | past perfect continuous<br>*Ed said (that) he **had been playing** the piano.* |
| *will/can*<br>*'I will/can play the piano.'* | *would/could*<br>*Ed said (that) he **would/could play** the piano.* |
| *must*<br>*'I must play the piano.'* | *had to*<br>*Ed said (that) he **had to play** the piano.* |

**!** We sometimes **don't** need to change the verb tense:

| | Direct speech | Reported speech |
|---|---|---|
| scientific facts / situations that are still true | *'The piano is made of wood.'* | *Ed said (that) the piano* ***is*** *made of wood.* |
| somebody just said something, so it's still true | *'I'll be there in five minutes.'* | *He's just texted and said (that) he* ***will*** *be here in five minutes.* |
| the reporting verb (e.g. *say*) is in a present tense | *'I love music.'* | *Ed* ***says*** *(that) he* ***loves*** *music.* |

**!** With reported yes/no questions, we use *if* or *whether* and change the tense and word order:

| Direct speech | Reported speech |
|---|---|
| *'Do you play the piano?'* | *Ed asked me* ***if/whether*** *I* ***played*** *the piano.* |

**!** With questions using *who, why, how*, etc., we repeat the question word and change the tense and the word order:

| Direct speech | Reported speech |
|---|---|
| *'Why did you choose the piano?'* | *Ed asked me* ***why I had chosen*** *the piano.* |

**!** Time and place words are often different, because of the different perspective:

| Direct speech | Reported speech |
|---|---|
| *here* | *there* |
| *today* | *that day* |
| *now* | *then / at that moment* |
| *tomorrow* | *the following/next day* |
| *next week/month/year* | *the following week/month/year* |
| *yesterday* | *the day before / the previous day* |
| *last week/month/year* | *the previous week/month/year* |
| *ago* | *before* |
| *this/that* + noun | *the/that* |
| *this/that* (subject/object) | *it* |
| *these/those* + noun | *the/those* |
| *these/those* (as a subject) | *they* |
| *these/those* (as an object) | *them* |

## Reporting verbs

Apart from *say*, there are lots of other verbs we can use to report what someone said. They each have their own grammar, so be careful when using them. They include: *claim, command, deny, order, promise, refuse, state, suggest, tell, warn* and many others.

# GRAMMAR REFERENCE | Unit 9 | Indirect questions

**USE:** Indirect questions are a way of being more polite when asking a question. We can use indirect questions in spoken and written English.

**FORM:** Although all indirect questions are questions, some have a question mark at the end, and some don't. It depends on the introductory phrase that you use.

## Introductory phrases which need a question mark at the end

*Can/Could you tell me/us/*etc. */ let me know …?*

*Do you know / think you could tell me …?*

*Would/Will you tell us …?*

**!** The basic rule is that if it starts like a question, it ends in a question mark.

## Introductory phrases which don't need a question mark at the end

*I'd be grateful if you could tell me/us,* etc. …

*I wonder if you could tell us / let us know …*

*I wonder if you know …*

*I'd be interested in hearing if you …*

*I'd like to know …*

**!** The basic rule is that if it doesn't start like a question, it doesn't end in a question mark.

## Word order

We don't use question word order in the main question.

| Short, direct questions (less formal) | Longer, indirect questions (more polite) |
|---|---|
| *Why did you choose the guitar?* | *I'd be grateful if you could tell us* ***why you chose*** *the guitar?* |
| *What is that instrument?* | *Do you know* ***what that instrument is****?* |
| *When is my next violin lesson?* | *I'd like to know* ***when my next violin lesson is****.* |
| *Where can I find a music shop?* | *I wonder if you know* ***where I can find*** *a music shop.* |
| *Are you a famous musician?* | *Could you tell me* ***if/whether you're*** *a famous musician?* |

## GRAMMAR REFERENCE | Unit 10 | Result clauses: *so, such, too, enough*

### *so* and *such*

**USE:** to talk about amounts, and their results and effects:

| | |
|---|---|
| *so* + adjective/ adverb + (*that*) clause | *It's **so difficult** (that) not many runners finish.*<br>*She ran **so fast** (that) she finished first.* |
| *so* + *many/much* + noun + (*that*) clause | *There are **so many** races (that) I can't choose.*<br>*There's **so much** snow (that) it's difficult to run.* |
| *such* + *a(n)* + adjective + singular noun + (*that*) clause | *It's **such a difficult race** (that) I didn't finish.* |
| *such* + adjective + plural noun + (*that*) clause | *They're both **such difficult marathons** (that) not many runners finish.* |
| *such* + *a lot of* + noun + (*that*) clause (= *so many/much*) | *There's **such a lot of snow** (that) they've had to cancel the race.* |

**!** We can also use *so* and *such* without a *that* clause. This has a similar meaning to *really* or *very*, but it's more emphatic.

*It's **so** far! = It's **very/really** far!*
*It's **such** a difficult race! = It's **very/really** difficult!*

### *too*

**USE:** to criticise, to say that something is negative or bad, or to show that something prevents us from doing something:

| | |
|---|---|
| *too* + adjective/adverb + *for* (+ full infinitive) | *It's **too expensive** for me. She runs **too fast** for me.*<br>*It's **too expensive** for me (to do every year).* |
| *too many* + plural countable noun | *I ran slowly because there were **too many** people.* |
| *too much* + uncountable noun | *There's **too much** snow.* |

**!** *too* is not followed by a *that* clause.

**!** When the meaning is positive, we don't use *too*. We use other words and phrases, such as *really* or *extremely* (with adjectives or adverbs) or *lots of* (with nouns).

### *enough*

**USE:** *enough*: the right amount/number of; *not enough*: less than the right amount/number of:

| | |
|---|---|
| (*not*) *enough* + noun (+ full infinitive) | *Because **enough people** entered, the race went ahead.*<br>*Because **not enough people** entered, the race was cancelled.*<br>*I've (I haven't) got **enough money** (to pay the fee).* |
| (*not*) *enough* + noun + *for* | *There's (There isn't) **enough snow for** a great Ice Marathon.* |
| (*not*) + adjective/adverb + *enough* (+ *for*) (+ full infinitive) | *You're (not) **fast enough to be** in the athletics team.*<br>*It was (not) **far enough for me to feel** tired.* |
| (*not*) + *a(n)* + adjective + *enough* + singular noun | *I'm (not) **a good enough runner** to be in the athletics team.* |
| (*not*) + adjective + *enough* + uncountable noun or plural countable noun | *They're (not) **good enough runners** to be in the team.*<br>*It's **not good enough snow** for an Ice Marathon.* |

**!** The word *enough* is not followed by a *that* clause.

## GRAMMAR REFERENCE | Unit 10 | Conditionals (2): third conditional

**USE:** to talk about the hypothetical past (i.e. to imagine a past that didn't happen):

*If I'd known about the race, I'd have taken part.* = I didn't know about the race. I didn't take part.

**FORM:** As with other conditionals, a third conditional sentence has two parts: the *if* clause and the result clause. We separate the clauses with a comma when the *if* clause comes first: *If I'd known about it, I'd have entered. / I'd have entered if I'd known about it.*

**!** Both clauses in the third conditional are hypothetical (i.e. they didn't really happen).

**!** Instead of *would*, we can also use *might* and *could*: *If I'd known about the race, I **might / could have** taken part.*

**!** Be careful with verbs in the negative in third conditional sentences.

*She would have trained if she **hadn't** been ill.* = She didn't train. She was ill.

## GRAMMAR REFERENCE | Unit 11 | Modals (3): modal perfect

**FORM:** modal + *have* + past participle (*would have gone, should have seen*, etc.).

The continuous form also exists: modal + *have* + *been* + *-ing* (*would have been doing, should have been watching*, etc.).

**USE:** The modal perfect is used for a number of different purposes:

### Deductions about the real past

Past situations which are almost certainly correct: *must, can't, couldn't*

*He* ***must have left*** *work by now.* = I'm almost certain he's left work.

*He* ***can't have left*** *work yet.* = I'm almost certain he hasn't left work yet.

*He* ***couldn't have left*** *work yet.* = I'm almost certain he hasn't left work yet.

Past situations which are probably correct: *should, ought to*

*He* ***should have left*** *work by now.* = He's probably left work by now.

*He* ***ought to have left*** *work by now.* = He's probably left work by now.

Past situations which are possibly correct: *may, might, could*

*He* ***may have left*** *work by now.* = It's possible he's left work by now.

*He* ***might have left*** *work by now.* = It's possible he's left work by now.

*He* ***could have left*** *work by now.* = It's possible he's left work by now.

### Describing a hypothetical past

We use the modal perfect in this way in third conditional result clauses.

*I* ***would have applied*** *for the job but I forgot.*

*I* ***could have applied*** *for the job but I forgot.*

*I* ***might have applied*** *for the job but I forgot.*

**!** We use *could* + *have* + past participle to describe hypothetical past ability. For real past ability, we use *could* + bare infinitive:

*I* ***could type*** *when I was eight years old.*

### Criticising past behaviour

We can use the modal perfect with *should* or *ought to* to criticise past action and behaviour.

*You should have told me about your new job!* = You didn't tell me and that was wrong.

*She ought to have handed in her report yesterday.* = She didn't hand in her report yesterday and that was wrong.

**!** Be careful with *should* + *have* + past participle because it can be used for situations which happened and didn't happen:

*She* ***should have called*** *them by now.* = She's probably called them. (probability)

*She* ***should have called*** *them by now.* = She hasn't called them. (criticism)

### Unnecessary past actions

We can use *needn't* + *have* + past participle to describe a past action which turned out to be unnecessary:

*I* ***needn't have worried*** *– they offered me the job!* = I did worry but it wasn't necessary.

*You* ***needn't have asked*** *for a pay rise. We've already decided to give you one.* = You asked for a pay rise but it wasn't necessary.

## GRAMMAR REFERENCE | Unit 11 | The causative

**USE:** to talk about asking or paying someone else to do something for us. We can use it when the person who does the action is unimportant or obvious, in the same way as we can with the passive. We can also use the causative to put the topic (the thing we are talking about) first in a sentence and the new information later.

**FORM:** *have* (in the right form) + object + past participle

***We're having the house decorated*** *next week.*

We can also use *get* instead of *have*. *Get* is a little less formal.

*When* ***did you get your hair done****? I like it!*

**!** The causative can also be used to talk about (usually bad) things that happen to us, such as things being stolen, broken, etc. We don't usually use *get* with this meaning.

*Jade* ***had her car stolen*** *last week.*

### The causative and the passive

The causative has a number of things in common with the passive.

- We use *by* to show who or what 'does' the action: *I had my portrait done* ***by*** *a famous painter.*
- We can use *with* to describe tools and equipment: *We've had our carpet cleaned* ***with*** *a special chemical.*
- We often don't use *by* if we don't know who 'does' it: *Val had her car stolen ~~by someone~~.*
- We often don't use *by* if it's obvious who 'does' it: *We're having a new house built ~~by a builder~~.*
- We often don't use *by* if it's not important who 'does' it: *I got my car repaired last week ~~by John the mechanic~~.*

## GRAMMAR REFERENCE | Unit 12 | The future (2): continuous, perfect simple and continuous

### Future continuous

**FORM:** *will/won't + be + -ing* (*will be working, won't be travelling*, etc.)

**USE:** to talk about actions happening (in progress) at a point in the future. This use is similar to how we use the present continuous to talk about actions happening now and how we use the past continuous to talk about actions happening at a point in the past. (See Grammar reference, Unit 1 and Grammar reference, Unit 2.)

*At midday tomorrow, **I'll be collecting** money for charity.*

(Compare: *Now, I'm collecting money for charity. / At ten yesterday, I was collecting money for charity.*)

We can also use the future continuous to refer to future events that are expected to happen, in a similar way to how we use the present continuous for the future.

*Next week, **we'll be having** a discussion about voluntary work.*

### Future perfect simple

**FORM:** *will/won't + have* + past participle (*will have finished, won't have started*, etc.)

**USE:** to talk about actions completed at a time between now and a point in the future. This use is similar to how we use the present perfect simple to talk about actions completed between some point in the past and now and how we use the past perfect simple to talk about actions completed before a point in the past. (See Grammar reference, Unit 4 and Grammar reference, Unit 7).

*Lauren **will have finished** the report by five o'clock.*

**!** We can also use other modals with these tenses, including *may, might* (possible actions) and *should* (probable actions).

*This time tomorrow, I **might be working** at the animal rescue centre. I'll let you know.*

*I **should have finished** work by six o'clock this evening. I'll call you if I'm going to be late.*

### Future perfect continuous

**FORM:** *will/won't + have been + -ing* (*will have been living, won't have been working*, etc.)

**USE:** to talk about actions happening up to a point in the future. This use is similar to how we use the present perfect continuous to talk about actions happening up to now and how we use the past perfect continuous to talk about actions happening up to a point in the past. (See Grammar reference, Unit 4 and Grammar reference, Unit 7.)

*On Friday, I **will have been volunteering** here for exactly one year.*

## GRAMMAR REFERENCE | Unit 12 | Past tenses for the present/future

**USE:** We sometimes use the past simple and past continuous to describe the present, the future, or general situations. Often, these are hypothetical situations.

### *If* clause in second conditionals

(see Grammar reference, Unit 6)

*If she **had** a job, she wouldn't wander round town all day.* = She doesn't have a job at the moment.

*I couldn't do voluntary work full-time unless I **won** the lottery.* = except if I won the lottery in the future

### Unlikely hypothetical situations using *suppose, supposing, what if, imagine (if)*

*Suppose/Supposing you **wanted** a part-time job. What would you look for?*

*What if you **wanted** a part-time job? What would you look for?*

*Imagine (if) if you **wanted** a part-time job. What would you look for?*

### Present wishes about hypothetical situations with *wish, if only*

*I wish I **had** a job I enjoyed.*

*If only I **had** a job I enjoyed.*

### Expressing preference with *would rather*

*I'd rather you **gave** some money to a charity supporting guide dogs for the blind.*

**!** We can't follow this structure with *I*:

✘ ***I'd rather I** worked with elderly people.*

✔ ***I'd rather you/we/she/he** worked with elderly people.*

### Expressing preference or making suggestions with *It's (high/about) time*

*It's time we **left**.* = We should leave now.

*It's high time you **left**.* = You should leave now.

*It's about time they **left**.* = They should leave now.

### To be very polite in questions, requests, hopes, etc.

***Did** you want to see me now?*

*I **was wondering** if you had decided which hero you're going to write about.*

*I **thought** you might need some help with that essay.*

# VOCABULARY REFERENCE

## Introduction

This *Vocabulary reference* contains all the target vocabulary from *Optimise B1+* Student's Book. The words and phrases are arranged unit by unit, so you can refer to them as you work on vocabulary lessons throughout the book. You can also use the pages as a revision tool when you're preparing for a test or an exam.

The target vocabulary has been subdivided into six groups:

### Topic vocabulary

The **Topic vocabulary** sections focus on language connected to the unit topic. Learning these words and being able to use them correctly will help you in your exams. Having a wide vocabulary is particularly relevant for Use of English, Speaking and Writing exams.

### Word formation

The **Word formation** sections present you with all the different parts of speech – verbs, adjectives, nouns and adverbs – that come from root words that appear in *Optimise B1+* Student's Book. Most exams will test your knowledge of word formation, so learning all the forms of a word is a good way to make sure you are well prepared for your exam.

### Collocations

**Collocations** are phrases with combinations of words which naturally go together in English. Learning collocations will help you in exam tasks, such as open cloze, multiple-choice cloze and sentence transformations. It will also improve your productive English and therefore help you with speaking and writing.

### Idioms

**Idioms** are common phrases in a language, whose meaning is often not literal, so can be difficult or impossible to guess. You will find a good knowledge of idioms is particularly helpful in sentence transformation tasks.

### Word patterns

**Word patterns** are phrases which use specific grammatical structures. For example, phrases with dependent prepositions (*regardless of*), or phrases that require a certain verb form or sentence structure (*find* (sth) *strange* (+ *that*)).

### Phrasal verbs

**Phrasal verbs** consist of a verb (*take, come, look*, etc.) plus a particle. The particle can be an adverb (*away, down*, etc.) or a preposition (*in, on*, etc.). Remember that some phrasal verbs have more than one meaning; in the tables, the meaning given for the phrasal verb always matches the one used in the unit.

### These are the main types of phrasal verbs:

**Type 1: the verb is transitive (has an object). When the object is a noun, we can put the particle before or after the noun:**

*I'll **sort** the CDs **out**. / I'll **sort out** the CDs.*

And when the object is a pronoun, the pronoun **must** separate the two parts of the phrasal verb:

✔ *I'll **sort** them **out**.*
✘ *I'll **sort out** them.*

**Type 2: the verb is intransitive (does not have an object) and you cannot separate the two parts of the verb:**

✔ *It's hard to **get by** without a job.*
✘ *It's hard to **get** without a job **by**.*

**!** Some phrasal verbs may have different meanings when they are used transitively or intransitively:

*I started to **drop off** during the lesson. (= fall asleep)*

*I'll **drop** the money **off** at your house tomorrow. (= deliver)*

**Type 3: the verb is transitive (has an object) but you cannot separate the two parts of the verb:**

✔ *I **came across** some old photos in the cupboard.*
✘ *I **came** some old photos **across** in the cupboard.*

✔ *In the end Harley **went for** the black jeans.*
✘ *In the end Harley **went** the black jeans **for**.*

**Type 4: the phrasal verb is three words – verb + adverb particle + preposition:**

*Why do you **put up with** his behaviour?*

**!** These phrasal verbs are always transitive and you can never separate the words with an object or pronoun:

✔ *He **got away with** the robbery.*
✘ *He **got** the robbery **away with**.*

Throughout the *Vocabulary reference*, you will see various abbreviations. This key explains what they all mean.

**KEY:** adj = adjective; adv = adverb; n = noun; ex = exclamation; p = preposition; phr = phrase; pl = plural; sb = somebody; sth = something; swh = somewhere; US = American English; v = verb

# UNIT 1

## WORD FORMATION | Adjectives with *-able / -ible*

| Core word | Derivatives |
|---|---|
| **access** (n) | (in)accessible (adj), (in)accessibility (n) |
| **admire** (v) | admirable (adj), admirer (n) |
| **advise** (v) | (in)advisable (adj), advice (n), adviser (n), advisor (US, n) |
| **believe** (v) | (un)believable (adj), belief (n), believer (n), unbelievably (adv) |
| **fashion** (n) | (un)fashionable (adj), (un)fashionably (adv) |
| **horror** (n) | horrible (adj), horrific (adj), horribly (adv), horrifically (adv) |
| **identify** (v) | (un)identifiable (adj), identification (n) |
| **permit** (v) | permissible (adj), permission (n) |
| **reason** (n) | (un)reasonable (adj), reasoning (n), (un)reasonably (adv) |
| **reverse** (v/n) | (ir)reversible (adj) |
| **sense** (v/n) | sensible (adj), sensibility (n), sensibly (adv) |
| **terror** (n) | terrible (adj), terrific (adj), terribly (adv), terrifically (adv) |

## COLLOCATIONS | Collocations with *come, do, make* or *take*

| Collocation | Example sentence |
|---|---|
| **come to an agreement** | My parents and I came to an agreement about my internet use. |
| **come to a/the decision** | I've come to a decision. I want to be a vlogger. |
| **do (sb's) best** | I know maths isn't your favourite subject, but do your best. |
| **do (sb) a favour** | Could you do me a favour and take notes for me in tomorrow's lesson? I can't be there. |
| **make progress** | We haven't finished the project yet but we're definitely making progress. |
| **take (sb's) advice** | Take my advice and spend less time on your computer. |
| **take (sb's) point** | Yes, I take your point about how important it is to exercise ... but I'm lazy! |

## TOPIC VOCABULARY | Words connected with *technology*

| Word | Example sentence |
|---|---|
| **fix** (n) | Is there a college course on how to fix broken laptops and mobile phones? |
| **gadget** (n) | Rex's new tablet is his favourite gadget. |
| **limit** (v) | Mum makes me limit my internet usage to two hours a day. |
| **mend** (v) | Becki dropped her phone and it stopped working, so she's taking it to the shop to see if they can mend it. |
| **on the internet** (phr) | How long do you usually spend on the internet each evening? |
| **online** (adj) | I'm going to use an online dictionary to help me with my homework. |
| **post on** (v) | Will always posts photos of his dinner on Facebook. |
| **repair** (v) | It cost a lot for the technician to repair my broken laptop but it works perfectly again now. |
| **switch off** (v) | Remember to switch off the TV and your computer before you go to bed. |
| **turn off** (v) | How do I turn off the sound on this phone? |
| **upload to** (v) | Don't forget to upload the photos to Instagram so I can see them! |

# UNIT 2

## TOPIC VOCABULARY | Words connected with *education/learning*

| Word | Example sentence |
|---|---|
| **accomplish** (v) | You look busy – have you accomplished a lot today? |
| **achieve** (v) | Joe hopes to get 100% in maths? How is he going to achieve that? |
| **beat** (v) | We'll win the championship if we beat *City* on Saturday. |
| **come first** (phr) | I'm sorry you didn't run fast enough to come first this time, but you did really well. |
| **come last** (phr) | Dan didn't train at all, so it's not surprising that he came last in the swimming race. |
| **fail** (v) | Mia failed the science exam and has to take it again in September. |
| **lose** (v) | Sam's good at tennis; I'm sure he won't lose the match. |
| **manage (to)** (v) | Tess managed to finish her history project on time even though she was ill. |
| **overcome** (v) | I'm nervous about exams but I've tried to overcome my anxiety and stop worrying. |
| **progress** (v) | Lewis has worked hard and is progressing well in English this year. |
| **succeed in** (v) | Did you succeed in learning how to juggle with five balls at the same time? |
| **suffer** (v) | Joshua suffers from a fear of heights. |

## WORD FORMATION | Adjectives with *-ful / -ive*

| Core word | Derivatives |
|---|---|
| **act** (v/n) | activate (v), (in)active (adj), acting (n), (in)action (n), (in) activity (n), actor (n), actress (n), actively (adv) |
| **attract** (v) | (un)attractive (adj), attraction (n), (un)attractively (adv) |
| **create** (v) | creative (adj), creativity (n), creation (n), creator (n), creatively (adv) |
| **effect** (v) | (in)effective (adj), (in)effectual (adj), effect (n) |
| **harm** (v/n) | harmful (adj), harmless (adj), harmfully (adv), harmlessly (adv) |
| **pain** (n) | painful (adj), painless (adj), painfully (adv), painlessly (adv) |
| **play** (v/n) | playful (adj), player (n) |
| **product** (n) | produce (v), producer (n), (un)productive (adj), production (n), (un)productively (adv) |
| **secret** (n) | secrete (v), secretive (adj) |
| **stress** (v/n) | stressful (adj) |
| **thank** (v) | thankful (adj), thankless (adj), thankfully (adv) |
| **use** (v/n) | useful (adj), useless (adj), user (n), usefully (adv), uselessly (adv) |

## PHRASAL VERBS

| Phrasal verb | Meaning | Example sentence |
|---|---|---|
| **build up** (Type 1) | increase | Jack's started doing weights to build up the muscle strength in his arms. |
| **carry out** (Type 1) | follow, e.g. instructions | Employees have to carry out the orders their bosses give them. |
| **do without** (Type 3) | survive without having | There's no way I could do without my mobile phone for a whole week. |
| **end up** (Type 2) | eventually arrive/ reach/happen | We took a wrong turning and ended up by a river. |
| **get on with** (Type 4) | make progress | How are you getting on with your new vlog? |
| **get up to** (Type 4) | do | What are you girls getting up to? Are you behaving? |
| **go about** (Type 3) | start and continue in the right way | How should I go about finding a part-time job? |
| **put up with** (Type 4) | accept, allow | This school won't put up with any bullying. |

# UNIT 3

## WORD FORMATION | Nouns with *-ity / -ness*

| Core word | Derivatives |
| --- | --- |
| **active** (adj) | activate (v), inactive (adj), acting (n), (in)action (n), (in)activity (n), actor (n), actress (n), actively (adv) |
| **aware** (adj) | unaware (adj), awareness (n) |
| **clever** (adj) | cleverness (n), cleverly (adv) |
| **complex** (adj) | complexity (n) |
| **creative** (adj) | create (v), creativity (n), creation (n), creator (n), creatively (adv) |
| **happy** (adj) | unhappy (adj), (un)happiness (n), (un)happily (adv) |
| **open** (adj) | openness (n), openly (adv) |
| **original** (adj) | originality (n), origin (n), originator (n) |
| **popular** (adj) | unpopular (adj), (un)popularity (n), popularly (adv) |
| **simple** (adj) | simplify (v), simplicity (n), simply (adv) |
| **weak** (adj) | weaken (v), weakness (n), weakly (adv) |
| **youthful** (adj) | young (adj), youngster (n), youth (n), youthfulness (n) |

## COLLOCATIONS | Collocations with verbs

| Collocation | Example sentence |
| --- | --- |
| **do good** | Watching less TV is definitely doing me good! |
| **find (sth) funny** | To be honest, I don't find Dad's jokes funny. |
| **go online** | We need to go online to find more information for our media project. |
| **have a friend round** | Let's have friends round tomorrow instead of going out. |
| **make fun of** | Please don't make fun of the way I dance! |
| **take a break** | You've worked really hard; it's time to take a break now. |
| **take part in** | Eddie would love to take part in a film one day. |
| **tell jokes** | Belle's good at telling jokes; she always makes me laugh. |

## TOPIC VOCABULARY | *TV programmes*

| Word | Example sentence |
| --- | --- |
| **chat show** (n) | This chat show's boring because they never have any young guests on. |
| **cookery show** (n) | Mum watches lots of cookery shows then makes the recipes at home for us to try. |
| **documentary** (n) | My favourite documentaries are the ones about wild animals. |
| **game show** (n) | I don't like all game shows, but I love things like *The Cube* and *Who Wants to be a Millionaire*. |
| **music show** (n) | I think it's more fun going to see music shows at the theatre than watching them on TV. |
| **reality show** (n) | The best reality shows are the ones where the contestants have to do something dangerous. |
| **sitcom** (n) | Sitcoms are funny, but do you think they're true to life? |
| **soap opera** (n) | Mum never misses her favourite soap opera and she talks about the characters as if they're real. |
| **talent show** (n) | You've got a fantastic voice; you should enter a talent show. |
| **the news** (n) | It's important to watch the news and keep up to date with what's happening in the world. |
| **weather forecast** (n) | The weather forecast said it was going to be sunny today, so why is it raining? |
| **wildlife programme** (n) | What I love most about wildlife programmes is the amazing photography. |

# UNIT 4

## TOPIC VOCABULARY | *Places in the city*

| Word | Example sentence |
| --- | --- |
| **attraction** (n) | One of the main tourist attractions in this capital city is the London Eye, also known as the Millennium Wheel. |
| **block of flats** (n) | Billie lives on the tenth floor of that block of flats. |
| **car park** (n) | You will pay a lot to leave your car in a city centre car park overnight. |
| **city centre** (n) | Most of the best shops are in the city centre. |
| **department store** (n) | Bloomingdales is one of the most famous department stores in New York. |
| **office block** (n) | Is that building just an office block or are there some flats in there as well? |
| **parking space** (n) | You won't find any parking spaces on the roads near the centre of town. |
| **services** (n, pl) | In some cities, people pay a lot for services like rubbish collection and street lighting. |
| **shopping centre** (n) | Let's get a bus to that huge shopping centre in the suburbs and look for everything there. |
| **suburbs** (n, pl) | Niall lives in the suburbs so he cycles into the city centre to get to his office each day. |
| **the subway** (n) | Over 5 million people travel on the New York subway each week! |
| **the tube** (n) | I'd rather walk to Piccadilly Circus than go underground and get the Tube. |

## WORD PATTERNS | Words + prepositions

| Core word | Example sentence |
| --- | --- |
| **covered with** | My birthday cake was covered with delicious chocolate. |
| **fed up** (of/ about/with sth) | I am fed up of people telling me what to do. |
| **dispose of** | Where can I dispose of my old batteries? |
| **have no intention of** (doing sth) | I have no intention of doing any more studying today. |
| **find a solution to** | She helped me find a solution to the problem I was having with my laptop. |
| **regardless of** | I will play football tomorrow regardless of the weather. |

## WORD FORMATION | Adjectives/nouns/verbs

| Core word | Derivatives |
| --- | --- |
| **able** (adj) | unable (adj), capable (adj), ability (n), (dis/in)ability (n), capability (n) |
| **advantage** (n) | advantageous (adj), disadvantage (n) |
| **agree** (v) | disagree (v), (dis)agreeable (adj), (dis)agreement (n) |
| **appear** (v) | disappear (v), reappear (v), apparent (adj), (dis/re) appearance (n), apparently (adv) |
| **aware** (adj) | unaware (adj), awareness (n) |
| **believe** (v) | (un)believable (adj), belief (n), believer (n), unbelievably (adv) |
| **comfort** (v/n) | (un)comfortable (adj), discomfort (n), (un)comfortably (adv) |
| **secure** (v/adj) | insecure (adj), (in)security (n), (in)securely (adv) |

# UNIT 5

## WORD FORMATION | Verbs/adjectives with *-ate*

| Core word | Derivatives |
|---|---|
| **active** (adj) | activate (v), (in)active (adj), acting (n), activation (n), (in)action (n), (in)activity (n), actor (n), actress (n), actively (adv) |
| **affection** (n) | affectionate (adj), affectionately (adv) |
| **consider** (v) | (in)considerate (adj), consideration (n), (in)considerately (adv) |
| **décor** (n) | decorate (v), decoration (n), decorator (n) |
| **despair** (v/n) | desperate (adj), desperation (n) |
| **equal** (v/adj) | equate (v), (in)equality (n), equally (adv) |
| **fortune** (n) | (un)fortunate (adj), misfortune (n), (un)fortunately (adv) |
| **motive** (n) | (de)motivate (v), (de)motivation (n), motivational (adj), motivator (n) |
| **special** (adj) | specialise (v)/specialize (US/v), specialisation (n)/ specialization (US/n), specialism (n), speciality (n), specialist (n), (e)specially (adv) |
| **stimulus** (n) | stimulate (v), stimulating (adj), stimulation (n) |
| **value** (v/n) | undervalue (v), overvalue (v), evaluate (v), (in)valuable (adj), evaluation (n), valuables (n) |

## PHRASAL VERBS

| Phrasal verb | Meaning | Example sentence |
|---|---|---|
| **drop off** (Type 2) | fall asleep | Dad was watching TV and dropped off on the sofa. |
| **feel up to doing** (Type 4) | feel well enough to do sth | I felt so ill yesterday I didn't feel up to getting out of bed. |
| **get (sb) down** (Type 2) | make sb feel upset or depressed | Hearing that terrible news today really got me down. |
| **let (sb) off** (Type 1) | not punish | Mr Tibbs caught me texting in class but let me off with a warning. |
| **look back (on)** (Type 2) | think about sth from the past | When Dad looks back on his childhood, he's amazed by how little technology there was then. |
| **put (sb) down** (Type 1) | say negative things to/about sb | Don't put Ben down just because he's not very good at history. |
| **sort out** (Type 1) | solve, resolve | Let's sort out who's sleeping on the sofa and who's in the tent. |
| **stand for** (Type 3) | put up with, tolerate | I won't stand for rudeness in my classroom, Alex. |

## TOPIC VOCABULARY | *Hobbies*

| Word | Example sentence |
|---|---|
| **blogging** (n) | If you're interested in blogging, you need to think how to make your blog interesting. |
| **board game** (n) | My family and I love playing traditional board games like *Monopoly* and *Cluedo*. |
| **DJing** (n) | Joe's hobby is Djing, which means we frequently hear music coming from his bedroom. |
| **martial arts** (n, pl) | They say that doing martial arts is good for your body and your mind. |
| **mountain biking** (n) | Mum knows I want to go mountain biking but she's worried that I'll hurt myself. |
| **online gaming** (n) | How many hours do you spend at your computer online gaming each week? |
| **painting** (n) | I wish I was good at painting but unfortunately I'm simply not artistic at all. |
| **photography** (n) | Digital cameras have made photography a lot easier; everyone can take good photos now! |
| **programming** (n) | Becki is doing a course on programming then she hopes to get a job in the gaming industry. |
| **scuba diving** (n) | Have you ever been scuba diving and seen all the brightly coloured fish that live underwater? |
| **social networking** (n) | Flo's a big fan of social networking and says that it's helped her to make new friends all over the world. |
| **yoga** (n) | Yoga helps you to relax and it's good exercise as well. |

# UNIT 6

## WORD PATTERNS | Words + prepositions

| Core words | Example sentence |
|---|---|
| **addicted to** | George goes running every day – he's addicted to exercise! |
| **advise against** | Our PE teacher advises against exercising right after a big meal. |
| **allergic to** | I'm allergic to strawberries so when I eat them, my face goes red and spotty. |
| **approve of** | Do you approve of people who never do any exercise and eat fast food every day? |
| **based on** | Mum's plan for healthy meals is based on the idea that fruit and vegetables are good for you. |
| **cure for** | Do you think scientists will find a cure for all diseases one day? |
| **date back to** | Grandma says her recipe for apple pie dates back to the 19th century! |
| **get rid of** | What can I do to get rid of a headache without taking any pills? |

## WORD FORMATION | Adverbs formed from adjectives

| Core word | Derivatives |
|---|---|
| **accident** (n) | accidental (adj), accidentally (adv) |
| **anxious** (adj) | anxiety (n), anxiously (adv) |
| **automatic** (adj) | automatically (adv) |
| **basic** (adj) | basically (adv) |
| **believe** (v) | (un)believable (adj), belief (n), believer (n), unbelievably (adv) |
| **cheer** (v/n) | cheerful (adj), cheerfully (adv) |
| **comfort** (n) | (un)comfortable (adj), discomfort (n), (un)comfortably (adv) |
| **current** (adj/n) | currently (adv) |
| **day** (n) | everyday (adj), midday (n), today (n), daily (adv) |
| **easy** (adj) | (un)ease (n), easily (adv) |
| **fast** (adj/adv) | fasten (v) |
| **frequent** (v/adj) | infrequent (adj), frequency (n), (in)frequently (adv) |
| **good** (adj/n) | better (adj/adv), best (adj/adv), goodness (n/ex), well (adj/adv) |
| **gradual** (adj) | gradually (adv) |
| **happy** (adj) | unhappy (adj), (un)happiness (n), (un)happily (adv) |
| **hope** (v/n) | hopeful (adj), hopeless (adj), hopefully (adv), hopelessly (adv) |
| **ordinary** (adj) | extraordinary (adj), (extra)ordinarily (adv) |
| **regular** (adj) | irregular (adj), regularity (n), (ir)regularly (adv) |
| **relate** (v) | relative (adj/n), relation (n), relationship (n), relatively (adv) |
| **remark** (v/n) | (un)remarkable (adj), (un)remarkably (adv) |
| **short** (adj) | shortness (n), shortage (n), shortly (adv) |
| **surprise** (v/n) | (un)surprising (adj), (un)surprisingly (adv) |
| **tradition** (n) | traditional (adj), traditionally (adv) |
| **true** (adj) | untrue (adj), truth (n), truly (adv) |

## TOPIC VOCABULARY | Words connected with *health*

| Word | Example sentence |
|---|---|
| **allergy** (n) | Some of my classmates have an allergy to nuts. |
| **bruise** (v/n) | How did you get that bruise on your leg? |
| **burn** (v/n) | Be careful you don't burn your hand on the oven! |
| **cold** (n) | Mum says I should stay in bed and drink lots if I've got a cold. |
| **cramp** (n) | It can be dangerous if you get cramp while you're swimming. |
| **cut** (v/n) | Ollie cut his finger while he was chopping the onions. |
| **fever** (n) | I feel hot, then cold, then hot again – I think I've got a fever. |
| **flu** (n) | Callum was in bed for ten days when he had the flu. |
| **temperature** (n) | Your temperature ought to be about 37° Celsius, not 39! |
| **throat** (n) | It can be difficult to talk properly when your throat is sore. |
| **sprain** (v/n) | Katia can't walk because she sprained her ankle playing tennis yesterday. |
| **virus** (n) | Four of my classmates are off school today and they're all suffering from the same virus. |

# UNIT 7

## TOPIC VOCABULARY | Words connected with *friendship*

| Word | Example sentence |
|---|---|
| **admire** (v) | I think it's important to tell the truth and I admire honesty in a friend. |
| **appreciate** (v) | Thanks for all your help – I really appreciate it. |
| **confide in** (phr v) | If you're worried about something, you can confide in me and I'll try to help. |
| **count on** (phr v) | Robyn is a great friend and I know I can count on her if I have a problem. |
| **forgive** (v) | I can't forgive Frazer for saying those unkind things about me. |
| **get on** (phr v) | Grace is so nice that everyone at school gets on with her. |
| **gossip** (v/n) | Anna and Lisa always gossip about everyone, and now nobody wants to be their friend. |
| **lose touch** (phr) | Mylene and I are best friends and we'll never lose touch! |
| **make friends** (phr) | Sometimes it's hard to make friends when you start a new school. |
| **rely on** (phr v) | Can I rely on you to help organise Mum's surprise birthday party? |
| **share** (v/n) | I left my lunchbox on the bus but Harry shared his sandwiches with me. |
| **support** (v/n) | A good friend will support you when you're feeling sad or anxious. |

## WORD FORMATION | Nouns with *-ance / -ence / -ment / -ship*

| Core word | Derivatives |
|---|---|
| **assist** (v) | assistance (n), assistant (n) |
| **develop** (v) | developing (adj), (un)developed (adj), development (n), developer (n) |
| **encourage** (v) | encouraging (adj), encouragement (n) |
| **exist** (v) | existing (adj), existence (n) |
| **friend** (n) | (un)friendliness (adj), (un)friendly (adj), friendship (n) |
| **member** (n) | membership (n) |
| **partner** (v/n) | partnership (n) |
| **perform** (v) | performance (n), performer (n) |
| **prefer** (v) | preferable (adj), preference (n), preferably (adv) |
| **relation** (n) | relate (v), relative (adj/n), relation (n), relationship (n), relatively (adv) |

## PHRASAL VERBS

| Phrasal verb | Meaning | Example sentence |
|---|---|---|
| **drop in (on)** (Type 4) | visit, often on the way to somewhere else | I'm going to drop in on Mrs Wiggins on the way home and check she's OK. |
| **get along with** (Type 4) | have a good relationship with | Do you get along well with Leah? |
| **go round (to)** (Type 3) | visit | What time are you going round to Ryan's this evening? |
| **keep on** (Type 3) | continue | Simon, if you keep on talking, I'm going to have to report you to the headteacher. |
| **look up to** (Type 4) | admire, respect | I really look up to my grandpa. He's an amazing man. |
| **rip up** (Type 1) | tear into pieces | She read the note and then ripped it up so no-one else could read it. |
| **run after** (Type 3) | follow quickly | I had to run after the bus today and only just caught it. |
| **take after** (Type 3) | look or act like a parent, grandparent, etc. | Megan takes after her mother. They both have long dark hair. |

# UNIT 8

## TOPIC VOCABULARY | Words connected with *geographical features*

| Word | Example sentence |
|---|---|
| **cliff** (n) | This photo of the sea was taken from above when we were walking on the cliffs. |
| **coast** (n) | We're going to go to the coast next weekend so we can swim in the sea. |
| **mountain range** (n) | The Andes in South America is the longest mountain range in the world. |
| **path** (n) | We often walk along the path from our house to the river. |
| **slope** (n) | That looks like a good slope to ski down! |
| **stream** (n) | Sometimes you see small fish in this stream. |
| **summit** (n) | It took the climbers seven hours to get to the summit of the mountain. |
| **valley** (n) | You get a great view of the valley from that house on the top of the hill. |
| **volcano** (n) | Mount Fuji in Japan is one of the most famous volcanoes in the world. |
| **waterfall** (n) | Have you ever been to Niagara falls – it's a huge waterfall in Canada and America. |

## WORD FORMATION | Nouns formed from verbs

| Core word | Derivatives |
|---|---|
| **arrive** (v) | arrival (n) |
| **behave** (v) | misbehave (v), (mis)behaviour (n) |
| **choose** (v) | choosy (adj), choice (n) |
| **conclude** (v) | (in)conclusive (adj), conclusion (n), (in)conclusively (adv) |
| **decide** (v) | (in)decisive (adj), undecided (adj), decision (n), (in)decisively (adv) |
| **depart** (v) | departure (n) |
| **describe** (v) | description (n) |
| **solve** (v) | dissolve (v), solvable (adj), solution (n) |
| **vary** (v) | various (adj), (in)variable (adj), varying (adj), variation (n), variety (n), invariably (adv) |

## WORD PATTERNS | Words + prepositions

| Core words | Example sentence |
|---|---|
| **crash into** | You can borrow my bike but be careful you don't crash into anything! |
| **lack in** | Rylan is lacking in experience, so he'll need some help putting up the tent. |
| **optimistic about** | Do you feel optimistic about your trip or are you nervous? |
| **purpose of** | I know what this yellow rope's for, but what's the purpose of the red one? |
| **shelter from** | You're not wet! Where did you shelter from the rain? |
| **specialise in** | Our sports teacher specialises in running and swimming. |
| **warn against** | My parents warned me against going climbing because they were worried I'd get injured. |
| **wrong with** | This soup tastes strange – is there something wrong with it? |

# UNIT 9

## TOPIC VOCABULARY | Idioms connected with *music*

| Idiom | Example sentence |
|---|---|
| **as fit as a fiddle** | Granddad is 85 but he's as fit as a fiddle and still goes jogging! |
| **blow (your, his, etc.) own trumpet** | Max is always blowing his own trumpet and saying how good he is at everything. |
| **change (you're her, etc.) tune** | You've changed your tune – yesterday you said you hated fast food and now you're eating a burger! |
| **drum up support** | My friends and I are trying to drum up support for our local animal charity. |
| **face the music** | I know Mum will be cross but let's tell her what's happened and face the music. |
| **make a song and dance about** | When I told Dad I'd lost his mobile phone, he made a huge song and dance about it. |
| **play it by ear** | I'm not sure what we're doing on Saturday but we can play it by ear depending on the weather |
| **ring a bell** | I think you've told me about Lucia before because the name rings a bell. |

## PHRASAL VERBS

| Phrasal verb | Meaning | Example sentence |
|---|---|---|
| **come up** (Type 2) | happen soon | Your birthday's coming up, isn't it? |
| **drop out (of)** (Type 4) | leave, stop attending | Charlotte started at a local college, but didn't like it and dropped out after a couple of months. |
| **give away** (Type 1) | reveal | It's a fantastic film, but I don't want to give away the ending. |
| **go in for** (Type 4) | enter, e.g. a contest | I'm thinking of going in for the school music competition. |
| **go on to** (Type 2) | stop doing one thing and start another | He started by welcoming everyone, and then went on to introduce the new members of staff. |
| **knock out (of)** (Type 4) | defeat and remove from a competition | I took part last year but got knocked out in the semi-final. |
| **put on** (Type 1) | hold, perform, e.g. a show | Why don't we put on an end-of-term concert? |
| **take on** (Type 3) | accept, agree to do, e.g. responsibility, work, etc. | Have you got time to take on another small project, Caleb? |

## WORD FORMATION | Nouns with *-ant / -ist*

| Core word | Derivatives |
|---|---|
| **account** (v/n) | (un)accountable (adj), accountant (n) |
| **apply** (v) | reapply (v), applicable (adj), application (n), applicant (n), |
| **assist** (v) | assistance (n), assistant (n) |
| **attend** (v) | (in)attentive (adj), attendance (n), attention (n), attendant (n) |
| **consult** (v) | consultant (n) |
| **contest** (v/n) | contestant (n) |
| **cycle** (v/n) | cyclist (n) |
| **guitar** (n) | guitarist (n) |
| **journal** (n) | journalist (n) |
| **optimise** (v) | optimistic (adj), optimism (n), optimist (n), optimum (n) |
| **participate** (v) | participant (n) |
| **perfect** (v/adj) | imperfect (adj), (im)perfection (n), perfectionist (n), (im) perfectly (adv) |
| **piano** (n) | pianist (n) |
| **serve** (v) | service (v/n), servant (n) |
| **special** (adj) | specialise (v)/specialize (US/v), specialisation (n)/ specialization (US/n), specialism (n), speciality (n), specialist (n), (e)specially (adv) |
| **violin** (n) | violinist (n) |

# UNIT 10

## TOPIC VOCABULARY | *People in sport*

| Word | Example sentence |
|---|---|
| **captain** (n) | Aled's dream is to be captain of the England football team one day. |
| **coach** (n) | Our tennis coach makes us train hard every day. |
| **fundraiser** (n) | The charity has asked Lily to be a fundraiser and collect money for them. |
| **leader** (n) | William was the leader for the first 500 metres of the race then Rob ran past him. |
| **medic** (n) | Ellie has fallen and the medics are going over to make sure she's OK. |
| **participant** (n) | I'm watching the match because my brother is a participant. |
| **referee** (n) | Stop playing – the referee has blown his whistle! |
| **sponsor** (n) | Tod's running in the New York marathon and he needs sponsors. |
| **supporter** (n) | Amy loves animals and is a supporter of several animal charities. |
| **winner** (n) | Congratulations, Millie, you're the winner! |

## WORD FORMATION | Adjectives/nouns/verbs

| Core word | Derivatives |
|---|---|
| **deep** (adj) | deepen (v), depth (n), deeply (adv) |
| **high** (adj) | heighten (v), height (n), highly (adv) |
| **large** (adj) | enlarge (v), largeness (n), largely (adv) |
| **long** (adj) | lengthen (v), length (n) |
| **low** (adj) | lower (adj/v), lowness (adj) |
| **strong** (adj) | strengthen (v), strength (n), strongly (adv) |
| **wide** (adj) | widen (v), width (n), widely (adv) |

## IDIOMS | Phrases connected with running

| Idiom | Example sentence |
|---|---|
| **get off to a running start** | Ben seems to have got off to a running start in his new job. |
| **get (sth) up and running again** | We're trying to get the school blog up and running again. |
| **hit the ground running** | We need someone who knows the job, can start immediately and will hit the ground running. |
| **run a mile** | If Mum sees that spider, she'll run a mile! |
| **run off my feet** | We've been run off our feet all day and now we're exhausted. |
| **run the risk of (+ *-ing*)** | If you don't practise your lines for the play, you run the risk of forgetting them! |
| **running around in circles** | Everyone is running around in circles trying to organise tonight's party. |
| **try to run before (she, you, etc.) can walk** | I know you're keen to go out in a kayak on your own, but stop trying to run before you can walk! |

# UNIT 11

## WORD FORMATION | Nouns with *-er / -or*

| Core word | Derivatives |
|---|---|
| **act** (v/n) | activate (v), (in)active (adj), acting (n), activation (n), (in)action (n), (in)activity (n), actor (n), actress (n), actively (adv) |
| **administer** (v) | administrate (v), administration (n), administrator (n) |
| **advise** (v) | (in)advisable (adj), advice (n), adviser (n), advisor (US, n) |
| **build** (v) | rebuild (v), building (n), builder (n) |
| **comment** (v) | commentate (v), commentary (n), commentator (n) |
| **conduct** (v) | conductor (n) |
| **counsel** (v) | counsellor (n) |
| **direct** (v) | indirect (adj), direction (n), director (n), (in)directly (adv) |
| **edit** (v) | unedited (adj), edition (n), editorial (n), editor (n) |
| **inspect** (v) | inspection (n), inspector (n) |
| **invent** (v) | inventive (adj), invention (n), inventor (n) |
| **lecture** (v/n) | lecturer (n) |
| **manage** (v) | mismanage (v), (mis)management (n), manager (n), manageress (n) |
| **operate** (v) | operational (adj), operation (n), operator (n) |
| **present** (v/n) | presentation (n), presenter (n) |
| **produce** (v) | product (n), producer (n), (un)productive (adj), production (n), (un)productively (adv) |
| **report** (v/n) | reporter (n) |
| **sail** (v/n) | sailing (n), sailor (n) |
| **supervise** (v) | supervision (n), supervisor (n) |

## PHRASAL VERBS

| Phrasal verb | Meaning | Example sentence |
|---|---|---|
| **come (a)round to** (Type 4) | change your mind, start to like and value sth, or end up liking it after not liking it at first | I didn't want to go to a pizzeria for my birthday at first, but I'm coming round to the idea now. |
| **come up** (Type 2) | arise, appear, happen | A problem's come up at work so I'll be home late tonight. |
| **get by** (Type 2) | survive (often in terms of money, food, etc.) | It's very hard to get by if you don't have a job. |
| **get through** (Type 3) | succeed, finish | It was a three-hour exam, but I got through it without too many problems. |
| **put forward** (Type 1) | suggest, offer | Would anyone like to put themselves forward to be team captain this season? |
| **put through** (Type 1) | connect, e.g. on a phone | Excuse me, could you put me through to the complaints department, please? |
| **stand in for** (Type 4) | replace temporarily and represent | Mrs Pye's ill so Mr Barker's standing in for her today. |
| **take over** (Type 1) | take control of a company or organisation | Will we lose our jobs if another company takes over? |

## TOPIC VOCABULARY | Words connected with *work*

| Words | Example sentence |
|---|---|
| **be made redundant** (phr) | Tom was made redundant last week so he's looking for a new job. |
| **full-time** (adj) | Lexy's job is full-time and she has to work some weekends, too. |
| **give sb the sack** (phr) | If you don't do the job properly, the manager will give you the sack! |
| **overtime** (n) | Do you get paid extra if you stay late and work overtime? |
| **part-time** (adj) | Having a part-time job at weekends has helped Emma save up for her holidays. |
| **permanent** (adj) | Poppy isn't going to look for a permanent job until she gets back from her gap year. |
| **salary** (n) | Who gets a higher salary, police officers or teachers? |
| **shift** (n) | Mum is a nurse and this week she's working night shifts so we won't see her much. |
| **temporary** (adj) | You might find a temporary job at the farm over the summer. |
| **unemployed** (adj) | Since leaving college, Rose has been unemployed. |
| **vacancy** (n) | Are there any vacancies in the factory where you work? |
| **wages** (n, pl) | I don't think people who work in shops get very high wages. |

# UNIT 12

## WORD FORMATION | Nouns with *-ism*

| Core word | Derivatives |
|---|---|
| **capital** (n) | capitalism (n), capitalist (n) |
| **critic** (n) | criticise (v), critical (adj), criticism (n), critically (adv) |
| **favourite** (adj) | favour (v/n), favouritism (n) |
| **friend** (n) | (un)friendliness (adj), (un)friendly (adj), friendship (n) |
| **hero** (n) | heroic (adj), heroism (n), heroine (n), heroically (adv) |
| **ideal** (adj) | idealism (n), idealist (n), ideally (adv) |
| **race** (v/n) | racism (n), racist (n) |
| **tour** (v/n) | touristy (adj), tourism (n), tourist (n) |
| **vegetarian** (n) | vegetarianism (n) |

## COLLOCATIONS | Collocations with *do* and *make*

| Collocation | Example sentence |
|---|---|
| **do good** | Working as a volunteer will do Francesca good. |
| **do harm** | Hard work won't do you any harm! |
| **do the right thing** | Orla is a kind and considerate person who always tries to do the right thing. |
| **do (my, your, etc.) duty** | Helping to clean local parks is one way of doing your duty for your community. |
| **make a difference** | Even a small donation to the charity will make a difference. |
| **make an excuse** | Jordan forgot her homework again and made another silly excuse. |
| **make (sb) proud** | James made his parents very proud the day he received an award for bravery. |
| **make sense** | Studying when you feel tired doesn't make sense. |

## TOPIC VOCABULARY | Words connected with *describing people*

| Word | Example sentence |
|---|---|
| **careful** (adj) | Olivia loves bikes but she's a very careful cyclist. |
| **caring** (adj) | The best nurses are the ones who are caring towards their patients. |
| **famous** (adj) | Many vloggers have become famous as a result of their online videos. |
| **infamous** (adj) | Police have arrested a member of the infamous gang of computer hackers. |
| **kind** (adj) | The residents at the home where Oscar works really love him because he's so kind to them. |
| **ordinary** (adj) | Despite being rich and famous, famous, they live like ordinary people. |
| **polite** (adj) | The teacher insists that we're always polite to each other in class, even when we disagree. |
| **popular** (adj) | Alfie is the most popular boy in the class; everyone likes him. |
| **sensible** (adj) | Poppy's sensible and always gives good advice. |
| **sensitive** (adj) | She is very sensitive to changes in temperature. |
| **typical** (adj) | Is there really any such thing as a typical teenager? |
| **unknown** (adj) | An unknown man who rescued two children child from a house fire received an award. |

# WRITING REFERENCE

## AN ARTICLE | Example task

**You see this announcement on a website for teenagers:**

> **Articles wanted!**
>
> Do you live in a tourist destination?
>
> What does your local area have to offer tourists?
>
> Tell us why someone might want to visit your local area and what attractions they might enjoy.
>
> The best articles will appear on the website!

**Write your article.**

*Always give your article a title.*

*Rhetorical questions are a good way of engaging your reader.*

AN UNEXPECTED TOURIST DESTINATION

Do you always spend your holidays in the same old places? It's time to try something a bit different. My home town of Bolton, in the north of England, has lots to offer the adventurous tourist!

*Use a friendly, conversational style.*

*Use exclamation marks to add a sense of excitement where appropriate.*

The first stop on our tour of the town is the local museum. This dates back to 1939 and has a fantastic natural history section, with lots of animals and birds to look at. If you're interested in ancient history, you'll find the museum's collection of objects from Ancient Egypt absolutely fascinating.

*Speak directly to your readers, using 'you' and 'your' where appropriate.*

*Use a variety of sentence types, including conditionals where appropriate.*

After visiting the museum, perhaps you'd like to go shopping! The Market Place is a large shopping centre, which has all the big names. You can find some real bargains, as well as souvenirs of your visit.

*Use linking words and phrases.*

Finally, when you get hungry, Bolton is a great place to eat out. Whether you like Indian food, Chinese food or traditional British food, you'll find everything in Bolton town centre. Your only problem will be deciding which restaurant to choose!

*Give your opinion where appropriate.*

Bolton might not be on everyone's holiday list, but give it a chance and I'm sure you won't be disappointed!

**USEFUL PHRASES**

| Rhetorical questions | Introducing points in order | Introducing further points | Introducing your opinion |
|---|---|---|---|
| *Do you usually …?, Are you one of those people who …? Have you ever …? Do you ever …?* | *Firstly, First of all, To begin with, Secondly, Next, Finally,* | *Also, In addition to that, Having done that, Another point is that …, Apart from that* | *I'm sure that …, I tend to think that …, Personally, I believe that …, I'm sure you'll agree with me that …, In my view, In my opinion, If you ask me, …* |

# A REVIEW | Example task

**You see this advert in an international music magazine:**

## Reviews wanted!

We're looking for reviews of music websites. Do you know any bands that have a great website? What's good about it? What's not so good? Would you recommend the website to other young people?

The best articles will appear in the magazine!

**Write your review.**

*Always give your review a title.*

*Give background information and explain what you have done/seen/visited/etc.*

THE MAYDAYS' WEBSITE

The Maydays are a popular group that many young people love. Like many groups, they have their own website. I decided to check it out to see if it's as good as their music.

*Use linking words and phrases.*

*Use a friendly, conversational style.*

First of all, when you go to the website, you can easily see what's available. There are links to interviews with the band members and links to music videos. I thought it worked really well. However, I know the Maydays have released a new song and the video wasn't on the website yet, which was a little disappointing.

*Give your judgement and opinion where appropriate.*

*Mention negative points as well as positive points.*

There are also links to an area where you can buy merchandise – T-shirts, CDs and other things connected to the band. Although there were a lot of interesting products, I found the prices to be rather high. Their CDs are available for much less in other places online. Having said that, they had T-shirts that are only available from this website, and I expect some fans will pay whatever they ask.

*Use a variety of sentence types.*

I would certainly recommend this website to any young person who likes the Maydays. You need to be a true fan to pay some of the prices, though.

*Give your recommendations where appropriate.*

**USEFUL PHRASES**

| Expressing likes | Expressing dislikes | Making recommendations | Reviews of books | Reviews of films/TV programmes/plays | Reviews of shops, hotels, etc. |
|---|---|---|---|---|---|
| *I really liked …, I thought X worked well, I was really impressed by …, I was pleasantly surprised by …* | *I found X disappointing, I didn't really like …, I wasn't impressed by X at all* | *I would certainly recommend, I'm happy to recommend this X to …, I think young people would really enjoy this …* | *is based on, is set in, main character, written by, plot, ending* | *It stars, is set in, action, drama, X plays a …, the lead role, written by, plot, ending* | *location, good/poor service, good/poor range, run by, overpriced, reasonable prices, have to book in advance* |

# AN INFORMAL LETTER/EMAIL | Example task

**You have received a letter from your English-speaking penfriend.**

> I need your help! My teacher has asked me to write about a public holiday in another country. Can you tell me about a public holiday you like? What traditions do you have connected to that day? What happens? Why do you like it?
>
> Thanks for your help, and write soon!
>
> Oliver

**Write your letter.**

*Use an informal greeting with your friend's first name.*

*Don't start giving information immediately. Be polite and refer to something that has happened to your friend. Use your imagination.*

Hi Oliver!

It was great to hear from you. I'm so happy you had a good birthday. And I'm glad you got my card!

*Use informal language, including contractions and exclamation marks where appropriate.*

*Present any information you have been asked for.*

You asked about a public holiday. I'd say that Independence Day is my favourite public holiday. It takes place on 12th July each year and we celebrate the day my country became independent. That was 200 years ago, and Independence Day has been celebrated every year since then.

*Use a variety of tenses and sentence structures.*

On Independence Day, it's traditional to go to the mountains with your family and have a picnic. We eat a special cake, called a Victory Pie, which is baked with a coin inside. The person who gets the coin is supposed to be lucky for a year! After that we play games such as football.

*Add any further points you've been asked for. Check the question carefully to make sure you don't miss anything.*

I guess I like this holiday in particular because it's a time when the whole family gets together. Everyone is off work and off school and the weather is usually good because it's the summer. I love being with my family in the mountains, enjoying the sun and playing games.

*Give your personal response if the question asks for it.*

Anyway, I hope that helps!

Write soon!

Lots of love,

Alex

*Use informal closing expressions.*

*End the letter/email with your first name.*

**USEFUL PHRASES**

| Starting the letter/email | Referring to someone's news | Introducing points | Ending the letter/email |
|---|---|---|---|
| *Hi Oliver!, Dear Oliver,* asking about health: *How are you? I hope you're well. How are things?* | *I'm so glad to hear you passed your test / had a good birthday / got a new pet / had a good party / etc., I was very happy to read that …, Great news about your …* | *You asked about …, I'd say that …, First of all, Firstly, Secondly, Also, Oh, and another thing!, By the way, Guess what!* | *I have to go now. Got to go. Take care! Write soon! Love, Lots of love, All my love, Best wishes, All the best, Yours,* |

# A FORMAL LETTER/EMAIL | Example task

**You have a received this email from your school principal, Mrs Carter. Read this part of the email and then write your email to Mrs Carter.**

> **From:** Sue Carter
> **Subject:** Suggestions for end-of-year event
>
> As you know, we usually hold an end-of-year event for school leavers on the final Friday afternoon and evening of term. Each year, I ask students for their suggestions regarding what to do. Please email me before next Friday with any suggestions you have. Explain why I should choose your idea!

**Write your email.**

From: Izzy Hopkins Year 12
To: Mrs Carter

Dear Mrs Carter,

I'm writing in response to your email asking for suggestions for this year's end-of-year event for school leavers. I believe I have a great idea which everyone will enjoy.

Last year, you held a formal ball in the Sports Hall. As I understand it, everyone enjoyed it but people found buying or hiring their clothes very expensive.

I would like to suggest that this year we hold a dancing competition to raise money for a local charity. It would last from 2pm until 9pm, and people could be sponsored for each hour they keep dancing. Several of the students in Year 11 are good DJs, so they could bring their devices and provide the music. It could be a lot of fun, and raise money too. I have discussed this with all my friends in Year 12 and they fully support the idea.

Please let me know if you have any questions, or would like to discuss this further.

I'm looking forward to hearing what you decide.

Yours,
Izzy Hopkins
Year 12

*Use a formal greeting.*

*It is acceptable to use some contractions (e.g. I'm, I'll, etc.), particularly if you know the person you're writing to. However, your vocabulary, grammar and spelling should be more formal than in an informal letter.*

*Give your reason for writing in the first paragraph.*

*Make sure you fully answer the question.*

*Indirect questions sound more formal and polite than direct questions.*

*As appropriate, ask if they need further information, etc. in the final paragraph. It is acceptable for this paragraph to be very short – even just one sentence.*

*We often have two formal closing expressions.* I'm looking forward to *is slightly less formal and serious than* I look forward to. *It's fine to use with your school principal.*

*End the letter/email with your first and last name. Add any other relevant information, such as what year you're in at school, if it's appropriate.*

## USEFUL PHRASES

| Starting the letter/email | Explaining why you're writing | Making suggestions | Inviting | Asking if they need anything | Ending the letter/email line 1 | Ending the letter/email line 2 |
|---|---|---|---|---|---|---|
| *Dear* + *Mr/Mrs/Miss/Dr* + surname, followed by a comma | *I am writing with regard to …, I am writing regarding …, I'm writing in order to …, I am writing in response to…* | *I would like to suggest (that) …, You may/might wish to consider …, One option would be …, Could I suggest …?* | *I would like to invite you to …, We would be very grateful if you'd consider attending …, I wonder if you would be able to attend …* | *Please let me know if you …, If you …, please let me know immediately.* | *I look forward to hearing from you., I'm looking forward to hearing from you soon., I am looking forward to hearing what you decide.* | *Yours, Yours sincerely, Regards, Warmest regards, Best regards,* |

# A STORY | Example task

**You have seen this announcement in an international magazine for teenagers.**

> ## Stories wanted
>
> Write a story for our magazine. Your story must begin with this sentence:
> *William put down his mobile phone and wondered what to do.*
> Your story must include:
>
> - a disagreement
> - a solution

**Write your story.**

*If you are given the first sentence, you can't change it in any way.*

*Always give your story a title.*

*Don't start writing until you've worked out the plot. Here, the writer noted this down before starting on the second sentence:* just got a text message – concert – wants to go but can't – disagrees with person texting/calling him – solution: Skype the concert

THE CONCERT

William put down his mobile phone and wondered what to do. Unable to make a decision, he looked at Callum's text message again: 'The Cowgirls have just turned up in the town square. Come down now! They're about to give a free concert!'

The Cowgirls were William's favourite band in the world. He had posters of them all over his bedroom wall. The problem was that he had promised to stay with his little sister Bella, who was ill in bed, while his parents went shopping.

William's phone rang. It was Callum. 'Come on, Will! They're starting in a few minutes. You've got to come.' William made his decision. He couldn't leave his sister.
'I can't, Callum. Sorry.'
'You're crazy! Don't be stupid! You've got to come!' said Callum.
'Callum, I can't.'
'Well, I think you're mad – but if you won't come, let's try this. I'll Skype you, and you can watch the concert live.'

And that's what they did. William – and his little sister – watched the Cowgirls sing all their hits live, from Bella's bedroom. It wasn't quite as good as being there – but nearly.

*Use appropriate tenses, such as past simple, past continuous and past perfect, and a range of grammatical structures, such as relative clauses.*

*Try to include some direct speech in your story if you can. Use speech marks. Remember that direct speech is usually informal.*

*Where appropriate/ necessary, show who said something.*

*If you have a conversation in direct speech, start each speaker on a new line. Even though it's a new line, you can still consider it part of the same paragraph.*

*The question said you have to include a solution. Make sure you remember to include what you have to. Plan this carefully before you start writing.*

*The question said you have to include a disagreement. Make sure you remember to include what you have to. Plan this carefully before you start writing.*

**USEFUL PHRASES**

| Time phrases | Creating drama | Verbs with direct/indirect speech | Concluding |
|---|---|---|---|
| *It had all begun …, Shortly afterwards, Some time later, Eventually, Finally, In the end,* | *All of a sudden, Without warning, Suddenly, Just like that* | *ask, cry, lie, promise, say, scream, shout, tell, think, whisper, wonder* | *In the end, And that's what they did., When it was all over,* |

# AN ESSAY | Example task

**In your English class you have been talking about education. Now your English teacher has asked you to write an essay for homework.**

**'Everyone should stay in education until at least the age of 18.'**
**Do you agree?**

**Notes**

Write about: 1 different types of skill/ability
2 earning money
3 .......................... (your own idea)

**Write your essay using all the notes and giving reasons for your point of view.**

*Create a serious and formal tone by using formal grammar, vocabulary and punctuation. This is not an article for your friends. It's a piece of academic writing for your teacher.*

*Introduce the topic in the first paragraph.*

Countries have different rules about when school leavers are allowed to leave the education system. In some countries, such as Angola, students can stop attending school from the age of 12. In Germany and Turkey, for example, they have to remain in some kind of education until 18.

*Give examples, and use appropriate phrases to do so.*

*Make contrasts, and use appropriate phrases to do so.*

Some people are very academic and succeed in traditional subjects at school, whereas others are more practical. They may not be good at maths, but they might be fantastic builders or DJs. If they stay at school until 18, they might waste time and become bored. Secondly, some teenagers would prefer to start earning money from the age of 16.

*Make a number of points, and use appropriate phrases to do so.*

*Express your personal opinion, or the opinions of others if required, and use appropriate phrases to do so.*

Because of this, I believe that not everyone is suited to school until they're 18. In my view, however, the government should provide them with more practical education if they want it until they're 18.

*Give reasons, express results and draw conclusions as required. Use appropriate phrases to do so.*

*Make sure you include your own idea if you're asked to.*

To conclude, I would argue that not every teenager should have to stay at school until the age of 18. However, in my opinion, every teenager has the right to some kind of relevant education up to the age of 18.

*Come to a conclusion, and use an appropriate phrase to do so, in the final paragraph.*

**USEFUL PHRASES**

| Listing points | Giving examples | Expressing contrast | Expressing results, giving reasons, drawing conclusions | Expressing your opinion | Expressing someone else's opinion | Concluding and summarising |
|---|---|---|---|---|---|---|
| *First, Firstly, First of all, To begin with, Second, Secondly, Third, Thirdly, What's more, Additionally, In addition (to this), Apart from that, Moreover, Furthermore* | *such as, like, for example, for instance* | *However, In contrast, Having said that, but, although, even though, in spite of, despite, On the one hand …, On the other hand …* | *Because of this, Consequently, For this reason, As a result, so, Therefore, This is the main reason why …,* | *In my opinion, In my view, To my mind, Personally, It seems to me (that) …, It is my view (that) …, I would argue (that)* | *According to …, Some people say (that) …, It is said (that) …, It has been said (that) …* | *To conclude, In conclusion, To summarise, To sum up, In summary …* |

# IRREGULAR VERBS REFERENCE

| Bare infinitive | Past simple | Past participle |
|---|---|---|
| be | was/were | been |
| beat | beat | beaten |
| become | became | become |
| begin | began | begun |
| bend | bent | bent |
| bite | bit | bitten |
| blow | blew | blown |
| break | broke | broken |
| bring | brought | brought |
| build | built | built |
| buy | bought | bought |
| catch | caught | caught |
| choose | chose | chosen |
| come | came | come |
| cost | cost | cost |
| cut | cut | cut |
| deal | dealt | dealt |
| do | did | done |
| drink | drank | drunk |
| drive | drove | driven |
| eat | ate | eaten |
| fall | fell | fallen |
| feed | fed | fed |
| feel | felt | felt |
| fight | fought | fought |
| find | found | found |
| forget | forgot | forgotten |
| get | got | got |
| give | gave | given |
| go | went | gone |
| grow | grew | grown |
| hang | hung | hung |
| have | had | had |
| hear | heard | heard |
| hit | hit | hit |
| hold | held | held |
| hurt | hurt | hurt |
| keep | kept | kept |
| know | knew | known |
| lead | led | led |

| Bare infinitive | Past simple | Past participle |
|---|---|---|
| leave | left | left |
| lend | lent | lent |
| let | let | let |
| lie | lay | lain |
| lose | lost | lost |
| make | made | made |
| mean | meant | meant |
| meet | met | met |
| pay | paid | paid |
| put | put | put |
| read | read | read |
| ride | rode | ridden |
| ring | rang | rung |
| run | ran | run |
| say | said | said |
| see | saw | seen |
| sell | sold | sold |
| send | sent | sent |
| set | set | set |
| shine | shone | shone |
| show | showed | shown |
| sit | sat | sat |
| sleep | slept | slept |
| speak | spoke | spoken |
| spend | spent | spent |
| spring | sprang | sprung |
| stand | stood | stood |
| steal | stole | stolen |
| stick | stuck | stuck |
| swim | swam | swum |
| take | took | taken |
| teach | taught | taught |
| tell | told | told |
| think | thought | thought |
| tread | trod | trodden |
| understand | understood | understood |
| wear | wore | worn |
| win | won | won |
| write | wrote | written |

Macmillan Education Limited
4 Crinan Street
London N1 9XW

Companies and representatives throughout the world

ISBN 978-0-230-48860-1


Written by Malcolm Mann and Steve Taylore-Knowles



First published 2017



Designed by Designers Collective
Cover design by Designers Collective
Cover photograph by **Getty Images**/Lisa Gagne; **Shutterstock**/ mexrix(background)
Picture research by Victoria Gaunt, Emily Taylor

Authors' acknowledgements
Malcolm and Steve would like to thank the team at Macmillan and all the many teachers and students around the world who helped make this wonderful project possible.

The publishers would like to thank the course consultant Karen Ludlow.

The authors and publishers would like to thank the following for permission to reproduce their photographs: **Alamy**/Dan Atkin p125, Alamy/Blend Images p126, Alamy/ephotocorp p63, Alamy/Hero Images Inc p141(br), Alamy/Juniors Bildarchiv GmbH p129, Alamy/Kzenon p97, Alamy/Marc Macdonald p106, Alamy/MBI p130, Alamy/Michael Spring p39, Alamy/Stock Connection Blue p95, Alamy/Alireza Teimoury p82, Alamy/Tetra Images p75, Alamy/Steve Vidler p109, Alamy/David White p29, Alamy/YAY Media AS p34(icon); **Cater News**/QMI p5; **Corbis**/ Markus Altmann p132(t), Corbis/Ian Lishman/Juice Images p120(l); **Getty Images** p66, Getty Images/AFP p104, Getty Images/Ascent/PKS Media Inc. pp26(tm), 81, Getty Images/Ezra Bailey p71, Getty Images/ Mehmet Hilmi Barcin p62, Getty Images/Bigshots p141(tl), Getty Images/ Blend Images - KidStock p56, Getty Images/Lisa-Blue p61, Getty Images/ Paul Bradbury p127, Getty Images/BSIP/UIGCA p131, Getty Images/ Buena Vista Images pp53, 86, Getty Images/Peter Burnett p52, Getty Images/Susan Chiang pp20(A), 55, Getty Images/chictype p110(br), Getty Images/Diane Cook And Len Jenshel p43, Getty Images/Andy Crawford p51, Getty Images/Deux p121(tl), Getty Images/Digital Vision p15(tcm), Getty Images/DreamPictures p120(cl), Getty Images/Scott Dudelson p27(tr), Getty Images/Duel p94, Getty Images/E. Dygas p72, Getty Images/Caiaimage/Sam Edwards p147, Getty Images/EyeWire p28, Getty Images/gilaxia p92, Getty Images/gjohnstonphoto p15(bl), Getty Images/sola deo gloria p73, Getty Images/Daniel Grill p139, Getty Images/Jamie Grill pp4, 74, Getty Images/Mike Harrington p18, Getty Images/Heritage Images p49, Getty Images/Hero Images p105, Getty Images/Hill Street Studios p141(bl), Getty Images/Dave J Hogan p99, Getty Images/Imagesource pp42(bl), 48, Getty Images/Juanmonino p59(cm), Getty Images/Nico Kai p64(B), Getty Images/Ronnie Kaufman/ Larry Hirshowitz p20(B), Getty Images/Mike Kemp p98(B), Getty Images/ Dan Kitwood p121(r), Getty Images/Jutta Klee p70, Getty Images/Lynn Koenig p59(br), Getty Images/Chelsea Lauren p27(bl), Getty Images/ Jean-Pierre Lescourret p40, Getty Images/Malandrino p76, Getty Images/ Albert mollon p115(C), Getty Images/Morsa Images p120(A), Getty Images/Moxie Productions p114, Getty Images/Peathegee Inc p64(A), Getty Images/PeopleImages pp116, 108, 119, Getty Images/Hannah Peters p96, Getty Images/Lewis Phillips p83(bl), Getty Images/Vincenzo Pinto p98(A), Getty Images/Monty Rakusen p124, Getty Images/Luca Sage p12, Getty Images/Schedivey Pictures Inc p11, Getty Images/ Ariel Skelley pp77, 128(tr), Getty Images/Michael Steele p107, Getty Images/sturti p54, Getty Images/Kris Ubach and Quim Roser p19, Getty Images/Gandee Vasan p26(tl), Getty Images/ Pierre Verdy p110(tr), Getty Images/vintagerobot p117, Getty Images/VisitBritain/Britain on View p83(cl), Getty Images/VisualCommunications p88, Getty Images/ Dougal Waters p26(tr), Getty Images/Cultura RM Exclusive/Marcel Weber p26(br), Getty Images/Roberto Westbrook p15(bm), Getty Images/ Westend61 pp59(tr), 80, 137, 122, Getty Images/Nick White p120(B), Getty Images/Chris Winsor p26(bm); **Imagesource** pp33, 132, Image Source/Rudi Kennard p87(br); **The Kobal Collection**/Working Title Films p100; **Photoshot**/Tim Robbins p42 (ml); **Rex Features**/Cultura pp15(tm, bc), 98(tr), Rex Features/Juice p22, Rex Features/LNP/Mike King pp102, 103, Rex Features/Steve Meddle p38, Rex Features/Mood Board p115(b), Rex Features/Erik Pendzich p44, Rex Features/Daily Mail/Mark Richards p21; **Science photo library**/PlanetObserver p84; **Shutterstock**/ antoniodiaz p9, Shutterstock/archetype p53, Shutterstock/Blend Images p15(c), Shutterstock/Claudia K p34(foreground), Shutterstock/Claudio Photography p16, Shutterstock/Vereshchagin Dmitry p30, Shutterstock/ Lenka Horavova p6, Shutterstock/Izf pp14, 15(tl), Shutterstock/junpinzon p8, Shutterstock/Amy Johansson p78, Shutterstock/Lightspring p118, Shutterstock/Maxx-Studio p5(l), Shutterstock/Joshua Resnick p65, Shutterstock/Roobcio p34(background), Shutterstock/TTStock p36, Shutterstock/Uber Images p58, Shutterstock/YanLev p32; **Stockbyte** pp41, 59(tl), 93(t); **Superstock**/Michael DeYoung p87(t); **Thinkstock**/ Todd Arena p7, Thinkstock/Monkey Business Images Ltd p128(tl), Thinkstock/Polka Dot RF p115(A), Thinkstock/subinpumsom p31, Thinkstock/Dimitri Zimmer p115(B).

The authors and publishers are grateful for permission to reprint the following copyright material: Adapted material from 'Teenage violinist given £1m Stradivarius to take on tour' by Hannah Furness © Telegraph Media Group Limited, 2014. Reprinted with permission. www.telegraph.co.uk (p95)



Printed and bound in Argentina

2021
16